Catholic Confederates

THE CIVIL WAR ERA IN THE SOUTH
Brian Craig Miller and LeeAnn Whites, Series Editors

Bushwhackers: Guerrilla Warfare, Manhood,
and the Household in Civil War Missouri
Joseph M. Beilein Jr.

Catholic Confederates: Faith and Duty in the Civil War South
Gracjan Kraszewski

Catholic Confederates

Faith and Duty in the Civil War South

GRACJAN KRASZEWSKI

The Kent State University Press

KENT, OHIO

© 2020 by The Kent State University Press, Kent, Ohio 44242

ALL RIGHTS RESERVED

Library of Congress Catalog Number 2019054932

ISBN 978-1-60635-395-0

Manufactured in the United States of America

LIBRARY OF CONGRESS CATALOGING-IN-PUBLICATION DATA

Names: Kraszewski, Gracjan Anthony, 1987- author.

Title: Catholic Confederates : faith and duty in the Civil War South / Grajan Kraszewski.

Other titles: Civil War era in the South.

Description: Kent, Ohio : The Kent State University Press, [2020] | Series: The Civil War era in the South | Includes bibliographical references and index.

Identifiers: LCCN 2019054932 | ISBN 9781606353950 (cloth) | ISBN 9781631014017 (epub) | ISBN 9781631014024 (pdf)

Subjects: LCSH: Catholics--Southern States--History--19th century. | Christianity and politics--Southern States--History--19th century. | United States--History--Civil War, 1861-1865--Religious aspects. | Confederate States of America--History.

Classification: LCC E489 .K73 2020 | DDC 973.7/3013--dc23

LC record available at https://lccn.loc.gov/2019054932

24 23 22 21 20   5 4 3 2 1

For Katy

Contents

Acknowledgments

This book would not exist without David Nolen: associate professor, assistant editor, reference librarian, veritable polymath, and, truly, one of the nicest people anyone could hope to meet. I first met David in the fall of 2012 while I was a graduate student at Mississippi State, seeking his advice on a seminar paper on nineteenth-century Southern Catholics. Up to that point, I had found little. In what couldn't have been more than twenty minutes of searching, David opened a floodgate of information, not the least of which was the Civil War diary of William Henry Elder, bishop of Natchez, who would become a central figure of my work. David lit the first spark to this project, and for that I am deeply thankful. That he is a die-hard Crimson Tide fan only detracts from my gratitude a little.

I am indebted to Alison Collis Greene, my advisor, for guiding this project from the preparatory phase through many revisions unto completion. I am even more grateful to have been able to observe how a first-rate scholar goes about her work. I extend similar thanks to the three other members of my committee: William Anthony Hay, Andrew Lang, and Anne Marshall, as well as the many other professors who helped me during my time at Mississippi State, in particular, Jason Phillips, Dennis Doyle, Mary Kathryn Barbier, Richard Damms, and Stephen Brain. I am grateful also for the friendship and support of my fellow graduate students, most especially Alan Harrelson, Rachel D'Addabbo, Karrie Barfield, and Cameron Zinsou. Thank you all.

Special thanks to MSU department head Alan I. Marcus. His deft leadership has enabled students like me to receive scholarships that finance their studies while simultaneously granting them invaluable teaching and research experience. I am likewise grateful to Emeritus Professor John F. Marszalek for selecting me to give the 2015 Marszalek Lecture at MSU, allowing me the opportunity to present a 1 percent distillation of my entire dissertation, which helped me focus the thesis and overall scope of my work.

Two travel grants enabled me to accomplish significant portions of my research. To Peter Ryan and the MSU Office of the Provost, thank you for funding my travel to the diocesan archives in Charleston, South Carolina; to the archivist in Charleston, Brian P. Fahey, a sincere thanks for all of your help. Since it would be wrong for a Catholic living in the United States to have never visited the American university that is literally named "Our Lady," I thank the University of Notre Dame Cushwa Center for a travel grant allowing me to come research at that institution's archives. (To Our Lady herself, I wish to extend the fullest measure of hyperdulia.) To everyone at Notre Dame, especially Senior Archivist William Kevin Cawley, thank you. In equal measure to the archivists at the Catholic University of America, those working in Emmitsburg, Maryland, at the Daughters of Charity–Province of St. Louise Archives, and those at the Ulysses S. Grant Presidential Library in Starkville, Mississippi: thank you all very much. Special thanks, too, to Rhett Lawson and his advisor, Molly Weathers, for their help with this project.

I am deeply grateful to James McCartin, Notre Dame PhD and current director of Fordham University's Center on Religion and Culture. I took his American history class the first fall of my first undergraduate year in college—at the time he and I were both at Seton Hall University—and it is no exaggeration to say this experience solidified my desire to become a professor myself. Years later, at MSU, he assisted me with a historiography paper and encouraged me to apply for the Cushwa Grant. For this, and everything, thank you, Jim. Additionally, I extend a very special thanks and warm greeting to Cristofer Scarboro of King's College, my undergraduate advisor and a man with whom I share my current institution, the University of Illinois at Urbana-Champaign.

I completed this book while working in the UIUC history department and want to extend warm gratitude to the department head, Clare Crowston, and all of the wonderful scholars and people at Illinois (especially my students) who have made my time there so pleasant. The warmest thanks, too, to Bill Sullivan, head of the UIUC Department of Landscape Architecture. I would be remiss if I did not also thank the assistant chaplain at the UIUC Newman Center, Father Chase Hilgenbrinck, for all he has done for my family and me during our time here. I also thank Fr. Chase for his work at Deportivo Ñublense and elsewhere and for best embodying the joie de vivre reminiscent of a young Karol Wojtyła.

I extend a special thank you to Will Underwood, Brian Miller, and everyone at and associated with the Kent State University Press. From the first moment my manuscript fell into their hands, I have believed there was no better place for it. Everything they have done in bringing this project to fruition has been both necessary and greatly appreciated, and, I am certain, the book would not be what it is without their expertise. The same goes for the archives and depositories that granted me permission to use the photos in this book; it is thanks to them that the characters who grace these pages come to life and can forge that important bond between the reader and the subject. Thank you all.

Finally, especially, and most importantly, I thank my family. To my father, Charles, and my mother, Aleksandra—no son could have better parents. No son could have better role models and friends. (To read Chanameed but once is to understand the English language as it was meant to hum and snap.) Bardzo was kocham. The same thanks and love to my brother, Konrad, who has one of best baseball swings I have ever seen and put that to use to practically singlehandedly down the Swiss on their own turf in Zurich. He is intelligent and funny in a way hard for me to describe. Konrad, suffice to say: you're a boss.

Thanks and love to my grandparents, John and Barbara; my Aunt Claire, who may not be officially canonized yet but is a living saint, and Uncle Carl; Wujek Jurek i Ciocia Iwona; Uncle Bill; Przemek and Kasia; and all my family in Często-chowa, especially Dziadek and Babcia. Thanks and love to all my brothers and sisters: Agata, Michał, Karolina, Colby, Anson, Colin, Liam, Lars, Molly, Sean, Amy, and Mat; the same to my parents-in-law, Bill and Theresa. I love you all.

The most profound thanks to my wife, Katy. You are my best friend, an amaz-ing mother to our boys, Søren and Bjørn, and my better half in academia as well as in life. I love you.

Introduction

To say things looked bleak for the Confederacy in the fall of 1863 is to be guilty of a severe understatement. Two years following the jubilation of chasing the Yankees from Fort Sumter and then defeating them on the field at First Manassas, Confederates had witnessed New Orleans captured by the Union; arguably their most tactically gifted general, Stonewall Jackson, killed by friendly fire; and a first invasion of the North fail. Lincoln subsequently issued the Emancipation Proclamation, giving new meaning to a war begun to save the Union—by now aiming to create a more perfect one. Soon afterward, a second invasion of the North failed at Gettysburg, this defeat made all the more devastating paired with the simultaneous fall of Vicksburg. In addition to the Twin Defeats, the Confederacy's faced many inner civil wars raging on the home front; bread riots throughout the South—in Mobile, Atlanta, and Richmond, where starving citizens, many of them women, stormed the streets demanding food at gunpoint—but one example.

The outlook was hardly better abroad. Jefferson Davis, though cognizant of his country's outmanned and outgunned reality from the start, could take heart that the American Revolutionaries had been in similar dire straits during their own secessionist experiment eighty years prior. Did not France's intervention following the Battle of Saratoga make all the difference? Were there not more Frenchmen fighting the British at Yorktown than Americans? Could not, rather *would not,* similar succor come to the Confederacy?

Davis's sanguine hopes proved barren. Neither Britain nor France nor anyone else was interested in helping the Confederacy outside of empty gestures of respect, such as when Britain and France labeled the Confederates *belligerents* rather than *rebels,* thus recognizing a struggle between two countries rather than a treasonous act against legitimate authority. When the Confederacy broke off diplomatic relations with Britain in autumn 1863, it seemed the end was near and that Davis's next move, trying to win the support of Pope Pius IX, was little more than desperation. Why would the pope even be open to receiving Confederate envoys, of having any role within this distant conflict? Surely, Davis and his government could not have been expecting much.

"[His] Holiness received these remarks with an approving expression," Confederate agent Ambrose Dudley Mann reported, having just handed Pius IX a letter from Jefferson Davis. Finally, perhaps, a Confederate diplomatic breakthrough had materialized. Mann was party to one of "the most remarkable conferences ever a foreign representative had with a potentate of the earth. And such a potentate!" he exclaimed, one "who wields the consciences of 175,000,000 of the civilized race . . . the viceregent of Almighty God in his sublunary sphere." Mann was not a Catholic. His enthusiasm did not flow from theological inclinations. Rather, as envoy of a government that had ceased hoping aid might come from traditional sources, Mann, as did the Confederacy in full, placed his diplomatic faith in the Roman Catholic Church.[1] Maybe there was a chance for papal support. And did it not follow that any kind of papal support might produce *some* kind of positive effect for the Confederacy?

Perhaps it could cause the Catholic nations of Europe to recognize the Confederacy, maybe complicate matters for Northern Catholics fighting for the Union, or even just confirm for Davis that the South was the "Christian side" warring against a secular and materialistic North. "The moral effect of the action of the Catholic Pontiff will be very valuable to us," the *Memphis Daily Appeal* claimed, for Northern Catholics "cannot fail to be influenced by the sentiments of the Pontiff, and will become less willing to cry war when he counsels peace." Because Pius had christened Davis "Illustrious President," Northern Catholics would be "less eager to deny our right to a separate name and place among the nations, when it is so frankly conceded by one commanding their reverence in so eminent a degree . . . while to our Catholic fellow-citizens it cannot fail to be peculiarly gratifying."[2]

Following contact with the Vatican, Davis appointed two clergymen, Bishop Patrick Lynch and Chaplain John Bannon, to official diplomatic posts. While this might seem surprising, further reflection reveals a long-standing connection between Catholicism and the Southern United States. A veritable deluge of European immigrants produced a significant majority for Northern Catholics in nineteenth-century America, but, according to Bannon, the faith had deeper roots in the South, "natural ally of the foreigner and the Catholic." The Catholic faith was congenital to the South, brought to Florida, the Gulf Coast, and up the Mississippi River by Spaniards and Frenchmen at the same time Englishmen were landing at Jamestown and Plymouth Rock. Catholicism was an innate part of the Southern religious landscape, even as Catholics remained a statistical minority in the Protestant-heavy Bible Belt.[3]

What would prove interesting during the war years for this variegated, multiethnic Southern Catholic conglomerate was the leveling effect Confederate devotion would have on potential ethnic divisions and/or distinctions. As is explained more precisely in chapter 2, while, or because, Southern Catholics of French origins did not lose their "Frenchness" during the war—the same being true for Southern Catholics of Irish descent, German descent, and so on—it is noteworthy how people preferring to be identified by their religion and citizenship in a new nation coming into being, the Confederate States of America, often relegated the ethnic nationalities of Southern Catholics to a secondary importance.

This favoritism of a new nationality at the expense of one's ethnic origins is nothing new in American history. Easily recalled are the stories of myriad immigrants into the Northern United States who desired to become "as American as possible" as quickly as possible, often changing last names to sound less ethnic or forsaking a mother tongue, even at home, so as to be fully immersed in the English language and American culture. A similar phenomenon occurred for Southern Catholics during the Civil War, the majority of whom tried to become "as Confederate as possible" as quickly as possible. And if they did not forsake native languages or change surnames, their ethnic stories, when taken in sum, are much more prejudiced toward amalgamation and ascent to a common, cohesive national identity—citizen of the Confederacy—than taking refuge in particular ethnic groups.

This true, issues pertaining to Southern Catholics' ethnic origins are to be found throughout the work.[4] French and Irish soldiers, for example, often explained their Confederatism using familiar nationalistic paradigms from their own traditions. The Confederacy was justified in its self-determination, as the Irish were justified in trying to escape British rule. This exact line of thinking was one reason Davis selected Bannon for his diplomatic post, believing, correctly, that the priest-diplomat would easily succeed in translating the Confederate revolution into the local language of Irish opposition to home rule. As Augustin

Verot, a bishop of French origins once argued, the Confederacy should seek European diplomatic aid with France first, because France, obviously, was the land whose own values of *liberté, égalité,* and *fraternité* most mirrored, or should be the proper inspiration for, the national values the Confederacy was hoping to develop. But while Southern Catholics often referred to their ethnic backgrounds, they preferred to put their faith and Confederate identity first, often speaking of ethnic origins in direct service of this new national identity, employing the aforementioned "familiar nationalistic paradigms from their own particular traditions" as a tool to better argue for what had become most important to them: defending, and winning the independence of, the Confederate nation.

Southern Catholics were indeed a minority, but they were a unique one, for while the more hierarchical Protestant denominations had exiguous ties to Europe and an appreciation for ecclesiastical structure, only Catholics had a pope, esteemed by the faithful to be Christ's vicar on earth. Southern Protestants did not confront the same dilemmas Southern Catholics did. A Mississippi Baptist's church community was strictly local. No ministerial authority from outside the state, let alone in the North or Europe, held jurisdictional power over him. But a Mississippi Catholic was part of a religious body that had not split along the North-South fault line. He was deeply entwined in a united, extra-sectional, and international religious fabric. As such, being constituents of a particular Confederate state and the Confederacy proper while simultaneously members of the universal Church in Rome, Southern Catholics held a theological and political dual citizenship.

Many prominent Confederates were Roman Catholics or had strong ties to the Church—included in this number are Gen. P. G. T. Beauregard; "poet of the Confederacy" Father Abram J. Ryan; R. Adm. Raphael Semmes; Secretary of the Navy Stephen Mallory; Gen. James Longstreet, a postwar convert; and even Lincoln assassin John Wilkes Booth, rumored to have converted to Catholicism.[5] Davis, an Episcopalian who in his youth was educated by Dominican friars and had asked to become a Catholic, remained sympathetic toward the faith his entire life. During his postwar imprisonment, Davis received a signed picture of the pope bearing the biblical inscription "Come unto me, all ye who are weary and heavy laden, and I will give you rest."[6]

And yet what is certainly, at minimum, an interesting relationship between Roman Catholics and the Southern Confederacy remains largely unknown. As recently as 2001, historians expressed dissatisfaction that Confederate religion was still being studied in an almost exclusively Protestant light.[7] It is a fair criticism.[8] A few books published in the first two decades of the twenty-first century have remedied this to a degree.[9] But while all these are excellent works, none offers a comprehensive or exclusive look at Southern Civil War Catholics.[10] As such, Randall Miller and Jon Wakelyn's assertion in *Catholics in the Old South* remains in force, albeit with an addendum: "Too little has been written about [*Southern*] Catholics and the Civil War."[11]

Catholic Confederates enters into the middle of this multifaceted historiographical thicket. Catholic commitment to and involvement in the Confederacy is at the heart of this narrative, one treating the beliefs and actions of bishops, chaplains, sister-nurses, soldiers, diplomats, and Pope Pius IX. The vast majority of Southern Catholics were deeply committed to the Confederate nation. Almost all were somehow involved in the Confederacy, even the largely apolitical sister-nurses, who were immersed in the war as field medics.

Navigating the spiritual and secular realms was a challenge for all Southern Catholics. Bishops participated in both spheres, tempering their politicization with a preeminent focus on religious matters. They displayed an indefatigable dedication to their congregations' needs, both the physical (providing food, clothing, and shelter and assisting in hospitals and orphanages) and the spiritual (celebrating Mass and dispensing the sacraments). Their calls for peace were often colored by political considerations, namely that peace would be "favorable" for the South, an arrangement whereby the Confederacy secured its independence. This common denominator aside, the way bishops advocated for such a settlement was nuanced. For some, such as Martin John Spalding, of Louisville, and Francis Patrick Kenrick, of Baltimore, preference for the spiritual was so pronounced that politics counted for significantly less. Others, like Patrick Lynch, of Charleston, and John Quinlan, of Mobile, were so acutely politicized they can, without exaggeration, be termed ardent Confederates. Still others straddled the middle with impressive equanimity. William Henry Elder, of Natchez, was so balanced that in some moments he seemed as involved as Lynch and in others as detached as Kenrick.

Chaplains and soldiers were highly politicized. To some degree, this is due to their proximity to the war. It is hard to remain indifferent to a cause when one is daily risking death for it. Furthermore, the majority of chaplains and soldiers were volunteers. While, owing to their priestly station, the chaplains' religiosity is fairly obvious, many soldiers were devout, possessors of strong prayer lives, regular attendees at camp prayer meetings, and practitioners of various Catholic devotions who undergirded their spiritual lives with frequent reception of the sacraments.

Sister-nurses were slightly different, an exception to the politicized, pro-Confederate rule. Their selfless dedication to wounded men transcended political partisanship, and they appear to have been solely concerned with healing wounded bodies and helping souls find God. The dichotomies of North versus South and Confederate versus Yankee were largely irrelevant. But that the sisters did not support the Confederate nation politically is not code for wartime withdrawal or apathy. On the contrary, they were deeply involved and highly visible, serving in hospitals as medics, psychological supporters, and religious instructors. Sister-nurses were prolific Catholic converters who, while seldom pushing their religious views, were happy to discuss their beliefs, should men ask. Many did ask, and many of these same men later became Catholics.

The nuns' unique role during the war cannot be overstated, nor should it be overlooked. The sister-nurses were on the battlefield, but unarmed; they were as close to danger as any soldier, but possessing neither weapons nor rabid political passions. Their willingness to provide medical and spiritual succor were their sole motivations. Furthermore, their wartime story complicates assumptions that *noncombatants* means actors far from the centers of action, at home, or, at minimum, out of harm's way. Most importantly, the sister-nurses' "participation without politicization" unveils the all-encompassing nature of Catholic involvement in the Confederacy.

Pope Pius IX is featured within this narrative as well, along with the Catholic diplomats Davis's government sent to him. That the Confederacy employed Catholic clergymen as official representatives to Europe shows its diplomacy sometimes had a distinctively religious quality. And as for the primary cause of the Civil War, slavery, there is ample discussion of the topic, scattered in pockets throughout each chapter—with two episcopal pamphlets penned on the subject, from Bishops Lynch and Augustin Verot, of Savannah, of particular importance.

Southern Catholics learned to balance their Catholicism and Confederatism throughout the war. For the vast majority, these identities were not in tension; rather, they mutually reinforced each other, making it possible for one to be both a devout Catholic and a devoted Confederate. I term the phenomenon by which Southern Catholics became involved in the Confederate nation *Confederatization.* Confederatization—the active ingredient for the leveling process that propelled Southern Catholics toward prioritizing a new national identity above older ethnic ones—serves as the connecting thread of this work, framing the discussion around each chapter's expositions concerning how and why Catholics were involved in the Confederacy. By demonstrating how thoroughly immersed Southern Catholics were in the Confederacy's culture, politics, and war, Confederatization calls attention to the fact that Southern Catholics are important components of the scholarly conversations in Civil War religious studies as well as within the larger, more general, history of Catholicism in America.

Confederatization is ultimately *what this book is about.* Bishops eagerly supported the Southern cause in inter-episcopal correspondence and in pastoral letters and sermons to their congregations. They encouraged men to join the Confederate army and resisted Union encroachments at home. Soldiers volunteered to fight for the cause while chaplains, although they were noncombatants, bore the same physical hardships soldiers did. Many Catholics displayed their Confederatization by refusing to take oaths to the Union. One soldier, Henri Garidel, essentially chose the Confederacy over his loved ones, as interminable separation from his family was the price for not compromising his Confederate loyalty. A chaplain, James Sheeran, would not take the oath even as harsh conditions during imprisonment threatened to kill him. He claimed to be a citizen of the South and stated that he had no other home. He was eventually released from Union captivity without having relented, his loyalty, and pride, intact.

Confederatization knew no geographical boundaries. Bannon and Lynch jumped at the opportunity to serve their nation overseas as diplomats. And even sister-nurses, while almost wholly apolitical, were still so completely involved in the Confederate war effort, aiding wounded men by the thousands on battlefields all across the South, that their "participation without politicization" makes it accurate to state that *almost all* Southern Catholics were *somehow* involved in the Confederate nation during the war.

The Confederatization thesis is directly related to, and challenges, the Americanization thesis within Catholic historiography. Per the Americanization thesis (which here is admittedly, and intentionally, only briefly sketched, and only as is relative to this book's arguments), nineteenth-century Catholics could not resolve their identities as both Americans and Catholics; they could not harmonize the two. Catholics neither assimilated into American culture nor did they contribute much to that society. They remained, in various historians' formulations, "outsiders." Beset by myriad prejudices, they withdrew into their own institutions, a prime example being the fight for a strong parochial school system, which reinforced stereotypes that Catholics were an insulated people. The turn-of-the-century papal proclamations against Americanism and modernism added to this perception, labeling Catholics retrograde and anti-American.[12] Assimilation into American society—*Americanization*—would not occur until the twentieth century.[13]

Confederatization contests this framework, challenging the assertion that Catholics did not assimilate into American society until long after the Civil War and, especially, that they were not integrated members of nineteenth-century Southern society. The reverse was true in both cases. The hope is to turn back the clock on Americanization and show that one need not skip over the nineteenth century in order to see widespread Catholic involvement in American, albeit Confederate American, culture and society.

To be clear, it is true Catholics faced extreme hostility from American society throughout the nineteenth century. They did often withdraw into their own institutions. They were treated with suspicion by a society that often viewed them as still essentially European and therefore "other." And there is no question that the twentieth century—especially in the 1960s, by way of the combined effects of John F. Kennedy's election and the Second Vatican Council—witnessed the apex of Catholic assimilation.

None of these truths are disputed. Confederatization leaves Americanization's twentieth-century claims untouched, confirming their validity, while making a corrective solely regarding the nineteenth century, this being, perhaps ultimately, the prime intention of this work: shifting the focus on Confederate Catholicism from the periphery to the center of Civil War religious history while simultaneously producing similar awareness of the importance of both the American South and, specifically, the nineteenth-century Civil War South, to the larger story of Catholicism in America.

In addition to simply presenting American Catholics, and Americans of various denominations, with a practically unknown feature of their own history, *Catholic Confederates* has three focused historiographical goals: first, to add a Catholic component to Civil War religious scholarship and, second, add a Southern Civil War facet specifically to nineteenth-century American Catholic historiography.[14] These two contributions likewise engage the larger field of American Catholic literature, which largely favors topics such as European immigration into the North, Latino immigration, ethnic and racial tensions in urban environments, moral issues such as contraception, evolving modes of prayer, and, especially, the post–Vatican II era.[15] The third and final goal is to join the already voluminous, and still growing, body of Civil War scholarship treating Confederate allegiance, loyalty, and nation.[16]

The Confederacy was a nation, not simply a loose conglomerate of rebelling states, and Southern Catholics were committed to the Confederacy precisely because of this nationalistic understanding. The Confederate nation was birthed from a revolution in the service of reaction, a looking back in the hope of resuscitating an imagined, idyllic past, something fundamentally different from progressive upheavals that seek to construct novel utopias.[17]

As such, the Confederacy compared its struggle for independence to the romantic nationalism of nineteenth-century Europe, not so much to the progressive avant-garde of 1848, in France, for example, as to those groups fighting for self-determination so as to restore the supposed glories of a bygone age; the stateless but culturally rich Poles, seeking to escape Tsarist domination, for example. Nationalism was as much a theme in the nineteenth-century United States as in Europe. And American nationalism was arguably most pronounced in the Southern states, where Christianity was a prime building block.[18]

Catholicism fit almost seamlessly into the Confederate restorationist-revolutionary paradigm. That the Church is often more conservative than radical is common knowledge, and if Southern Catholics did believe the Confederacy stood for tradition and the "best ideals" of European civilization, it is easy to see the connections. For almost two millennia the Church has stood against all manners of "progressive" causes. Not just the myriad heresies of the early centuries AD, but modern movements such as the Protestant Reformation, the Enlightenment and French Revolutionary era, and the nineteenth century's "secular religions": socialism, communism, scientism, and positivism. The Church's opposition has often been couched in a defense of tradition, be it ecclesiastical or cultural.[19]

Unfortunately, included in the Catholic and Southern cohesion around "cultural traditionalism" was the support of slavery. Just as Southern Catholics became practically indistinguishable from Southern Protestants in endorsing the Confederacy's war, politics, and national aspirations, so, too, did they often uphold typical societal views on slavery. As is discussed in detail throughout the book, most especially in the bishops' interactions with African Americans on the home front, the Catholicism-slavery wartime narrative is a complex one, fraught with ambiguities, but one that, in the end, has a disappointing bottom line. Many Southern Catholics did believe African Americans and whites were spiritual equals before God, yet societally, that was not the case. Catholics often joined the majority opinion in the South that found little, if not nothing, wrong with slavery in the temporal realm. Catholic bishops issued many jeremiads denouncing sin as the prime cause of the war, but as to the glaring sin of slavery, they said little. And near the end of the war, in a last-ditch effort to gain papal support, it was a Catholic bishop who tried to remove the Vatican's reluctance to help the Confederacy—this reluctance directly stemming from the CSA's open endorsement of human bondage—not by disavowing the South's connection to slavery but, rather, by claiming that the South's "peculiar institution" was not that bad, certainly nothing like the horrors Northern abolitionists claimed. In sum, Southern Catholics viewed slaves much as Southern Protestants did: inferior, second-class persons in need of paternalistic guidance from whites.

Ultimately, as Southerners viewed their nascent nation as the true heir to the Constitutional principles of 1776, so, too, did Southern Catholics. Bishops as well as soldiers and chaplains were constantly looking back in time to defend the future of the Confederate nation. Perhaps in its success or failure they saw the success or failure of their religion in America. Often alongside a Southern Catholic's political defense of the Confederate nation was the Catholic faith. While not lost on all scholars, this connection between Southern conservatism and Catholic traditionalism remains, underappreciated.[20]

Many Southern Catholics saw the natural symbiosis between Southernism and Catholicism and then sought to live it out within Confederatization's devout Catholic-devoted Confederate paradigm. It is the primary reason Southern Catholics supported the Confederate cause and were so eager to participate in the Confederacy's politics and war. Southern Catholics saw in the South the "most Catholic" part of America, a stark contrast to what many believed an increasingly materialistic and secular society metastasizing in the North. The American Civil War provided the opportunity for the fashioning of a new national identity. Southern Catholics jumped at the opportunity to become committed Confederates.

Regarding style, this work gives preference to a deeper focus on main characters instead of a plethora of actors who, naturally, must be given less individual attention. Chapter 1, which investigates all Southern bishops, focuses dominantly on three or four prelates. Three chaplains and three soldiers are the primary characters of chapters 2 and 3, just as the final chapter, on Confederate diplomacy, features two Catholic diplomats and the pope above all others. While sister-nurses are largely studied in tandem in chapter 5, individual personalities do break through. In the consideration of bishops during the war, in chapter 4, one man, William Henry Elder, dominates the narrative in near-biographical fashion. This preference for the sustained voice of the few over fleeting snippets from many is also adequately flexible to permit a zooming out for the purpose of statistical appreciation when needed.

Attention has been paid to scope, to the disciplined recounting of the "Southern Catholic story" as it happened during the war so as to avoid diluting the importance of this narrative with distractions broader than the intended focus. In addition to presenting the wartime histories of the expected figures—the bishops, chaplains, and soldiers—the Confederatization thesis challenges two common misconceptions: that the Civil War was exclusively a domestic event, by way of an entire chapter dedicated to Catholic-Confederate diplomacy, and that when scholars speak of Civil War women they necessarily mean home front actors. The sister-nurses show that some Southern women could be found on battlefields, as close to the danger as any soldier.

The goal in demonstrating the depth of Catholic commitment to the Confederacy is to prompt some reconsiderations about nineteenth-century Catholicism in the South and the relationship of those Catholics to the social and political causes of the day and, in turn, to help scholars of Civil War religion and American Catholicism better understand the place of Southern Catholics within their respective fields and American history writ large. Historian James Woods writes that while many important events have been covered, "an overall narrative of Southern Catholicism beyond that remains to be written." While in no way pretending to be a comprehensive history, even of a small portion of the Southern Catholic story, in its exclusive focus on the Confederacy and the war years *Catholic Confederates* will hopefully be a positive step toward a thorough understanding of Southern Catholicism.[21]

CHAPTER ONE

The Bishops Respond to Secession and the First Year of the War, 1860–1861

Immediately following South Carolina's secession from the Union in December 1860, Patrick Lynch, bishop of Charleston, declared the state "henceforth not only our Mother but our only Sovereign, who has sole right to our allegiance." South Carolinians should give a "whole, undivided loyalty" to this new nation, even taking up arms if necessary. That same month, Archbishop of Baltimore Francis Patrick Kenrick claimed it would be "suicidal" for the South to leave the Union. The bishop of Louisville, Martin John Spalding, agreed with Kenrick and hoped the crisis might yet be resolved: "God grant us peace!"[1]

The bishops' views on pertinent societal matters were important to Southern Catholics. It is still so today. But, with American Catholicism in a nascent, although developing, phase during the Civil War, this relevance was even more pronounced. The ultramontane temperament of the nineteenth century strengthened prelates' authoritative roles, and a theological congruity with Rome produced a generally unified ecclesial community at home and abroad.

This chapter traces Southern Catholic bishops' responses to the secession crisis into the war's first year, demonstrating what these responses were in an analysis of inter-episcopal letters, peace pastorals, and other assorted correspondence. Many of the bishops shared the general *augusterlebnis* of their fellow Southerners, firmly believing their state proper (and later on, the Confederacy in sum) was an independent nation possessing the right to secede so as to recapture a foundational sovereignty. Thus, many eagerly looked forward to what they believed would be a short and glorious victory over a tyrannical North.

All bishops were clergymen first, tending to religious matters above all. But even those of a more reticent stripe, content to distance themselves from the growing sectional issues before the war had officially begun in April 1861, were found, once this line had been crossed, quickly moving into fervent support of the Confederate nation. Catholics were not simply involved members of the Confederate nation; they were *just as devoted* to the cause as their Protestant neighbors.

Indeed, Southern Catholics proved to be, like their episcopal leaders, Confederatized partisans throughout the conflict, but what were the statistical realities of this Southern Catholic community by 1860? Although Catholicism was indigenous to the South, Northern Catholics, many of them recently arrived immigrants, were far more numerous. Alabama, home to an estimated ten thousand Catholics, a paltry 1 percent of the state's population, presented a typical story in a region were Catholic churches made up a tiny fraction of a state's houses of worship, with Tennessee (ten Catholic churches, 0.4 percent of all churches in the state), Georgia (eight, 0.3 percent), and North Carolina (seven, 0.3 percent) of like character.[2]

The "most Catholic" Southern states were Louisiana, Kentucky, and Maryland.[3] Louisiana boasted the largest number of Catholic churches in the South, ninety-nine, and an impressive statewide percentage of 17.3 percent. Kentucky, with eighty-three Catholic churches, and Maryland, with eighty-two, lagged behind at 3.8 percent and 8.0 percent. New Orleans, home to the highest cluster of Catholics in any American city, possessed a robust eighteen Catholic churches, with a combined seating capacity exceeding twenty-five thousand people and an aggregate property value of $1.04 million. It is unsurprising that five of this book's main personalities were Louisiana Catholics of some connection; soldiers Felix Poche and Henri Garidel, Chaplain Louis Hippolyte-Gache in his service with the Tenth Louisiana, and the archbishop of New Orleans, Jean-Marie Odin, along with Chaplain James Sheeran, each prewar Louisiana immigrants.[4]

In between conspicuously Catholic New Orleans and Baltimore and the Catholic wilderness in Georgia, Alabama, and North Carolina stood a middle ground of Confederate states. Texas was home to approximately 120,000 Catholic citizens who could celebrate Mass in thirty-three statewide churches. Although Mississippi had nearly an identical number of Catholic citizens as Alabama (approximately 10,000), it had almost twice the number of churches (seventeen). Florida also had seventeen, and while South Carolina had but eleven, it was home to Charleston, one of the most important centers of Southern Catholicism.[5]

Despite these at times paltry numbers, the Catholic faith made significant strides during the antebellum period, progressing markedly since the nation's founding. In 1776, the faith was illegal in every colony except Maryland and Pennsylvania—which was unsurprising, given Maryland's foundational Catholic roots and Pennsylvania's widespread religious toleration. The Church possessed few members and less societal import. Church infrastructure was miniscule, and a frontier, almost missionary, character defined Catholicism in the South. Parish priests moonlighted as itinerant preachers, making the rounds to impoverished outposts at times beset by more than a five thousand to one parishioner-to-priest ratio. Churches often bore more of a resemblance to wooden shacks than majestic European cathedrals.[6]

But growth came, and much of it can be attributed to the establishment of Southern dioceses, which before the nineteenth century were limited to Baltimore (established 1789) and New Orleans (1793). Charleston and Richmond were established in 1820. The Diocese of Mobile was founded in 1829, followed by Natchez and Nashville, each in 1837. Little Rock, Arkansas, a diocese created in 1843, encompassed the entirety of a state that saw its Catholic population nearly triple in size between 1830 and 1850. By 1860, with the establishments of Savannah (1850) and Saint Augustine (1857), North Carolina remained the sole southern state without a Catholic diocese. A growing ecclesiastical nexus was starting to emerge, with the North having but seven more dioceses (twenty-two to fifteen) at the war's outbreak. As late as the 1840s, Southern dioceses were more numerous than Northern ones, lending credence to the idea of a more entrenched Catholicism in the American South.[7]

Catholic prewar societal integration, an evolving process Confederatization highlighted and firmly cemented during the war years, was visible throughout the South. In Charleston, Protestants financially contributed to Catholic hospitals, helped nuns care for orphans, and even sent their children to Catholic schools. In Louisiana, women religious ran numerous local academies, open to Catholics and Protestants alike, many upper-class women "learn[ing] their attitudes about God, dancing, and government from nuns." Catholic bishops drew large crowds; for example, the bishop of Mobile, John Quinlan, was known for often having many Protestants in his audience, something common across the Southern episcopate, especially during the war. Bishops preached in wholly secular places, the Louisville courthouse just one such setting. When another bishop was set to give the baccalaureate sermon at the University of North Carolina, one observer commented that the excitement was akin to "as great a rush to see the animal as if he were the big bull of Bashan or Pope of Rome."[8]

Many Protestants were drawn to Catholic worship, even if they ultimately remained apart from it. In Bardstown, Kentucky, a Protestant lawyer promised land for a new church, on the condition that the building be "attractive." Congregationalist preacher and abolitionist Henry Ward Beecher, brother to *Uncle Tom's Cabin* author Harriet Beecher Stowe, wrote that he was enraptured by the Church's "majestic and imposing ceremonies," the "dazzling" lights, ornaments, and vestments, along with "the power of music and the breathing marble and living canvas, and all the diversified contributions of art." After a European tour, Beecher explained, "I am bound to say, also, that I have been agreeably disappointed in the appearance of the monks and priests in Roman Catholic countries. As a general rule, they have appeared to be clear-faced, intelligent, and sincere men. Only once or twice did we meet the legendary type of monk—round, fat, and worldly. In Switzerland, and in Northern Italy, the general impression produced upon me by the priests has been highly favorable to them."[9] Although the Confederacy failed in its independence bid, it was not, as one historian notes, "for lack of sacrifices on the part of southern Catholics." Catholics' "support for the southern way of life and southerners' support for Catholic hospitals, schools, and churches were not unrelated."[10]

The Confederatization thesis demonstrates how numerous emergent factors present during the antebellum period only became more apparent, and more potent, during the war years. During the war, sisters who had operated hospitals throughout the prewar South operated on bodies and souls as sister-nurses; priests, who bore responsibility for souls, now assumed the added responsibilities of chaplaincies and diplomatic posts; laymen, whose children attended parochial schools alongside Protestant children, died alongside those same Protestants, serving together under the same flag, each wholly committed to the Confederate nation; and Catholic bishops, widely respected before the war, only saw their social profiles increase, as when Natchez's William Henry Elder refused a prayer request for Lincoln, winning him much admiration throughout the South and beyond.

Elder, Quinlan, and the whole of the Southern episcopate presiding during the Civil War were installed within a decade of the conflict.[11] The bishops had immediate experience with the characteristics of the Church in the South and, perhaps most importantly, the sectional tensions besetting antebellum America. Clerical paucity augmented their importance. Elder was the sole Catholic bishop in Mississippi, as was the standard reality elsewhere throughout what would become the Confederate States of America. During the war, the bishops participated in both the spiritual and secular realms. They worked, with varying success, to balance these loyalties. Peace initiatives are but one example. For the majority of bishops, peace advocacy included the stipulation that any settlement be favorable for the South. While the bishops did desire an authentically "Christian peace," one prioritizing the end of bloodshed, they found it difficult to untangle their Confederate commitments from their religion—because they, like many Southern Catholics, saw no contradiction in being both devout Catholics and devoted Confederates.

Bishops would discover that their roles as religious leaders often became inextricably entwined with political issues. Each bishop faced this reality uniquely, and as such the bishops' responses to secession differed somewhat. Yet all, with one debatable exception, were Confederate supporters.[12] Spalding, arguably the most peace-minded prelate, was thoroughly Confederatized even though he did not express this as forcefully as Lynch or Quinlan. Spalding was from a state outside of the Confederacy anyway; Kentucky, like Maryland had a thoroughly Southern spirit but nonetheless remained in the Union.[13]

Confederatized though they were, bishops refrained from bringing secular matters into sacred space. Political commentary was not heard during the Mass, and the political counsel given outside of Mass was often presented in negative or passive formulations. For example, Elder once stated that the faith *did not forbid* Catholics from advocating for secession but stressed they were in no way *obligated* to support it or the Confederacy. This approach enabled the bishops to avoid the appearance of partisanship while resting assured their congregants did not have to be told to be good Confederates.[14]

Regarding spiritual matters, however, the bishops did give active and unambiguous counsel. They encouraged their congregants to pray, fast, and live righteous lives—even demanded as much. And they did so often out of a penitential spirit, in reparation for what could seem countless sins. The contrast is important: while giving plentiful advice concerning what Southern Catholics they should do spiritually, the bishops restricted secular matters to the realm of the permissible. This balancing act between did not end with the secession crisis; it framed the entire Catholic Civil War experience.

As 1860 drew to a close, the United States stood on the precipice of war. In November, Spalding, deeply troubled, wrote to the archbishop of Cincinnati, staunch unionist John Baptist Purcell. "The South is assuming a very menacing attitude, & this time I fear these men are in earnest, & disunion is imminent. The Lord deliver us!" he added, as "the whole world seems to be getting out of joint." On December 1, Kenrick wrote in similar fashion to Richmond bishop John McGill, expressing his fear that secession would cause irreparable damage.

Nonetheless, he still believed the Union could be preserved and hoped "conservative men should step forward at this crisis, to save the country."[15]

Other bishops took similar approaches. They were worried but hopeful. Elder joined the public discourse by issuing a circular letter to his parish priests on November 25. The bishop of Natchez, who would later show himself to be a clear-cut Southern partisan, at first refrained from politicization. Priests should simply lead their congregations in the "first duty of the Christian Patriot;—which is to beg for the light and protection of Him, in whose hands are the hearts of men and the destinies of nations."[16]

Because the "present condition of our political affairs calls urgently for the most fervent supplications to Almighty God," Elder cautioned his priests it was "not for us here to discuss the question connected with our situation." He instructed his clergy to encourage congregants in "offer[ing] up to God Prayers, Fasting and Alms Deeds, for His merciful guidance and protection." The faithful should unite in a general Communion on December 9, within the Octave of the Immaculate Conception of the Blessed Virgin Mary, for "our Holy Mother is by excellence the Help of Christians." Elder desired that Mississippi Catholics attend Mass frequently, pray daily ("at least once the *Our Father,* the *Hail Mary,* and the *Glory be to the Father*"), recite the Rosary, adore the Blessed Sacrament, fast, give alms, and come to confession for "the most effectual means to obtain God's favor is to purify the soul from sin, and to receive worthily the Sacrament of the Blessed Eucharist: and no Catholic should imagine he has done his duty to himself and his fellow-citizens on this occasion, so long as these duties to God are left undone."[17]

Elder's first response to a possible war was a return to Catholic fundamentals. While clergymen were the letter's primary recipients, the prescriptions were not exclusively for them. These pertained to the laity as well. Elder, who believed faith should preempt, inform, and direct political decisions, expected the men of his parishes, who could become soldiers, to join him and their priests in praying and fasting for peace.[18]

On December 20, 1860, South Carolina became the first state to secede, though the opening shots of the war would not be fired for four more months. South Carolina delegates adopted a secession ordinance on Christmas Eve, appealing to state sovereignty and constitutional infractions as justification. The delegates drew heavily from the US Declaration of Independence. Each colony had been "and of right ought to be, FREE AND INDEPENDENT; and that, as free and independent States, they have full power to levy war, conclude peace,

contract allies, establish commerce, and do all other acts and things which independent States may of right do." Colonial sovereignty was analogous to state
sovereignty. As colonial ties to Britain had been sundered once the Crown's
rule had become "destructive of the ends for which it was established," so, too,
could South Carolina disassociate from Washington for similar reasons. For it
was "the right of the people to alter or abolish [the existing government], and
to institute a new government."[19]

On the night of December 20, shockwaves of excitement reverberated
through the streets of Charleston. Bells rang, artillery was discharged, houses
were decorated with candles and lamps, and impromptu parades marched
through the streets accompanied by music.[20] The *United States Catholic Miscellany,* organ of the Diocese of Charleston and edited by Bishop Lynch, gleefully declared:

> After years of patient endurance, of energetic yet friendly protest and remon-
> strance, South Carolina has, at last, in solemn convention of her people, re-
> sumed the portion of her sovereignty which she surrendered in 1789; and now
> stands before the world, a free independent Sovereign State.... South Carolina
> is henceforth not only our Mother but our only Sovereign, who has sole right
> to our allegiance. The whole, undivided loyalty of our heart and conscience,
> (we speak not only as a Carolinian, but as a Catholic theologian) must be hers
> and hers only. May the God of Peace guide her counsels and bless her with ever
> growing prosperity!—May the Lord of Hosts shield her, if need be, and bless
> with victory her arms, if they must be used to maintain her honour and her
> independence as a sovereign commonwealth![21]

Lynch's overt Confederatization was on display long before the official commencement of hostilities. Lynch believed the South, led by South Carolina's
example, would recapture the lost ideals of the American Revolution, ideals he
maintained had been betrayed by a wayward Union. As with many Southerners then pledging a new allegiance to the bourgeoning Confederate nation, at
first in piecemeal fashion via loyalty to one's own state, Lynch envisioned the
war as a restoration, not a revolution. He believed Catholicism would fit seamlessly within a project structured to reclaim the authentic design of American
independence.

In reading Lynch's article, it is striking to see how synergetic his thinking
was with his state's secession ordinance. Lynch used the word *sovereign* four

times in a dispatch just 150 words long. He alluded to South Carolina waiting patiently to reclaim an independence that was there all along. The secessionists were not creating sovereignty ex nihilo; such was South Carolina's original and proper state of being. With secession formally declared, Lynch was fully committed. South Carolina alone held any claim on his allegiance, the "undivided loyalty of [his] heart and conscience," which he specified was given by a man who spoke as both a Catholic and a Carolinian.[22]

While Lynch's note is brief, his reaction to secession is a fair distillation of standard Southern Catholic opinion on the matter. Roman Catholics were integrated and invested members of their surrounding culture. Their thoughts, feelings, and actions, especially in the political realm, were often indistinguishable from the accepted "Southern norm." Nowhere is this more evident than during the war, where Catholics, like their amply studied Protestant neighbors, rejoiced at the news of secession; viewed it as a licit action toward reestablishing their state's foundational right to sovereignty; gave their full loyalty, seemingly overnight, to a new nation; and, should war come, were prepared to fight, confident God's blessing would bring them ultimate success.

On January 4, 1861, Bishop Augustin Verot published a tract on slavery. It is significant for two reasons. In being an example of overt public Catholic support for the South's social mores, it demonstrated that pro-Confederate sympathies extended to the top of the Catholic hierarchy. The tract was also a distillation of previous Southern Catholic thought concerning slavery, serving as bridge from the antebellum writings of the first bishop of Charleston, John England, and Archbishop Kenrick to Lynch's wartime treatise—the bishop of Charleston's work written at Pope Pius IX's behest.

Verot began by referencing St. Augustine's *City of God*, arguing Rome's prosperity flowed from justice. He claimed the South would rise and fall along similar lines. For him, a just society included human bondage. "Slavery [has] received the sanction of God," Verot wrote, a view typical among slavery apologists, and one seconded by Augustus Marie Martin, bishop of Natchitoches, Louisiana, and the most extreme pro-slavery southern prelate, who likewise did not see the contradiction in championing slavery while telling his congregants, "Our first and most irreconcilable enemy is sin, however designated, arrayed or disguised."[23]

Verot, echoing Pope Gregory XVI's 1839 condemnation of the slave trade (*In Supremo Apostolatus*), forbid participation in the practice, calling it immoral and unjust.[24] Furthermore, slaves held a range of inalienable human rights. A master could not make a claim on a slave's life or soul, only his labor. Masters could not exploit their slaves sexually. Slave marriages were legitimate and had to be unconditionally respected. "Our Saviour's word on this cannot pass away," Verot wrote. "'What God has joined together, let no man put asunder.'"[25]

Slave families were sacrosanct. "Families ought never to be separated, when once established," Verot wrote. "It is unreasonable, unchristian, and immoral to separate a husband from his wife and children and to sell the husband North, and the wife South, and the children east and West." Masters' other duties included providing slaves with lifelong food and housing, medical care, and the "means of knowing and practicing religion." "This is a sacred, indispensible, burden of duty of masters," Verot added, cautioning that "the neglect of which alone, if they had committed no other fault, would expose them to eternal damnation." Per Verot, slaves were spiritually equal before God. They were entitled to standard human rights, including the rights to worship, marry, and have families. The glaring hypocrisy is that slaves were to be denied their fundamental right to freedom.[26]

On January 6, Lynch wrote to the archbishop of New York, John Hughes. "If we are not now in a state of war we are very like it and very near it." Lynch claimed secessionists were guiltless because these delegates wished only to proceed in a way that would avoid conflict, settling matters by a peaceful "dissolution of a partnership." Secession was a legitimate action, Lynch argued, justified by four factors: abolitionist agitation, Northern violations of constitutionally guaranteed state sovereignty, the inflammatory and disunion-catalyzing speeches of Northern senators, and, finally, its economic benefits for the South.[27]

Lynch added that while he did "not claim to be a Union man myself," he would, nonetheless, regret to see "this government [the Union], after a glorious, though brief ascent, burst like a rocket, and leave only . . . some fragments. I fear too," he stated, "future civil wars, strifes, and miseries. . . . I hope . . . the Constitution will be saved and the infractions of it will be addressed." Here, Lynch sounded like Kenrick, but with a twist. The archbishop of Baltimore was wholly for peace, whereas Lynch did not want the Union saved if certain "infractions" went unaddressed. For Lynch, these transgressions were gaping wounds growing more infected by the day. As such, he believed other states would soon follow South Carolina's lead. Should this transpire, "such a disruption could never be healed." Other prelates concurred. Archbishop Odin wrote, "The election of Lincoln, abolitionist candidate, to the presidency, has put all the states of the South in a state of anxiety. . . . Civil War is expected."[28]

Lynch's prediction came true only three days after his letter to Hughes. Mississippi seceded from the Union on January 9.[29] By the end of the month, four other states had joined the first two: Florida, January 10; Alabama, January 11; Georgia, January 19; and Louisiana, January 26. In Louisiana, Catholics were conspicuously present in the midst of formal secessionist proceedings. A Catholic priest opened the state convention with prayer, and this became a common occurrence for other official functions. Texas's secession, on February 1, made the number of departed states seven.[30]

Southern Catholics were, generally speaking, enthusiastic supporters of secession. Such was the case for Catholics in Charleston, the *Memphis Daily Appeal* claimed in a February 1861 article, titled "Catholics for Secession," based on findings printed in the *New Orleans Catholic Standard.* The same was true in New Orleans, with "our entire Catholic population, a very large majority of whom voted the secession ticket." In Baton Rouge, a majority of Catholics and Jews supported secession. To support this claim, the local newspaper *Sugar Planter* cited the most recent issue of the *Israelite:* "With every passing day, we [the Jewish community] get more and more convinced that the Secessionists are right." The *Memphis Daily Appeal* further stated that the "Irish, as a body, all over the Union, have ever been true to the South." Religion and patriotism went hand in hand, "throb[ing] together . . . and [Catholics] are ready for the struggle whenever the arrogant North shall presume to force it upon us."[31]

An already tenuous political situation was getting more delicate by the day. But the bishops, at least for the time being, attempted to insulate themselves from external events. On February 4, Bishop McGill issued a pastoral letter in this vein. The Richmond prelate reminded his congregation that the upcoming Lenten season was a time of "rendering satisfaction for our many sins." He encouraged the faithful, especially when "the displeasure of God seems to weigh heavy upon the nations," to humble themselves and by "prayer, penance and good works" make atonement for their faults.[32]

Nothing in McGill's letter touched on secession or politics. McGill never mentioned an obligation to take up arms. His sole focus was getting Catholics to place their faith in God and to seek spiritual remedies for preventing war. "The fortunes and fate of our beloved country are now trembling," McGill wrote, "we know not what ruins and disasters may be impending." Yet, "the Redeemer came to bring peace on earth to men of good will. Let us pray for union and peace."[33]

The day McGill's pastoral letter appeared, Elder wrote the editor of the New Orleans newspaper *Le Propagateur Catholique,* Fr. Napoléon-Joseph Perché, who would later be the archbishop of New Orleans (1870–83). Elder outlined what he believed were the motives for secession. Only three months had passed since his apolitical circular. Now, he was beginning to identify with the Confederate cause. "I have heard three distinct grounds given for our separation from the Union," the bishop of Natchez wrote. First, "some say the Union was a kind of free association, which any state had the right to forsake whenever she judged it conducive to her interests—the right of secession." Second, others claimed the Union had been a perpetual compact but was rendered null and void by "other parties" (Northern states and abolitionism). Finally, Elder surmised, even if no violation necessitating secession had occurred, the South still possessed "the right of self-preservation," for "it was impossible for us to live in the Union."[34]

Elder did not go beyond "what he had heard." However, the man who later became famous for his public refusal of a prayer request for Abraham Lincoln was a natural Confederate who only became more ardent over time. He believed the Confederacy was the only legitimate government in Mississippi. He counseled his congregants to be good citizens and to support this government, while simultaneously demanding they place spiritual matters before politics. So, too, did the other bishops, many of whom, like the archbishop of Baltimore, tried to remain optimistic. Kenrick wrote to McGill on February 14 declaring he was still "full of hopes for the Union." He added, "Much is due to Old Virginia." If Virginia remained within the United States, war might yet be avoided. In the meantime, he hoped for peace for the simple reason that "folks need to be kept from doing themselves and others harm."[35]

On February 18, when Jefferson Davis was installed as president of the Confederacy's provisional government, it became more likely that folks would do harm. In his inaugural address, Davis argued that the South's separation from the Union was equivalent to the colonists' revolt against Great Britain. Confederate secession was merely exercising a right "the Declaration of Independence of July 4, 1776, defined to be 'inalienable,'" that the consent of the people is the crux on which legitimate government rests. The consent of the people had formed a government and the consent of the people could disband a government. The Confederacy was rightful heir to the heritage of 1776, Davis further claimed, its foundation built on conservatism, agrarianism, and a palpable religiosity attractive to Christians of various denominations, including those desirous of some updated version of Middle Age, pre-capitalist Europe.[36]

On March 2, a pastoral letter by John Quinlan, bishop of Mobile, appeared in the *Charleston Catholic Miscellany.* Quinlan began in step with his brother

bishops' call for peace and unity. He expressed sorrow at the way passions had
gotten out of hand and had led to an irreversible course toward war. He regret-
ted "the dismemberment of this great Republic" and added, "Heaven knows
we would do all we could to legitimately prevent it."[37]

Quinlan then presented his view on what was driving the ongoing crisis. His
contention—unlike Lynch's four-point justification of secession or Elder's three
motives for Southern withdrawal, both of which focused on political and economic issues—was that spiritual matters were the prime cause of disunion. He
was not speaking of some vaguely defined "Christian values" Americans had
drifted away from. Rather, the problem was that America had not fully incorporated the Catholic faith into its political philosophy. The only type of America that could stave off disunion was an authentically Catholic one. Had more
people listened to the Church, there would be no threat of war. "The Catholic
principle," Lynch explained, called for "obedience to the highest recognized authority, and assent, without appeal to its decisions." This was the only method
by which "States rights and Congressional power can move in harmony together." Catholicism was the one necessary ingredient, the glue that could hold
the country together.[38]

While Quinlan was maximally Catholic, he was an ardent Confederate too.
He rejected any reunification that would leave the South, *his South,* in a sub-
servient position to the North. "Better that the instrument of confederation
should be rent in pieces and scattered to the winds than that it should become
a cloak of malice or a bond of iniquity." Quinlan's assent to the reactionary
quality of Southern nationalism was clear: better for the Union to be completely blown up than continue on its current course. Should the South be able
to begin anew on its own, even if this meant rebuilding out of the rubble, the
sadness of this potential reality might be greatly mitigated.[39]

Elder, writing to James Duggan, bishop of Chicago, in February, claimed that
since the Confederacy was the only "government which exists here [Mississippi]
de facto," Catholics were bound, as "good citizens . . . not only to acquiesce in it
but to support it & contribute means & arms & above all to avoid weakening it by
division of counsel without necessity." This positive position on the Confederate
war effort was outside the norm of the usual discourse. The standard counsel
implied Catholics *could* fight, that they were permitted but not required to do so.
Yet in a March 5 letter to Duggan, Elder further cemented his growing Confederatization, agreeing with Jefferson Davis that labeling Confederates *rebels* was
incorrect and that *disloyalty* was not an appropriate term. Elder's subtle evolu-

tion from cool support to clear advocacy was typical of the Southern episcopate and shows how early the bishops Confederatized.[40]

Nonetheless, in a letter to Kenrick at this same time, Elder soon returned to focusing on what Catholic teaching allowed, without overt partisanship. "My course, & I believe the course of my clergy, has been not to recommend secession—but to explain to those who might inquire . . . [that] their religion did not forbid them to advocate it." However, "since secession had been accomplished, I have advised even those who thought it unwise still to support our State government and the new Confederacy—as being the only government which exists here."[41]

In Mississippi as throughout the South, not everyone supported the Confederate nation. There were alternate Souths within the Confederacy, factions large and small, and the fissures took on many forms: the poor versus the rich, the hill country versus the coast, women versus men (see the Southern Bread Riots of 1863). As Stephanie McCurry writes, "the Confederate war ripped liked an earthquake through the foundation of southern life."[42] This true, numerous other historians argue that while contradictions did exist they were sufficiently smoothed over to engender a strong national identity and one adequately resolute to wage four years of war.[43]

Catholic bishops contributed to this process, to the crystallization of the Southern nation. Their pastoral letters, along with general advice to priests and parishioners, helped shape Southern Catholic approaches to the questions of the day, especially for those men who journeyed from the pew to the battlefield. Catholic bishops joined Confederate Protestants in a religiously tinged nation-building process. Furthermore, since a preponderance of white Mississippians were committed Confederates, Elder's point about "existing governments" corresponded to reality; a reality where the vast majority viewed the Confederacy as Mississippi's sole extra-state authority.

On April 11, Spalding wrote prophetically to Purcell: "If a blow be struck at Charleston or Pickens [Pensacola, Florida], we will all be compelled to go out of the Union in less than three months." The next day, Confederate forces, led by Gen. Pierre Gustave Toutant-Beauregard, a Catholic, fired on Fort Sumter in Charleston Harbor. Confederate guns enfiladed the enemy from multiple positions—including Fort Johnson, Fort Moultrie, Cummings Point, and batteries on Sullivan's Island—sending shells on their target every two minutes. By midday, a significant number of the wooden buildings in the fort were on fire. "Quarters in Sumter all burned down," Beauregard wrote to Davis. With no chance of repelling the Confederate assault, at 2:00 P.M. on April 13, Union major Robert Anderson, who, coincidentally, had instructed Beauregard in artillery at West Point, agreed to a truce. Fort Sumter was surrendered the following day.[44]

With many of its citizens watching the bombardment from a variety of vantage points, Charleston erupted into jubilation at the decisive victory. "We write these lines amidst the booming of cannon all over our harbor," the *Charleston Catholic Miscellany,* meaning Lynch, wrote on April 13. "May God in his mercy protect our homes, avenge a righteous cause, and put to speedy flight the hirelings who already occupy, or are on the point of invading, our soil!" Lynch—widely noted for his fervent Confederatization and often thought of as, in precisely the term the newspaper the *New South* once selected, a "hot rebel"—ordered a *Te Deum,* the classic Christian hymn of thanksgiving, sung in the Cathedral of St. John and St Finbar after the fall of Sumter. He did so in gratitude for the Confederate victory and because no life had been lost during the bombardment. There is no reason to doubt Lynch was glad victory had been secured without bloodshed. It is also clear thanksgiving was, in ample measure, for the sweeping triumph attained by the side he believed was providentially guided.[45]

The *Catholic Mirror,* organ of the Archdiocese of Baltimore, assumed a somber tone. It reprinted an excerpt from the *Richmond Whig* titled, "The Horrors of Civil War." Over the coming four years, this dire warning would prove dolorously prescient, as hundreds of thousands of men lost their lives, not to mention the multitudinous other tragedies beyond the scope of statistical analysis. "Those who are investing in epaulettes and swords, and, for the sport they expect from a civil war, are sparing no pains or effort to get one up," the paper noted. But should people get what they want, they would find "civil war abounds more in horror than in pastimes, and that blood and misery, [rather] than pleasure and profit, are its horrible fruits."[46]

Perhaps thinking of horrible fruits to come, Kenrick wrote to Lynch on April 16 expressing the "intense anxiety" that had descended on Baltimore and his enduring hope that "God may spare the country, and grant peace." Intense anxiety was not just a Southern phenomenon. James Frederick Wood, bishop of Philadelphia, wrote Lynch on April 18: "All we can do is pray to God to save us from the dreadful . . . consequences of civil war." On April 21, Spalding told Purcell, "The times are truly awful." Five days later he noted, "Wars & rumours of wars . . . the country is on the verge of dissolution and ruin. *Dona Nobis Pacem!*" "We all deplore the war which threatens to assume a frightful character,"

Kenrick wrote to Hughes. "Life is scarcely desirable if we are to witness the horrors of civil war." Kenrick's words proved tragically accurate. He would die unexpectedly in the summer of 1863, a victim of stress-induced heart failure.[47]

While Fort Sumter was devastating for those hoping for peace, an equally important step toward all-out civil war was Virginia's departure from the Union on April 17. The tipping point had been Lincoln's call for seventy-five thousand volunteers immediately following Anderson's surrender. No less crucial was Robert E. Lee's decision to turn down the American president's offer to command an army called into the field to "enforce the Federal law." Although opposed to secession and war, Lee famously claimed he could not "take part in an invasion of the Southern States." He resigned from the US Army on April 20 and soon thereafter accepted the position of "Commander of the military and naval forces of Virginia," along with the rank of major general. The basis of Archbishop Kenrick's hope for the preservation of the Union, "Old Virginia" refusing to join the seceded states, was dashed.[48]

In May 1861 Bishop Lynch received three letters in six days from his fellow Southern prelates, each written in light of the events at Sumter. On the ninth, Elder explained, "We are continually offering up our prayers for peace. God grant it to us." In this letter, he was as desirous for peace as Kenrick and Spalding. "The times are evil," Elder wrote, and remedies were "only in the hands of God." The "best thing we can do for our country is to go forth to work to sanctify ourselves and our flocks." Had there been "more Saints among us there wd. have been more charity, patience & wisdom & more guidance from God," Elder continued, speculating that maybe Americans would have been spared a coming chastisement. As Elder believed spiritual laxity was a root cause of the conflict, he reciprocally believed religion could most effectively repair the damage, the "active prayer and sanctification of the faithful." On May 12, Lynch heard from Kenrick: "Public spirit is completely crushed." Perhaps Baltimore's archbishop had finally abandoned his hope for peace, realizing the Union could not be saved and that war, one already under way, was inevitable.[49]

The third letter Lynch received, on May 15 from Bishop McGill, was of a different tone. McGill asked for Lynch's advice on the crisis: "This is all *entre nous,* and a mere expression of thoughts which force themselves on my mind." The letter was a stark contrast to McGill's politics-free February pastoral. Chronology was certainly the differentiating factor. In February, the war had not yet begun. In May, it had and it was time to take sides. McGill was now wholly Confederatized. "Give me your views on some of the moral questions presented by the present circumstances of our poor country!" the bishop of Richmond demanded of Lynch. He then posed three questions: was not justice on the side of the South, was not the North acting unconstitutionally, and could a person volunteer in Lincoln's army without this constituting a sin? Why McGill would think enlisting in the Union army could be sinful is initially confusing. The Church took no official position on the war. But viewed from the perspective of his Confederate loyalty, it becomes clear why he would say this.[50]

McGill argued the North came as "an invading enemy." Virginia was under attack, and "I cannot be blind as to which side seeks to domineer and oppress, and which presents just claims." McGill's assertion that he continued to pray and hope for peace might have been sincere, yet, owing to the context, it is unlikely politics was not part of his calculations. By "peaceful arrangement," he did not mean Kenrick or Spalding's peace. His was more in the vein of Lynch or Quinlan's thought, a peace in which the Union allowed the South to go its separate way to begin charting its own national destiny.[51]

Although many Catholic clergymen shared McGill's conviction, the proper balance between church and state had to be maintained. No matter how Confederatized the bishops became, their faith came first. On May 11, Elder published a statement to this effect in the *Charleston Catholic Miscellany*, chastising those who would preach politics from the pulpit. The letter foreshadowed his own defiance of a prayer request for Lincoln later in the war.

> No Catholic, no Irishman of the South need vapor or make a fool of himself to prove his loyalty; and the Catholic priest or Bishop who would read political harangues or military proclamations from his pulpit, or display the Confederate Flag from his steeple, would be suspected of unsound mind. Were any foolish mob to make such a demand, neither priest nor person amongst us would comply it.[52]

Peter Richard Kenrick, the bishop of St. Louis and brother of the archbishop of Baltimore, held similar views. When asked to fly the US flag over his cathedral, he demurred. "No other banner may be placed there, for already there stands one which alone shall stay, the banner of the Church." These attitudes are crucial to understanding the religious prioritization inherent to Catholic Confederatization. As devout Catholics and devoted Confederates, the bishops could appear to have an equal dedication to both causes. But while a prelate might be conspicuous in his support for the Confederacy, there was a spiritual boundary political devotion did not cross.[53]

By the end of May, many clerics were assigning war guilt solely to the North. Bishop Quinlan called for the South going its separate way, permanently. "We must cut adrift from the North," he wrote to Lynch on May 18. "We of the South have been too long on 'leading strings.'" Perché wrote to Elder the following day, saying it was Southern Catholics' "duty to rebuke" a fanatical, abolitionist Catholic clergy in the north and western United States. Elder would eventually hold this position too. On July 16, the feast day of Our Lady of Mount Carmel, he wrote Lynch that Southern clergymen should do "anything we of the South can & ought to . . . to abate the war fever among the clergy & Catholic laity of the North." By this time in the war, only two Southern bishops—Spalding and Whelan of Nashville, for Kenrick had lost hope—still clung to any vestiges of neutrality, uncertainty, caution, or the desire for unconditional peace that had characterized much of the episcopate in late 1860.[54]

A detached, pacific position would become even harder, if not altogether impossible, to hold following the events of July 21, 1861. That day, Union and Confederate forces met near Manassas Junction in northern Virginia. The North struck first, breaking through the Southern lines and sending Confederates fleeing in retreat. The Confederate forces coalesced on a plateau known as Henry Hill House. During the ensuing fight, Gen. Bernard Bee noticed the positional strength of a Virginia Military Institute professor's brigade and encouraged his troops: "There stands [Thomas J.] Jackson, like a stonewall. Rally behind the Virginians!"[55]

Jackson was thus given a new, significantly recognizable, name. Soon after uttering his famous phrase, Bee was mortally wounded. Although he died the following day, his directive was heeded, contributing to the Confederate victory. Intense fighting continued throughout the day. Finally Jackson, at 3:30 P.M., ordered a bayonet charge. It worked, giving the Confederates command of the immediate position. Beauregard then successfully swept the Federals off the field. No pursuit of the Union army followed.[56]

The victory was celebrated as a great military triumph in the South. It was, but its psychological effects were of even higher significance. Following the battle, there could no longer be any doubt that the war would not be some short and tidy affair. "The details of the battle fought on Sunday last are full enough to enable us to judge its result," the *Catholic Mirror* reported on July 27. "We now see that the war which we are waging is one which will task our utmost strength and . . . we cannot hope to escape from it." The *Mirror* did not view the future with hope: "We now see that it is destined that the people of this once happy country should agree together to cast into this fearful fire of civil war, their own lives and the lives of their children."[57]

Soon after First Manassas, a debate over the Civil War, specifically its causes, took place between Bishop Lynch and Archbishop Hughes. With his "Letter of the Bishop of Charleston," published on August 4, Lynch instigated the exchange. "All the hopes cherished last spring of a peaceful solution have vanished before the dread realities of war," he began, before asking, "What is still before us?" He predicted a massive, all-out war, with the two belligerent sections "marshaling hundreds of thousands of men" against one another. Who was to blame? Lynch argued, "Responsibility falls, should fall, on those who rendered the conflict unavoidable."[58]

"The South years ago, and a hundred times, declared that the triumph of the abolition or anti-slavery policy would break up the Union," Lynch wrote. Most grievous was the "dogged obstinacy of the Black Republicans at Washington [who] last winter made all the South secessionists." Referencing the popular southern position that secession was externally triggered by inflammatory abolitionist rhetoric, Lynch soon moved his argument into the economic realm. "Even a child could see the vast benefits to all from this cooperation," he stated, adding that Southern production of cotton, tobacco, sugar, and rice, when coupled with Northern manufacturing and grain generation, produced a system of mutual harmony and prosperity.[59]

The Union, "taking up anti-slavery, making it a religious dogma, and carrying it into politics," had caused disunion and war. "What could the South do but consult its own safety by withdrawing from the Union?" Lynch asked, faced with "unconstitutional laws and every mode of annoying and hostile action," the culmination of which was Lincoln's election. Remaining in the Union would mean cowing to the North's "tame submission." The South "desired to withdraw in peace," but the war had been thrust upon it. And this war, "unnecessary in the beginning, will only bring ruin to thousands in its prosecution. It will be fruitless of any good." Lynch finished:

> At its conclusion . . . the parties will stand apart exhausted and embittered by it;
> for every battle, however won or lost, will have served but to widen the chasm
> between the North and South, then to render more difficult, if not impossible,

any future reconstruction. This mode of attacking the South can effect nothing beyond the loss of life it will entail. . . . The separation of the Southern States is un fait accompli. The Federal Government has no power to reverse it. . . . Why preface the recognition by a war equally needless and bloody? Men at the North may regret the rupture as men at the South may do. The Black Republicans overcame the first at the polls, and would not listen to the second in Congress. . . . They are responsible. . . . [L]et those who voted the Black Republican ticket shoulder their muskets and bear the responsibility. Let them not send Irishmen to fight in their stead when . . . they care little which of the combatants destroys the other.[60]

Lynch's final remarks are a standard defense of the Southern position, save for a tiny addition at the end, one speaking to Catholic North-South spiritual unity. Lynch argued that not only was the Union at fault for the war, the war was tragically pointless because countless lives would be lost in futile resistance to the inevitability of permanent separation. The Union's sole course of action was to allow the South to go in peace before all this came to pass. Yet should the North fail to perceive common sense, Lynch claimed, Catholics would be among the primary sufferers, in particular Northern Irishmen, who would be sent to their deaths by the thousands in the name of a hostile Republican ideology. Father John Bannon, on his diplomatic mission to Ireland, employed the same argument: the North, replete with anti-Catholic and anti-Irish bigotry, wanted Irishmen simply for cannon fodder, to be the advance guard in winning a war that would simultaneously eliminate them.

Lynch's complaints about "Black Republicans" were especially indicative of his full immersion in secessionist rhetoric. "We call the attention of our citizens of the Catholic faith . . . and warn them against the incendiary principles which form the future programme of the *Black Republican party,*" the *Memphis Daily Appeal* wrote in an article titled "The Catholic Church to Be Assailed by the Black Republicans." For Northern politicians, slave emancipation was only a step toward the ultimate goal of ridding America of Catholicism. "We will get after that other abomination, the Catholic church, and drive it out," the paper added, quoting an unnamed "leading" Republican. "We shall then have a free and Protestant North."[61]

Archbishop Hughes's reply came three weeks later, on August 23.[62] He thanked Lynch for his letter, surprised mail routes had remained intact, as in "happier years," when all states had found meaning in the words *E Pluribus*

Unum. Hughes met Lynch on common ground, claiming to be an advocate for states' rights and agreeing, for example, that neither South Carolina nor Massachusetts had any right to interfere in the other state's internal affairs. Yet those same states gave consent to a Federal government and its laws by signing the Constitution. This was a free choice, uncoerced. No state had the right to secede on a whim, and certainly not under the arbitrary reasons Lynch stated. It was "a great mistake," Hughes asserted, to assume "the Federal Government and the people of the North are determined to conquer and subjugate" the seceded states. The South was in rebellion and so needed to manufacture victimization to rationalize its actions. "I would say that the mind of the North looks only to the purpose of bringing back the seceded States to their organic condition," Hughes concluded, "ante bellum."[63]

Lynch and Hughes's exchange well illustrates how American Catholic bishops understood allegiance. Just as the Church did not split over slavery, it did not differ in spiritual matters. Lynch and Hughes equally, indiscriminately, and consistently discharged the religious duties of their episcopal station. As Catholic bishops, they were practically indistinguishable. Politically they were at odds, with each man's decision to side with his respective section a natural choice.

On September 9, Bishop Verot presented a pastoral letter, returning once more to the theme of a sin-induced national calamity. "We feel it a duty incumbent on us to exhort you to earnest and frequent prayer," he wrote, "in view of the calamitous times which have come upon us." Everywhere there was "grief, distress, misery, and intense suffering." Verot encouraged his congregation to "pour fervent supplications to the throne of grace, that the Almighty may shorten the days of our affliction, quell the waves that have risen against us and threaten to engulph us, and grant to us once more the blessings of an honorable, lasting peace." For Verot—as for Lynch, McGill, Quinlan, Elder, and the majority of the Confederatized episcopate and laity—"honorable" had become as important as "peace." Verot further believed the war was punishment for a people gone astray, yet Southerners, Catholics and Protestants, differed from Northerners in identifying what sins were to blame. For the North, Southerners' societal cornerstone (as CSA vice president Alexander Stephens infamously put it) was the primary sin, and many believed there would be no peace without this issue's final resolution.[64]

Peace was a constant hope for American Catholics, including those overseas. Thomas Sim Lee, a nineteen-year-old Marylander studying at the North

American College in Rome, who would be ordained a priest in 1866, wrote his father in November 1861 with this in mind. Lee began his letter in high spirits, explaining that Rome was "a very good place" for someone studying for the Church, as "the richest marbles and the finest paintings" adorned the churches and art and culture was in the very air he breathed. But, Rome and America were each enveloped in peril, and this pervaded his thoughts even more. "When I came here nine months ago," Lee wrote, "Rome was in as much danger as Washington is at present. . . . God send a speedy peace to America!"[65]

Many Catholics in America still held out hope God would indeed send this speedy peace, and soon. Even into autumn 1861, with nearly half a year having passed since Fort Sumter, Catholics in Leonard Town, Maryland, declared their intentions via the local newspaper, *Saint Mary's Beacon.* Maryland Catholics—of whom another paper would declare one year hence: "The[y] are almost unanimous for the South"—were, at this moment in time, of one mind concerning war: "peace first, peace last, peace ever."[66] This because war would bring despotism upon a fractured Union, as many would suffer as a result, especially the poor, but above all "because it is in consonance with the interests, and teachings, and charities, of our Holy Church—and peace, because the Divine Spouse hath said: 'Blessed are the peace-makers, for they shall see God.'"[67]

As the war's first year drew to a close, another type of disaster struck Bishop Lynch's Charleston diocese. In December, a fire broke out on the Cooper waterfront and strong winds soon swept the conflagration into the city. As Lynch went to warn the residents at the Convent of the Sisters of Our Lady of Mercy, soldiers rushed to assist frenzied citizens. There was no time to address the fire in the Cathedral. Lynch's residence and the seminary library were also destroyed, along with the bishop's miter, crozier, vestments, and the many personal valuables congregants stored within.[68]

Miraculously, no one died, which is truly remarkable, considering that 540 acres in Charleston, along with 575 homes, were affected by the fire. Unfortunately for Lynch and the diocese, the church's insurance policy had lapsed. Nothing was covered. Jefferson Davis sent a message to the Confederate Congress in response to the fire, "recommending an appropriation for the sufferers." Congress committed $250,000 toward this purpose, but, even with this help, and more to come in the future, Lynch would spend the rest of his life working to recover the near half-million dollars' worth of damage. In a letter from December 23, 1861, Verot wrote that he could not properly express "how much the calamity which has fallen upon you has afflicted me." In Augusta, Georgia, Verot took up a collection that netted $370. The money was enclosed with this letter, along with Verot's promise to solicit similar charity in Macon, Columbus, and Atlanta.[69]

At the conclusion of 1861, the war had reached an impasse. Secession had not resulted in amicable separation; secession was not an isolated action but a legitimate region-wide movement, one having birthed a de facto nation regardless of the lack of official recognition from the North and other countries. The hope that peace could still be attained following Fort Sumter was lost when Virginia seceded. First Manassas was an eye-opening battle, removing lingering notions that the war would be any combination of short, bloodless, or gamelike. For all its moving parts—political and military, social and religious—1861 ended without anything resolved, save that the war was here to stay. Union soldier James B. McPherson was right, and among the few prescient prognosticators, when he wrote to his friend, Confederate soldier E. P. Alexander, following Fort Sumter that both sides were in "deadly earnest" and primed to fight until "the bitter end."[70]

The Southern episcopate was sympathetic to the Southern cause. The bishops largely identified with their surrounding culture. Lynch is perhaps the best example of this. He was Confederatized from the start of the conflict, even before it, actively celebrating South Carolina's secession and the events at Fort Sumter. His brief article in the *Charleston Catholic Miscellany* following his state's secession in December 1860, similar to his two letters to Archbishop Hughes in January and August 1861, employed arguments for secession and defenses of the Southern position that could have been written by any rabid Confederate. Lynch was indeed a rabid Confederate, his views standard Confederate fare because he, like the majority of Southern Catholics, was a standard Confederate.

Even when much of the Southern episcopate watched the unfolding events of late 1860 and early 1861 with something of a spiritual detachment, desiring peace regardless of political outcome, the bishops openly joined in supporting the Confederacy once the war began. Elder, the model for Catholic Confederatization's prioritization of the spiritual over the political, progressed from penning a November 1860 circular solely spiritual in nature to, three months later, claiming the United States had no authority in Mississippi while encouraging Mississippians to be loyal citizens and fight for their new nation.

McGill quickly moved from a February 1861 pastoral letter focused on preparing his congregants for Lent to three months later telling Lynch he plainly saw the righteousness of the Southern cause and that fighting for the North, an "invading enemy," was sinful. Even the truly pacific bishops, Spalding and Kenrick, who actively hoped for peace longer than anyone else, supported the South and did not always keep this out of view. Throughout the war, the bishops, who began the balancing act between their faith and their politics during the secession crisis, remained deeply attuned to the daily workings and cause of their new country.

CHAPTER TWO

Confederatization on the Battlefield

Catholic Chaplains and Soldiers, 1862–1864

"Before them let the nations tremble at the subjugation of the South, and Archbishop Hughes prepares to chant the requiem of the Catholic church!" blared a *Memphis Daily Appeal* article in November 1862. The fates of the Confederacy and Catholicism were linked, with the Western Hemisphere's social and religious structures hanging in the balance. Should the Union triumph, "Mexico and Cuba will follow after the South; Catholicity will perish in America; and Catholics will be known in the empire only as helots and peons!!"[1]

Even if Catholic chaplains and soldiers did not share such alarmism, they worked feverishly to prevent the above scenario, or any other type of Union victory. One of these men was John Bannon. During the siege of Vicksburg, Bannon worked with an artillery team, assisting with a variety of duties, including firing the cannon himself. He was willing to join the Confederate defenses even though as a priest he was expressly forbidden to use weapons in any capacity. Bannon was maximally Confederatized from the start of the war to the end. He volunteered to join the cause and served as both chaplain and diplomat.[2]

And yet, this same man who believed his side was fighting a crusade against Yankee infidels was above all a devout Catholic. Bannon, who "joked and laughed with them [the troops]" before battle, found his action largely consisting of ministering to "the dying on the battlefield." He was a priest whose first concern was saving souls, one who spent countless hours in the confessional, baptized the living and the nearly dead by the hundreds, and for every projectile loosed from his hands, a crucifix or a Bible passed through a thousand times more. How could a priest fire cannons at the enemy while otherwise spending the majority of his time dispensing the sacraments and tending to men's spiritual needs? How could a man participate in trying to end the lives of an enemy whom, if he found near death, he would do all in his power to prepare him to die, politics left aside? The answer lies in the devout Catholic-devoted Confederate Confederatization paradigm, to be explored over chapters 2 and 3.[3]

Chaplains demonstrated their Confederatization by assuming the same hardships as soldiers. They endured long marches over rough terrain, extreme weather, food shortages, and the ever-present specter of death. Many identified with the Confederacy's reactionary ideological blueprint. In the Confederacy, they imagined a nation embodying Western Civilization's best qualities, an authentic America in line with the Founders' original ideas, set upon a Christian foundation.

Catholic soldiers by and large chose to fight and die for the Southern cause. Many joined the armed forces long before conscription was enacted and thus showed their Confederatization in perhaps the most straightforward way possible. To fight was the natural choice. As to precisely *why* they chose to fight, historian James M. McPherson explained it best: "The motives of many volunteers were mixed in a way that was impossible for them to disentangle in their own minds." A plurality of factors funneled into a somewhat cohesive group identity, and this, combined with myriad other personal factors, ultimately led them to join the Confederacy.[4]

Six men play central roles in this chapter: chaplains Bannon, James Sheeran, and Louis-Hippolyte Gache and the soldiers John Dooley, Felix Pierre Poche, and Henri Garidel, though, naturally, other chaplains and soldiers appear throughout. At times, the soldiers are presented en masse, the findings drawn from group rather than individual experience. Where the concentration of Catholic soldiers was high, at large outdoor Masses for example, one can see a united religious fabric and infer a communal spiritual intention.

In sum, soldiers and chaplains were deeply involved in, and passionately supported, the Confederate nation. This chapter shows various ways this fealty manifested, from the basic—volunteering to fight, volunteering for the chaplaincy—to the more nuanced, at times even complex, intellectual defenses of the Southern position, this alongside plentiful anti-Northern polemics. Catholics' vitriolic attitude toward the enemy was as potent as any other Confederates for, as the following exposition lays bare, Confederatization was a passionate, if not obsessive, attachment to an ideal Catholics readily signed up to defend and die for.

Although small in number, Southern Catholics heartily supported the Southern cause. They were, in other words, highly Confederatized. In Mississippi, it was not long before nearly every congregation had members serving in the Confederate army. A priest reported to Bishop Elder that twelve married men from his congregation volunteered for service, willingly leaving behind wives and children to fight for their country. Seminarians interrupted their theological studies to fight; physicians in training put residencies on hold to fight; even underage Mississippi Catholics—such as fourteen-year-old Dennis Mulvihill and thirteen-year-old Baldasero Genasci—fabricated stories, or simply ran away from home, to join the fight.[5]

Such patriotic enthusiasm was not unique to Mississippi. A contingent of Southern Catholic students at Georgetown resigned en masse in the spring of 1861, informing Father John Early, "Our presence here any longer would be attended but with little good to us, for . . . our County (the Confederacy), our parents and our brethren call loudly upon our presence at our respective homes." Catholics in Georgia "heartily supported the war." In Louisiana, the Mettoyer family of Cane River, French Catholic *gens de couleur libre,* supported the "doomed cause of the Confederacy" like any other planters, regardless of skin color, and likewise suffered "the depredations of war." Many French Jesuits supported the war because they believed Catholic participation would heighten the social profile of Southern Catholics and improve their social position. And approximately 70 percent of all Irishmen in the South—the region's largest Catholic ethnic group, numbering about 139,000 persons, with many viewing *Irish* as synonymous with *Catholic*—served in the Confederate army.[6]

Nonetheless, even with so many Southern Catholic laymen entering the Confederate service, firsthand accounts are scarce. With thousands of Catholic soldiers in the Confederate ranks, a representative analysis is difficult at best.[7] As such, this chapter focuses on a handful of chaplains and soldiers and how they understood the relationship between their faith and their service to the Confederacy. The narrative keeps to a chronological structure but is thematic in approach and moves freely between the eastern and western theaters. Quality has been selected over quantity, with the goal being a documentary-style window into the life of the Catholic-Confederate soldier and chaplain, a "day in the life" of these six men extrapolated over the course of the war.

For Father John Bannon, Southerners were nothing less than "crusaders" fighting a "holy war" in defense of their homes and families. Why not then support this cause personally? And so Bannon left St. Louis in December 1861, wearing a false beard to avoid Federal authorities, before joining the First Missouri as its Catholic chaplain. Bannon made an immediate impression, soon being found "everywhere in the midst of the battle when the fire was heaviest and the bullets thickest." Because he believed "no men fight more bravely than Catholics who approach the sacraments before battle," he willingly exposed himself to danger in order to bring men closer to God, providing Holy Communion and Confession amid heavy gunfire and bursting shells. This single-minded dedication led a non-Catholic Confederate general to call him "the greatest soldier I ever saw." Regarding his own bravery, Bannon was modest and unperturbed. "If I am killed, I am not afraid to meet my fate. I am in God's keeping. His holy will be done."[8]

In February 1862, a time when the Union army had attained signal victories in Tennessee at Forts Henry and Donelson followed by the capture of Nashville on the twenty-third, one day after Jefferson Davis was elected to a six-year term as Confederate president, the Church leadership in the South was busy trying to furnish chaplains like Bannon for the many Catholics within the army. Twenty-eight chaplains, out of a South-wide total of 278 priests, would serve during the war. All of these men were well educated, often beyond the university level. For their service, Southern chaplains were paid fifty dollars a month.[9]

Two of them, Sheeran and Gache, were as committed to the Confederacy as Bannon. Sheeran once encountered a Union prisoner who claimed he did not support Lincoln. He was fighting only to uphold the Constitution. For Sheeran, this stance was problematic. "My parting advice," he wrote, was "before going to bed every night try and recall to your memory the number of times Abe Lincoln has perjured himself by violating the Constitution since his introduction into office." "Then," he added, "put your hand to your breast and ask yourself in the presence of God if in fighting for your perjured President, you are fighting for the Constitution of your country."[10]

Another time, Sheeran castigated a prisoner from New York for saying he had joined the Union ranks to "put down this rebellion, and I will fight till I die for the flag of my country!" "I told him plainly that such talk was mere nonsense," Sheeran noted, because there was "*no* Union" to fight for and no rebellion to put down. The Southern people were "merely defending their national and constitutional rights." For Sheeran, the Confederacy was no rebel sect but a sovereign nation, one acting in accord with the prerogatives flowing from that status. In a parting blow, he added that he did not believe the New Yorker's pledge to die for the American flag was sincere, considering "his present condition as a prisoner showed that he did not mean what he said."[11]

Gache once claimed that pursuing retreating Federal troops was "the greatest thrill of my life," while gleefully reveling in the sight of "shells exploding in the midst of those confused and terrified troops." Gache's service to wounded men, particularly in the spiritual realm, is without question, but he did not always leave off politics when engaged in religious duties. He was once relieved when a dying Union Catholic soldier told him he was "a Democrat too"; thus he "had done nothing to merit Southern wrath."[12]

In the midst of a sacred priestly duty, preparing a dying soldier to meet God, Gache was so invested in Southern politics he could not restrain expressing "relief" that this Northerner was not also an abolitionist—as if such a thing could matter at that moment. But for Gache, it did. For many Catholics, chaplains and soldiers alike, it did. Nonetheless, this is one of a sparse collection of examples involving a priest bringing politics into the sacramental realm. Even the most Confederatized priests almost always abstained from political discourse when dispensing the sacraments.

For chaplains, as George Rable notes, "it came down to a willingness to live with soldiers and share their hardships." Sheeran, once described as "the most dedicated of Southern patriots," slept in the same places soldiers did, often the ground of a battlefield; marched alongside them; and partook of their rough fare. He once reflected, while "laying down on a bed of gravel" to sleep, that for inspiration he wished to think of "those heroes of mortification, whose names adorn the calendar of the Church." He mentioned Saint Rose of Lima, who chose a "log of wood for a pillow and the bare ground for a couch." "Happy would we have been or at least thought ourselves that night had we a round log for a pillow, or smooth ground for a bed," Sheeran wrote. "Just think of it! A sharp fence rail under your head and rocks from the size of an egg to that of a cannon ball under the wearied body." Sheeran conceded his mediations were profitless because he "considered these very mortifications as child's play compared with what Confederate soldiers had to endure and I, of course, among the latter."[13]

In these moments, Sheeran fused the Confederate cause to his Catholic faith. To serve God was to fight for the Confederacy, and vice versa. Such proclamations were not unique to Sheeran. Garidel once plainly noted in his diary, "God is on our side. I am sure that ours is a just cause." After Mass, having just gone to confession and received Holy Communion, Poche, now "prostrate at the altar of my Saviour," offered special prayers that "the justice of God" would be satisfied by the Confederacy—"our young nation[, which] has suffered enough"—being granted "her independence and an honorable peace."[14]

These men often raised battlefield sufferings to an almost spiritual level, arguing that to fight and die for the Confederacy was to fulfill a religious as well as a political duty. Sheeran believed he and Southern soldiers were almost saints in the making, the bearers of a type of dual redemptive suffering for God and country. Many Southerners, Catholics included, began to see the Confederacy as a new Israel, a chosen people providentially guided. When considering how old this idea is within the American intellectual tradition, dating back to Winthrop's "City on a Hill," it is readily apparent why the Confederacy imagined its restorationist revolution to be more continuum than rupture.

Sheeran once recounted the story of an Irishman named Pennyman, a "dyed in the wool" unionist, who claimed he could demonstrate, using mathematical calculations, why the North would conquer the South. Sheeran didn't explain how this proceeded. He did write, however, that he was the one who provided adequate support for his position, proving to Pennyman that the North had as much right to coerce the South into remaining in the Union as England could justifiably dominate Ireland. He then chastised Pennyman, a Virginia immigrant, to "obey the laws of your adopted State. . . . But should you not feel disposed to take this advice, take a trip to the North and never come back."[15]

Gache shared Sheeran's penchant for anti-Northern spiels. In a letter to the Reverend Phillipe de Carriere, his colleague at Spring Hill College in Mobile, Gache wrote, "The Yankees are just no good," and he could not "abide them." For Gache, a *Yankee* was not just a Northerner fighting for the Union but anyone opposed to Southern values and the Confederacy. For some unspecified reason, he suspected Carriere of Yankee sympathies: "Make haste to become once more a true and loyal Southerner." Unsatisfied with Carriere's progress, Gache wrote again two months later. He expressed his disappointment in learning that Carriere, whom he had thought was "only a skin deep Yankee," was in fact "a double-dyed Yankee . . . right to the very substance of his soul." Carriere was all but anathema to him, reprobate not from the religion each held in common but from the political cause to which Gache cleaved so dearly.[16]

That Confederates had nothing good to say about Northerners, or the Union, is not news. It is one of the most obvious and banal facts of the war. But that acerbic language is found so *plentifully* in the writings of Southern Catholic chaplains and soldiers serves as further evidence of their Confederatization. According to John Dooley, the North was "the land [led] by a party of brutal men, uneducated, unrefined, unprincipled, inhuman, criminal, and perjured." Yankees were fanatics and brutes, and to be a "friend of Yankeedom" one had to likewise be fanatical, brutal, and, above all, hypocritical. Sheeran once described a squad of Union prisoners as "these unfortunate subjects of King Abe

1st." Poche ridiculed Lincoln as "[King] Abraham 1st," other sobriquets including "very illustrious father Abraham I" and "his majesty." Union soldiers were "Yankee vandals" or "infernal Yankees," not content to fight the Confederate army but bent on persecuting the average Southern citizen at every opportunity.[17]

Conversely, Poche openly proclaimed his Confederate patriotism. He referred to himself as a "rebel" and a "good Confederate," while gushing with pride that his sixteen-year-old brother, Clidamont, had joined the Confederate service, evidence that he had become "a good Confederate and excellent patriot." Poche once claimed to have greatly enjoyed a dinner because his hosts were women who had "always [been] good Confederates." Another soiree did not receive his approval because the hosts, although providers of "a good dinner," were "still most ignorant, benighted," and, worse still, "unpatriotic." Poche would term Lincoln's assassination "consoling news." Dooley would refer to the late US president as the "monster [who] was got rid of."[18]

Union forces, led by Adm. David Farragut, whom Garidel called a "scoundrel," captured New Orleans in April 1862. "The reported occupation of New Orleans by the Federal troops is now fully confirmed," the *Catholic Mirror* noted laconically. Mary Ann Murphy, a New Orleans girl who would become Sister Marietta of the Sisters of Loretto, surmised that Northern control of her city, with Gen. Benjamin F. Butler in command, signaled a time when "the clouds grew darker" in the South. It is well known that Southerners detested the man whom they derisively nicknamed "Spoons" (for his supposed appetite for pilfering the silverware of New Orleans' wealthy, now occupied, class) or "Beast."[19] Garidel mockingly referred to him as "celebrated" and questioned the general's courage, recalling that during a charge Butler was sure to be found "very far behind his troops because he isn't man enough to take the lead. He should try it so that we may capture him and drag the wretched coward to Richmond."[20]

By June 1862, Mary Ann Murphy's "dark clouds" grew darker still, with the Western Confederacy almost fully occupied by the Union. When Memphis fell on June 6, Vicksburg remained the lone major Western city still in Confederate hands. Portions of Alabama and Mississippi, much of Tennessee, and all of Kentucky were Union possessions before the summer got under way. The Confederate military apparatus was desperate to enlist any help it could find to aid an undersupplied army deficient in munitions. Thus, an article appeared in the *Memphis Daily Appeal* advertising "Church Bells for Cannon." It was a follow-up to a previous declaration that Gen. P. G. T. Beauregard had requested church bells be melted down into weaponry. The appeal—whether owing to the Catholic clergy's Confederate patriotism or to the fact that the request was being made by a Catholic general, perhaps both—was successful, and "responded to with great alacrity. The right spirit, we perceive, is amongst our clergy."[21]

With Catholics leading this project and Protestants sure to join in, the *Daily Appeal* continued, "Can the South, the great South, be conquered or subjugated under these feelings of patriotism and devotion? Surely not." Church bells had "been consecrated with great solemnity to the service of God. They can never be used again for secular purposes unless, from motives of the greatest public urgency . . . from this it will be seen how great a sacrifice is made and how loyal a spirit exists among such an influential body of men." A subsequent article in the same newspaper noted, "The Catholic clergy of New Orleans have sent word to Gen. Beauregard that the bells of every Catholic church in New Orleans are at his disposal, to recast into cannon."[22]

Former church bells flying into enemy lines notwithstanding, it was events in the eastern theater that ultimately saved the Confederacy from defeat and disintegration. Once again, as at First Manassas, Stonewall Jackson played a critical role. His famous Valley Campaign stymied the North's plan of attack and compelled Lincoln to reroute troops earmarked for the Peninsula to the Shenandoah Valley. When Jackson arrived in eastern Virginia, in late June 1862, Robert E. Lee had assumed command of the Army of Northern Virginia. Lee turned the tide almost immediately, ending the Peninsula Campaign a month later. He then marched northward. By August, the Confederacy was fighting in northern Virginia, eyeing an invasion into Union territory.[23]

Dooley's and Sheeran's war journals both begin at this time, in August 1862. Dooley's first action was at the Battle of Cedar Mountain (August 8, a Confederate victory). Gache was also at Cedar Mountain. One evening, under the orders of Stonewall Jackson, who "was perfectly aware of the situation," Confederate troops embarked on a nighttime march through "a rather thick forest of pine and oak." Jackson knew there was a considerable force of Union soldiers hiding in the forest and so instructed his men to keep marching as if unaware, as if playing right into a Union ambush, while "he brought three pieces of artillery up from the rear and placed these in a hidden position."[24]

The fight soon commenced. "For thirty minutes bombs and shells were bursting in all parts of the woods. I won't go so far as to say that our shells fell as thick as hailstones, but during the entire time of the bombardment few of their troops could enjoy a single moment of safety," Gache explained to Carriere. "The affair was a success in every respect, except that the gathering darkness and the thickness of the trees prevented us from enjoying the sight of Yankees fleeing in panic from the very place where they hoped to entrap us."[25]

Later that month, Sheeran and Dooley were present at the important Battle of Second Manassas. For the still-green Dooley, the battle was filled with equal parts excitement and terror. He recalled the three days as replete with an intense sun, a burning heat. The smell of gunpowder was everywhere, and he was possessed by an acute personal fear. "Oh, how scared I felt! If I could only stay out of the fight with honor how gladly I would have done so!" Although Union troops couldn't see Dooley and his men, "they keep *a-feeling* for us." Not a pleasant thought, he wrote, especially when considering the high odds of being shot at any time. Dooley did not see much direct action. He did, however, witness the dread realities of war. "At every step" there were "piles of wounded and slain and their feet are slipping in the blood and brains of their comrades."[26] Gache had similar comments the week before: "I was overwhelmed by a profound sadness: so many men only a few hours before so full of life now lying wounded, mutilated and grotesquely contorted: some dead; some in their last agony; some struggling desperately for life; some still fully conscious and therefore able to suffer more keenly, were calling out for doctors, for wound dressers; for something to drink, for help."[27]

Sheeran's account of Second Manassas is rich in detail. "I was not long . . . in discovering the object of Jackson's visit to Manassa [*sic*]," he wrote on August 27, a day before the battle opened. It was all about provisions, stored on a parked train filled with a cornucopia of foodstuffs and supplies, a golden opportunity for famished and impoverished Southern soldiers to fill their stomachs and exchange their rags for something more resembling clothes. "Just imagine about 6000 men hungry and almost naked," Sheeran explained, "let loose on some million dollars worth of biscuit, cheese, ham, bacon, messpork, coffee, sugar, tea, fruit, brandy, wine, whiskey, oysters; coats, pants, shirts, caps, boots, shoes, socks, blankets, tents etc. etc." In a scene that "beggars description," Sheeran reported crowds of Confederate soldiers emerging from railway cars dressed in Federal army uniforms, wagoners and ambulance drivers with new equipment, and surgeons helping themselves to medicine and medical instruments. "I had often read of the sacking of cities by a victorious army," Sheeran noted, "but never did I hear of a railroad train being sacked."[28]

The army was "in a desperate condition" on the first day of the battle. And it was not just Gen. John Pope whom Confederates would have to contend with; possible reinforcements might come from the surrounding environs at any time to join the fight. Even still, "our men felt confident that Jackson knew his business and gave themselves no concern." Sheeran, stationed at a field hospital, took it upon himself to be something of a watchdog against lackluster troops. "I felt it my duty to rebuke them for their straggling propensities," he wrote. Yet, "when I looked down and saw some of these poor fellows barefooted, I felt more disposed to pity than scold." Sheeran tried to get as close to the action as possible. He ignored a Confederate general's order to fall back and rode out over the battlefield, between the opposing lines to see "if I could recognize any of our dead." He was then mistaken for a Confederate officer and suffered a close call. "A shell . . . passed directly over my head, and burst some hundred yards in advance." There was little time for reflection, for "another fearful missile" was fired in his direction, at which point he put his horse into full gallop "with a speed surpassing even any of Stonewall's flank movements," escaping into the woods while being chased by a hail of Union gunfire.[29]

Second Manassas was a decisive Confederate victory. On August 28, future Catholic convert Gen. James Longstreet arrived on the field in support of Jackson. The combined Confederate forces "fell upon the enemy with a savage ferocity," Sheeran noted. Afterward, "Gen. Lee began to make arrangements for a general engagement." The next day, Sheeran recorded the success of this effort. "About half an hour before dark we heard the glad tidings that the Yankees were flying in every direction, the battle was fought and the victory won." Making the usual post-battle hospital rounds, he wrote, "Never did men accomplish more, suffer more, and complain less."[30]

Lee's victory sent Pope and his army into retreat toward Washington. The US capital was stricken with panic. Many were beginning to see Lee as invincible, commanding an unstoppable force methodically marching northward toward inevitable victory. Returning soldiers gave hyperbolic accounts of great destruction, extra weapons and money were sent to New York as reinforcement against possible Southern attacks, and the fear of an imminent Confederate takeover was in the air. Jefferson Davis had earlier predicted Maryland, arguably the most pro-Southern Union state, would soon join the Confederacy. This was never closer to realization than following Second Manassas. Nothing was more indicative of Confederate prowess than the first Northern invasion. To date, the war had been contested exclusively on Southern soil, in Mississippi, Tennessee, Louisiana, and Virginia. Now it would be fought in Union territory.[31]

The Confederate army entered Maryland in September. Initially, Dooley saw the reception in Frederick as hostile. He reasoned this was because people were either outright unionists or afraid and therefore reluctant to display their Confederate sympathies. However, "many in Frederick [were] bold enough to cheer as we passed, feeling that we were the last representatives of free government." Dooley speculated that Marylanders believed if the Confederacy fell, "the right of self government or the rights of States and peoples to govern themselves would fall with us," and a "despotism more galling than any tyranny of Europe would be forced upon the land."[32]

Many newspapers would concur with Dooley's sentiments. The *Daily Confederate,* of Raleigh, North Carolina, claimed the Union was using slavery as a cover for a war on religion. "Religious freedom on this continent owes much to the South," the paper stated, "for had not Yankee fanaticism had slavery to combat, it would long since have been engaged in a life and death crusade against the Catholic rebellion." The North wished to impose upon the South "a tyranny more cruel and debasing than any that Europe has ever experienced." The Winston, North Carolina, *Western Sentinel* published a bluntly titled article: "Subjugation: What May Be Expected." The stakes were as large as they were simple: complete victory or complete servitude. "Nothing can be more certain than that we have before us either a complete military success in the war, or else the full measure of Poland's and of Ireland's grinding oppression and emaciating humiliation."[33]

Supposed "Yankee subjugation," especially pursuant to religious freedom, was an ever-present fear among Southerners, Catholics and non-Catholics alike. The Meridian, Mississippi, *Daily Clarion* saw "arrogant, subversive and really infidel" designs within Union war aims directed toward "subordinat[ing] the spiritual to the temporal." This "must shock in serious collision, not merely the large body of Roman Catholics," the paper noted, but "every Christian organization that claims for itself anything like dignity or sacredness in rite or discipline." While Sheeran did not express Dooley and the Southern press's fears, he did share their undiluted Confederate partisanship. "I grieved to think," he wrote, "that a Union, which was once the political idol of my soul, was now shattered forever." It had fallen into such abject disrepair because liberty had been employed as a "cloak for their disorganizing principles." The Union had "enkindled the fires of social and political discord." It alone was to blame for everything.[34]

Sheeran rejoiced at seeing the Confederate flag flying in Frederick and re-counted a humorous story concerning a local woman arguing with a Confed-erate soldier, he having "probably drunk *more* than was necessary," claiming he had stolen bacon from her. The woman proudly announced she was a "*Union-ist,* and must not be imposed on by any Confederate rebel." Sheeran aimed to impartially investigate the matter, but soon the woman soon changed her story and declared she had been mistaken about the supposed theft. "I told her she should not be so uncharitable as to accuse any person" of such a crime "but we would be willing to forgive her if she would give three cheers for Jeff Davis." While she refused to do so, Sheeran reported leaving her "in better humor."[35]

Frederick was a beautiful city, Sheeran explained. And he was grateful for a good supper, a clean shirt, and a hot, soapy bath, "luxuries I had not enjoyed for over three weeks." Staying that night with Jesuits, as opposed to his famil-iar place on the ground of a battlefield, he wrote, "I found myself within the peaceful walls of a convent. Before me was the image of my crucified Savior, near me was that of His Immaculate Mother."[36]

The Battle of Sharpsburg (Antietam) was fought less than two weeks later, September 14–17, 1862. The South's failure there, and subsequent retreat, ended the first invasion of the North and threw a cog in Lee's war machine. The fighting was legendarily brutal. Dooley recounted the battle as a frightening mélange of explosions, frayed nerves, and horror. As the Union army barraged the city on September 16, he wrote, "The men around me said it was the severest shelling they had ever witnessed. Every shell went screaming, whistling, whining over our heads, and not a few burst near by us." He confessed that as he had never seen something like this before, the spectacle was "perfectly thrilling."[37]

Dooley's journal is full of reflections like this. He demonstrated his Con-federatization by not just volunteering to fight but doing so with passion, al-most joy. He "gave his best" at soldiering, no empty platitude in a war filled with many who shirked battle, straggled behind, or even deserted. Even when Dooley was scared—and he often was—he seemed a natural soldier, and if not fully at home on the battlefield, eager to do his part. He also demonstrated his Confederatization in near-groveling estimations of Robert E. Lee. It is no secret Southerners liked Lee, Southern Catholics no less than others. Gache called Lee "Our 'Great Man' *par excellence* . . . he'll be our second president, provided the Good Lord spares his life and provided our republic lives beyond its infancy." Lee was an Episcopalian, yet "very favorable toward Catholics and he has the greatest esteem for them." Dooley took these sentiments much further. Lee was the Confederacy's "Beloved Leader." Who, he asked, "does not love Gen. Lee, who would not barter life for his smile? And now that he speaks in words of love and admiration to his wearied troops, who does not feel every syllable burning in his very heart's core?"[38]

Dooley penned those words following the battle's conclusion on September 17, a day that would "not be easily forgotten by those who participated in the sanguinary [event]. . . . The Yankee general opposed to our immortal Lee had," he noted, "100,000 men more than we had, of which more than 60,000 or 70,000 were fresh troops who had not struck a blow during the campaign. Such were some of the odds against us on this glorious day." Fighting in the cornfields, Dooley recalled his retreat that day as being about honor as much as sheer survival. As he fled the oncoming Federal soldiers, he made sure to turn around frequently so as to avoid being shot in the back, "so disgraceful a wound." The battle ended inconclusively. Sheeran, not present but in Harpers Ferry, and there complaining about "professional stragglers" on whom he looked "with contempt," claimed victory, disbelieving "the lying dispatches" of the Union.[39]

The battle's inconclusiveness, and Sheeran's incorrect assertion, aside, it is evident the effects—with the Confederacy's march on Washington repelled and with Lincoln issuing the Emancipation Proclamation, effective January 1, 1863—were monumental Union victories. It would become clear later in the war that the time immediately prior to Sharpsburg, with momentum on the South's side and no Emancipation Proclamation yet issued, the proclamation making the war decidedly about slavery and hamstringing any potential pro-Southern foreign intervention or assistance, not Gettysburg, was the true high-water mark of the Confederate nation's independence movement.

The Confederate invasion of the North had failed. Southern troops were sent reeling back across the Potomac and into Virginia. During the retreat, Dooley lamented the ruinous condition of his home state. "As we pass through the Shenandoah Valley I think how in the days of peace and prosperity every hamlet and stream, every vale and mountain, hilltop and mead, of our own loved Virginia, was teeming and resplendent with fertility, loveliness and grandeur." The war's dominant theme was proving to be destruction and devastation. "Scarce a farmyard that is not stained with human blood, scarce a stream but has been tinged with the life current of some of Virginia's bravest; scarce a field unpolluted by the enemy's touch." Even the most Confederatized Southerners were starting to weigh the cost of independence: "Oh war, war!

Cruel, bloody war!" Dooley wrote. "Little did they know who wished for this! Oh, may they never know peace in this life who have forced this diabolical alternative upon our noble land."[40]

The Confederacy rebounded from the disappointing Northern invasion with victory at the Battle of Fredericksburg in December. Dooley mentioned helping build a stone wall. Situated at the base of Marye's Heights, it proved devastatingly effective against the storming Union army. Assault after assault failed, until Union casualties approached twelve thousand men. During the final attack on Marye's Heights that day, the Confederate guns "redouble their angry howls, and shrieks, and thunderings for blood and life: crash after crash and volley after volley, roar after roar," Dooley explained, until "we have been victorious in this last act of the sanguinary drama." On his diplomatic mission to Ireland, Bannon would cite the decimation of Meagher's Irish Brigade against the stone wall as evidence the North viewed Irishmen as little more than cannon fodder.[41]

After the battle, an officer approached Sheeran, telling him a "Capt. V— had disgraced himself and his regiment by his cowardice and that the men publicly denounced him." That Sheeran was seen as a mediating figure, someone who could help settle disputes for Catholics and non-Catholics alike, further speaks to his integration and respected status within the army. Sheeran conversed with the accused party. The captain protested, claiming institutional mistreatment. Sheeran did not believe him and urged him to resign, and said "that his own self-respect required [it] . . . because the boys accused him of being a coward." The man brushed this off. He knew a few people openly disliked him and so was unsurprised a few had voiced their displeasure. But "he was mistaken," Sheeran recalled, "for it was not only a few who accused him of cowardice, but every man in the regiment." At this revelation, the man tendered his resignation. "And the 14th," he concluded, "got rid of the biggest coward that ever played soldier."[42]

Following Fredericksburg, both sides settled into a winter hibernation of sorts; one often endured with the help of alcohol. One cold winter night Sheeran asked a soldier for some whiskey. Prizing his limited supply, the man consented, on the condition Sheeran would not spill it: "I pledged my word that I would not." Gache claimed to drink primarily for medical reasons. "Do you know what I do to preserve my precious health?" he wrote to Carriere. "I'll tell you in a low voice. Now don't be scandalized, and whatever you do, don't tell anyone else. I've been taking w-h-i-s-k-e-y." Although he despised the actual taste, "certain trustworthy people assure me that it is a *sine-qua-non* for the life I lead," and so he made sure to "finish off a bottle every ten days." If nothing else, "it will never make me fat!" Dooley noted celebrating Christmas Day with a jug of whiskey his father had sent from back home. "We all get quite *agreeable* at night."[43]

Alcohol also chased away wartime blues. Garidel noted that Christmas away from home was a somber affair, filled with "marching in the mud and cold with empty stomachs," and therefore, many marked it with "drunkenness." Nonetheless, in the midst of sadness, there were moments were the spirit of the season broke through. On Christmas Day 1862, Sheeran noted hearing a rumor that the soldiers were going to get him a present. The chaplain spoiled the plan, telling them he didn't need anything, but "if they wanted to honor our Infant Savior they might bestow their charitable gifts to his representatives, the poor orphans of St. Joseph's Asylum in Richmond." Sheeran recorded that the donation was "a very handsome sum" of $1,206.[44]

Shortly after the New Year, Bishop Quinlan contacted CSA secretary of the navy Stephen Mallory, himself a Catholic. Quinlan asked that Bannon be granted an official chaplaincy within the Confederate army. Since leaving St. Louis, Bannon had been working in a volunteer capacity, living off the generosity of soldiers. "John Bannon of St. Louis," Quinlan wrote, "with a noble sacrifice of all self interest, relinquished his comfortable position of Pastor . . . ever since then, he has been the faithful Apostle to about 1,800 Catholic Missourians of Price's Army; he has been in the trying conflicts of Elkhorn, Farmington and Corinth & is yet with the same army." Quinlan also asked Mallory to backdate his commission to February 1862. "I know it does not belong to your department, but I am sure, for the Sake of our cause, and the spiritual interests of so many brave men you will do all you can to obtain the granting of this request." The request was granted. Bannon was made an official chaplain in February 1863.[45]

After months of a slow spring thaw, Port Gibson, Mississippi, fell to the Union on May 1, 1863. Fifteen days later, a crucial battle was fought at Champion Hill, twenty miles east of Vicksburg. Union victory there forced Pemberton to retreat into Vicksburg's fortifications. The stronghold soon became a prison, one he would emerge from in surrender. What Ulysses S. Grant wrote to Henry Halleck on May 25 would be accomplished in five weeks. "Vicksburg will have to be reduced by regular siege." As the action was raging about western Mississippi, Henri Garidel made his fateful decision to leave New Orleans, departing for Richmond aboard the ironically named schooner *United States*. The reason for Garidel's voluntary exile is simple: he quit New Orleans because he would not take the Union oath. Garidel was so Confederatized he willingly left behind all he loved. He would miss his family so much, stark depression and contemplating suicide became commonplace.[46]

If anyone *should* have compromised his Confederate patriotism, it would be someone like Garidel, an involved husband and father. But he did not. Like countless other Southern Catholics, he was fully invested in the Confederate nation. "My heart was very heavy and I wept as I thought of my dear wife Lolo and my dear children." The journey to Virginia was burdensome. Additionally, Garidel noted his frustration with a man named Joe Wagner, "even more of a nuisance because he is so huge." Garidel claimed to have "no personal grudge" against Wagner yet, for unspecified reasons, "I call him a *son of a bitch.*" Arriving in Richmond, "we got busy immediately looking for a place to stay." Garidel eventually made his way to an eighteen-by-twenty-foot room, rented from a Mr. and Mrs. Hester on Sixth Street between Clay and Leigh.[47]

At this time, May 1863, the Army of Northern Virginia suffered an irreparable loss in the eastern theater. Lee's Army had won a decisive battle at Chancellorsville (May 2–10), but it came at an enormously high cost. Returning from the fight on May 2, visibility poor in the late twilight, Stonewall Jackson was mistaken for the enemy and shot three times by friendly fire, twice in the left arm, requiring amputation. He died within a week. Jackson's death was felt deeply throughout the South, and Catholics expressed their grief as readily as anyone. "I'm sure that as true Southerners you all mourned the death of our brave General Jackson," Gache wrote to Carriere. "I don't have to tell you that our loss was a very great one; that he alone was worth 50,000 men."[48]

Gache made a religious exception for Jackson. If a Protestant was of great value to the Confederate war effort, his very Protestantism seemed mitigated. The late general was "a very good Christian," and Gache was hopeful concerning Jackson's salvation because "he was probably in good faith, one can hope that his pious sentiments must have led him to an act of perfect contrition. Surely, He who loves to bestow mercy, must have bestowed it abundantly on this man." Dooley asked, "Who indeed can ever replace our noble hero, so pure, so truly great?" Jackson's name would live on in great fame, Dooley correctly predicted, while, with far less accuracy, he also envisaged the demise of that "dastardly government against which he drew his unblemished sword, [which] shall for centuries have lain in ruin and disgrace." Sheeran was preoccupied with the gruesome scenes he had witnessed at Chancellorsville, the "dead bodies of the enemy lying in every direction, some with their heads shot off, some with their brains oozing out, some pierced through the head with musket balls." Jackson's death notwithstanding, the Confederates had won. Preparations were made for a second invasion of the North. It would prove to be the final Confederate offensive into Union territory.[49]

Back in the western theater, Bannon had made it safely inside Vicksburg's walls on May 18. Devoted Confederate he was, he engaged in warring activities outside the scope of his priestly duties, working as a cannoneer with an artillery team. He supposedly knew each man's job "as well as he knew the Bible." Bannon performed myriad tasks, including swabbing the barrel with a sponge, ramming down powder and canister, and even firing the cannon. He subscribed to an especially active philosophy concerning clerics and war, and he was not alone. The Baton Rouge *Sugar Planter* reported a story about two clergymen, an Episcopalian minister and a Catholic priest, taking up arms for the Confederacy in the Norfolk environs. "When God calls upon his ministry to defend the holy cause," the priest, Father O'Keefe, said, "it must prevail."[50]

By these types of actions, Bannon demonstrated possibly the strongest example of chaplains' Confederatization. He believed so ardently in the Southern cause that he was willing to overstep the bounds of his priesthood and become, for all intents and purposes, a soldier. Bannon's spiritual duties were not put to the side; he never *just* worked with cannoneers. But that he engaged in fighting at all is a remarkable, even scandalous, testament to his zealous Southern partisanship. This was scandalous because, as one priest explained why neither he nor his fellow clergymen could be drafted: "The Catholic Church forbid[s] their clergy from taking up arms in defense of any Government, and if they do, they would be incapacitated from exercising the duties of the priesthood."[51]

Vicksburg was fatigued and near capitulation when the Civil War's most famous battle commenced. Fought in southern Pennsylvania over three days (July 1–3, 1863), the Battle of Gettysburg began by happenstance when the armies crossed paths on July 1. Brief skirmishing followed. Much of the Confederate reluctance to attack has been blamed on Lee's ace cavalryman J. E. B. Stuart and his mysterious disappearance, depriving the army of valuable reconnaissance information. The second day's crucial engagement occurred at Little Round Top, a hill at the far end of the Union army's left flank. Two of Gen. James Longstreet's divisions led the charge up the hill, an attack that did not begin until 5:00 P.M. that day. Multiple times, the Confederates stormed the hill but could not take it. The fighting was intense, ending in hand-to-hand combat after Union colonel Joshua Chamberlain initiated a successful downhill bayonet charge. Chamberlain, a future governor of Maine, received the Medal of Honor for his actions that day and later in the war was promoted to the rank of major general.[52]

Pickett's Charge—the most famous portion of the most famous battle of, arguably, America's most famous war—took place on July 3. Lee ordered an attack against the center of the Federal line, across a mile of open ground, with the now celebrated clump of trees on Cemetery Ridge the objective point for the converging armies. The Confederate cannonade began at one o'clock. Dooley, who lay prostrate on the ground, waiting, wrote he would never "forget those scenes and sounds. The earth seems unsteady beneath this furious cannonading, and the air might be said to be agitated by the wings of death. Over 400 guns nearly every minute being discharged!"[53]

"How long we take to gain our position, what delays, what suspense!" Dooley wrote in the anxious final moments before the charge. Nerves were surely frayed for many men that day. And yet, on the precipice of this monumental charge, Dooley and his fellow soldiers found time for an apple fight. "Around us are some trees with very small green apples; and while we are resting here we amuse ourselves by pelting each other with green apples." When war narratives whitewash suffering, accentuating the glorious at the expense of the brutal and the tragic, something is lost. So, too, is something lost when scholars recount battles as if the participants were less man than machine; as if both sides consisted of robotic tin soldiers dutifully tending to the business of war. The crabapple story well illustrates that soldiers were, after all, people, and people never stop being so even in situations impossibly trying and serious.

These men were about to walk out over a swath of unprotected land into a hail of cannon fire and shrapnel. Their reward for making it safely to their objective would be volley after volley of musket fire, swords, and bayonets. They knew many of their number were going to die, even within the hour. But instead of trembling with fear, they acted like children playing carelessly on their grandparents' farm.[54]

When the guns fell silent, Dooley wrote, "there is no romance in making one of these charges . . . when you rise to your feet as we did today, I tell you the enthusiasm of ardent breasts in many cases *ain't there*," adding that safety, not glory, was the pressing concern. "The thought is most frequently, *Oh, if I could just come out of this charge safely how thankful would I be!*" Some soldiers fainted from the "suffocating heat and the terrors of that hour." But when the "time appointed for our charge is come," Dooley responded dutifully. He, alongside thousands of men, marched forward, toward the cannons, the "black heavy monsters" spewing "flame and smoke and storms of shot" upon the charging Confederates. Dooley pressed on, soldiers falling beside him and gore in every direction, party to the moments when men's "life blood bespatters your check or throws a film over your eyes!"[55]

Dooley soon neared the Federal position and saw Confederate officers Lt. Col. Thomas S. Garnett, Gen. James L. Kemper, and Lt. Gen. Louis Armistead closing in as well. Approximately thirty yards from the Federal guns, he was shot, one bullet through each thigh. As Dooley lay wounded on the battlefield, all he could do was wait to hear if the charge had been successful. "We hear a new shout, and cheer after cheer rends the air. Are those fresh troops advancing to our support?" he wrote. "No! no! That huzza never broke from southern lips. Oh God! Virginia's bravest, noblest sons have perished here today and perished all in vain! Oh, if there is anything capable of crushing and wringing the soldier's heart it was this day's tragic act and all in vain!"[56]

The day of Pickett's Charge, Grant was on the very precipice of victory in Vicksburg. The month-and-a-half siege had worn down the entrenched Confederates. Grant, telling Pemberton it was his choice when to stop "the useless effusion of blood," informed the Confederate commander he would march into the city at 8:00 A.M. the following day, July 4. After roll calls were made out, and paroles signed by the officers, the Confederates would leave. The "rank & file will be allowed all their clothing but no other property," Grant explained. Bannon left his chaplaincy immediately following the siege of Vicksburg. He traveled to Richmond and told Bishop McGill he would perform any duty assigned him. A few months later, he ran the blockade. Bannon, on his way to Europe and tasked with a mission directed at gaining foreign recognition for the Confederacy, would never again set foot on American soil.[57]

On Independence Day 1863, the North had attained a dual victory across both theaters, which the South would call the twin defeats. Lee would never again threaten Washington, and Vicksburg was in Union hands. This reality has led some scholars to identify a fatal blow.[58] Others believe the twin defeats were not "fatal," at least not fatal to Confederate morale. Confederate soldiers continued to fight. War weariness should not be interpreted as a withdrawal of support or the abandonment of hope. Rather, it was simply that: war fatigue.[59] Sheeran's experience at Gettysburg speaks to this position. He reported hearing "the loud laughter of the men," soldiers who had "fought hard . . . now falling back and wading to their knees in mud and mire." Such a scene, tremendous physical carnage mingled with the psychological impact of total defeat, was "calculated to depress the spirits of even the bravest men, [but] had no such effect on these Confederate heroes. They were as cheerful a body of men as I ever saw . . . you would think they were going to a party of pleasure instead of retreating from a hard fought battle."[60]

Dooley's compensation for surviving Pickett's Charge would be two years in prison camps. A prisoner for not even a day, Dooley asked an Irish soldier from Massachusetts "how could he consistently turn his back on his principles and for the pitiful hire of a few dollars to do all in his power to crush a brave people asserting their right of self government." By "his principles," Dooley meant the legacy of the 1848 Young Ireland movement, which had fought for home rule. It was self-evident to him that Ireland and the Confederacy were engaged in the same struggle. Just as the Irish were trying to escape British dominion, so the Confederates were trying to escape Lincoln's despotism. What "would Mr. Mitchel think of him," Dooley wrote, "now that he was engaged in the cause of tyranny, fighting against honesty, Justice and right, and moreover against those very gallant young men he was asking to hear of?" The Union soldier began to cry. "Perhaps we were too severe toward him," Dooley wrote, "but when we see the Irishman supporting so foul a tyranny as ever blackened the pages of any history, our indignation cannot be but moved."[61]

Dooley was not alone in harboring such opinions. An article in the *Memphis Daily Appeal* referred to any Irishman fighting for the Union as a "spectacle painful and humiliating," adding that this only furthered "a course of policy similar to that which expelled the natives of Ireland from their possessions and from their homes." How could Irishmen reconcile their faith with Northern anti-Catholicism and fight for a side that was drafting priests and "impressing them in the Abolition Army"? Raleigh's *Daily Confederate* encouraged New York City Irish Catholics to heed the advice of the *Metropolitan Record*, a paper "bold and defiant in its denunciations of the military despotism of Abraham Lincoln, and, representing as it does the Catholic sentiment of New York, must wield a powerful influence over the Irish members of that church."[62]

Charlotte's *Western Democrat* published an account titled "An Irishman's Opinion of the Irish Federalists," retelling an encounter between an Irish Federal officer and an Irish grocer in Washington, DC. The officer entered the man's store and declared his intent to purchase some supplies. "You are an Irishman, I believe?" the grocer asked. Yes, the officer said, adding that he was originally from Massachusetts. Perhaps he should have withheld this information, for the grocer said in reply, "Not three years ago the Legislature of Massachusetts passed a law prohibiting the military organization of Irish Roman Catholics and yet you are here to fight for these same Yankees and to oppress Southerners who are struggling for their independence." Understandably taken aback, the officer said nothing. "You and Bishop Hughes," the grocer said, along with other "Irish Catholic renegades, can buy nothing in this store."[63]

Ethnic identity mattered in nineteenth-century America, and many scholars have written fine books about this topic.[64] What is most interesting, however, is that while ethnic identity continued to matter throughout the war, it often manifested as a tool in the service of a fast-developing, supraethnic loyalty to the Confederate nation. Dooley, Bannon, and Sheeran would often mention their Irish heritage in light of how it squared with their Confederatism, arguing that Northern Irishmen were being "un-Irish" in supporting the tyrannical "British-like" Union oppressing the "Irish-like" freedom-seeking Confederacy. This was similar to why Bishop Verot placed diplomatic hope in the French; not just because he was French himself but especially because the fate of his new country rested on these questions. It would be great if help came from his birth country, but any help that would aid his new nation's independence bid ultimately mattered. The Confederacy was more important than France, as it was more important than Ireland for Irish Southerners. Without disavowing their ethnic backgrounds, many Southern Catholics began to identify, above all, with their new Confederate national identities.

By July 8, Dooley reported feeling better. At this time, he and his fellow inmates had been moved to Fort McHenry in Baltimore. There, in what another prisoner termed "the black hole of Calcutta," and where Sheeran would later be incarcerated himself, Dooley celebrated his twenty-first birthday. Convinced Marylanders were as staunchly Confederate as he was, he claimed the Fort McHenry guards, "by winks and nods," made clear they were Yankees in name only. "The colors under which they are maneuvering are not in accordance with the feelings of their hearts." Dooley would remain in captivity for essentially the remainder of the war, not paroled until February 1865. He, like scores of other prisoners North and South, endured horrible food and horrifying living conditions, moving from "the black hole of Calcutta" to the "black hole" of Johnson's Island in Lake Erie. Dooley nonetheless remained an ardent Confederate. Travails aside, there was time for recreation even in prison, a slight break from the daily ennui. Dooley mentioned regularly watching some type of game, one he didn't quite comprehend but still took enjoyment from.[65] He recalled, "The prisoners nearly every evening are engaged in a game they call 'base-ball,' which notwithstanding the heat they prosecute with persevering energy. I don't understand the game, but those who play it get very much excited over it, and it appears a fine exercise."⁶⁶

While Dooley adjusted to prison life and Bannon was out on Atlantic waters, Garidel begrudgingly settled into Richmond. "The vegetable market didn't have much," he wrote, "nothing compared with ours in New Orleans. The fruit isn't good, neither the peaches nor the apples." Of self-described "delicate tastes," Garidel was especially preoccupied with Richmond coffee, ridiculing it as "famed," "*alias* a cup of grain," and "*cafiot.*" Once, "we had a miserable breakfast with Confederate coffee. I don't know what it actually is." Another time he quipped, "The coffee they gave Henry [his four-year-old son] at home in the morning was much, much stronger . . . they don't know what good coffee is."⁶⁷ Food scarcity and lack of quality was a constant source of reflection for Garidel. Gache perhaps penned the final word on Civil War food: "As far as supper was concerned—well, we dined on dreams."⁶⁸

Perhaps humorous disparagement helped take Garidel's mind of his numbing, daily depression. "I got up at seven, thinking very dark thoughts. . . . I am close to going crazy," Garidel wrote in October 1863. "I went to the church today to see if I could find the bishop [McGill] to ask him to help me make peace with God. . . . Without that, I might end things badly. My thoughts are too black. I am not well." "If I didn't believe in the next life," he mused once, "I would be tempted to end my suffering. To chase these ideas away, let us kiss our children and say the rosary." Beneath all this was a Confederatized Catholic wholly devoted to the Southern cause. Garidel's oath refusal is far from the only manifestation of his Confederatization. In search of more nuanced information than could be gleaned from papers, he listened to speeches about the "state of the Confederacy" and visited "The Secession Club." He attended parties frequented by important Confederate leaders and made acquaintances with Jefferson Davis. "I went to pay a visit to the president," he wrote of a New Year's Day soiree hosted by Davis and his wife. "When he heard I was from New Orleans, he pressed my hand."⁶⁹

Garidel's Confederatization blossomed with his attempt to formally join the Confederate army in May 1864. He signed up to become a sharpshooter. On May 6, he explained that if "Yankees are there" he would leave along with several coworkers-turned-soldiers for Drewry's Bluff that evening. (Garidel was employed as something of a hybrid accountant, bookkeeper, and statistician.) As he waited, he noted seeing a family in town and that it made him "unbearably sad."

"My poor wife, my poor children," he wrote, "perhaps you will despise me. My only consolation lies in the Lord and the Blessed Virgin. And I pray to her with ardor." He remained at the office that evening and into the night, looking out onto the street where "all groups of people [were] . . . waiting for news." He felt privileged to "have the news firsthand because it is the Department of War, and my office is the Ordinance Bureau." Soon came a dispatch detailing fighting on the James River, men "blown to pieces," exploded gunboats, and other assorted mayhem. If he was going to be sent into battle, Garidel was to learn the following day. "I want to go," he wrote.[70]

The next day, Garidel woke at seven, attended Mass, and participated in Bishop McGill's special prayers "for the month of Mary." He then made his way to the office to await further orders. "The battle is still going on," he wrote, "the Yankees are surrounding us on all sides, but I think we are ready for them . . . we have the upper hand." The men were soon informed they were bound for Drewry's Bluff. While boarding the boat taking them there, Garidel recalled, "we could hear the cannon. My heart was beating fast." On arriving on the scene, however, "we were disappointed. There were no Yankees there. Our troops were fighting five or six miles away, and there was no way to join them."[71]

On May 8, he mentioned alarms in the city and that Union troops were fast approaching. "Big deal! They are still far away and are being beaten on every front." Later in the week, the enemy had come frightfully close. Garidel compared the cannon fire to crashing thunder. Richmond was under a "veritable rain of fire." The bombing was so intense it was difficult to write. "We hear the cries, the fusillades, the cannon, the bombs exploding," he wrote, "if by chance a bomb exploded here where I am writing, no one would ever know what had become of me, but I think that the Blessed Virgin will watch over us." Garidel was confident Beauregard, a hero to him as to countless French Catholic Southerners, would "make them pay dearly for their insolence."[72]

Garidel confessed all this stress left him exasperated. Additionally, his hemorrhoids were causing him severe pain. "I am bleeding like a steer, but, thank God, aside from that I am well." He saw the Confederate president "passing by with his staff to go to the battlefield as soon as daylight breaks." He feared the possibility of Davis being killed. "It would be very bad for the Confederacy," but "no one could stop him" from coming into harm's way. And then, it seemed his hero had come through. The battle appeared to be won, the Yankees vanquished. "Beauregard has put the enemy to flight and taken 2,000 or 3,000 prisoners."[73]

Garidel interacted with some of these men the following day, assisting in boarding Union POWs onto boats for transport to prison camps. His immediate response, claiming to witness rampant faux patriotism among Union soldiers, is nearly identical to Dooley's comments from the other side of the equation. When Dooley was imprisoned following Gettysburg, he believed his captors, by "winks and nods," signaled they were only nominally Union. Now Garidel, in the position of jailer, felt the same way about apprehended Union soldiers. Southern Catholics' Confederatization could be so blinding it clouded basic rationality. In Dooley's and Garidel's minds, there was not a single man, woman, or child in the whole of the Northern states who *really* supported the Union war effort, its government, or the tyrannical autocrat at the controls. It had to be a facade. The righteousness of the Southern cause was akin to scientific fact.

As they boarded the boat, the Union prisoners "were cursing the Yankees as hard as they could." Furthermore, "eight hundred of them at once had thrown down their rifles and run over to our side." Why this en masse desertion? Northern battlefield immorality, the callous wasting of lives just to gain inches of ground. Union commanders, Garidel wrote, got their soldiers "drunk so they will fight—it is truly horrifying—so they don't know what they are doing. They attack like lions and don't have the strength to keep up the fighting, so our men massacre them."[74]

Later on, he got into an argument with a woman because she sympathized with wounded Union soldiers. It stands to reason Garidel—having witnessed what he called "the most horrible spectacle in the world . . . everywhere you saw brains, arms, and legs . . . horrible, and it is impossible to describe it"— would feel the same. But he did not have any compassion whatsoever. "I disagreed with her," he noted, laconically. Washing up and saying good night "to my dear Lolo and my dear children," he went to bed.[75]

The near miss, or missed opportunity, at Drewry's Bluff was the closest Garidel would come to personal militaristic involvement in the Confederate war effort. He did, nonetheless, keep up a steady stream of anti-Northern vitriol, denouncing even those on his own side when they failed to meet his standard of rabid Confederatization. Should Richmond fall to Union forces, Garidel was sure a vast majority of the population would capitulate immediately and do what he, perhaps, believed amounted to treason: take the oath. When he crossed paths with Gen. John C. Pemberton—overseer of the Vicksburg debacle and a man whose case was not helped by being born in Pennsylvania, this fact making easy fodder for Trojan horse–type conspiracies—he did not hide his true feelings. "He is still wearing the insignia of a general," Garidel stated bitterly, having heard Pemberton was supposed to have already been demoted to "a simple lieutenancy." "May the Lord take pity on him, but I don't like his face."[76]

Poche, stationed more than a thousand miles west of Garidel, and much closer to the home of both men, was constantly in the saddle, often riding in between swamps, bayous, and hamlets up and down the Mississippi River Valley. His nearly three years of Confederate service (1863–65) are an ode to itinerant travel. While Dooley demonstrated his Confederatization in short, hot bursts with a palpable desire for the fight, Poche's Confederatization was more tepid and drawn out, a testimony to perseverance and a willingness to go anywhere, and to any lengths, in the performance of his duties.

Poche ventured as far west as Mansfield, Louisiana, and as far east as Meridian, Mississippi. He traveled as far north as Monticello, Arkansas, having come up from his southern terminus around New Orleans. He was assigned to essentially all of Louisiana, west-central Mississippi, and parts of southeastern Arkansas. Poche's territory comprised approximately 120,000 square miles; roughly the size of New Mexico. But it is not just how Poche traversed this distance but also the frequency of his travels that is indicative of his Confederatization, for if there was ever a time for someone not fully invested to jump ship and desert, unchartered bayous and swamps, where one was perambulating alone, would be the place to do it.[77]

A few of Poche's journal entries from October 1863 are a good microcosm of his quotidian difficulties. After breakfast one day, he and his men set out for their next stop. A large portion of the day was required to cover just fifteen miles. "We suffered very much from the cold," he noted, the journey made worse by having to make use of "very muddy roads." After a rushed dinner, the party still had ten miles to go before nightfall, a "miserable traveler's inn" in "the piney woods" their destination. They arrived but did not have much time to rest. The next morning the men rose early and departed immediately. They "took breakfast at another miserable inn" further down the road. The next day, Poche was struck with a bout "of my chronic colic, which made me suffer terribly." Sick or healthy, cold or warm, tired or well rested, the soldiers had to keep moving.[78]

Poche was often far removed from "infernal Yankees." But as the war touched all parts of the American landscape, even into remote areas of rural Louisiana, it found him too. On December 8, the Feast of the Immaculate Conception of the Blessed Virgin Mary, torrential rains and "a hard cannonade on the Mississippi" pummeled the area. The following day, Poche reported the effects of "another heavy cannonading." He claimed amazement at the destruction to local houses. One home was hit with 128 cannon balls, one piercing the house from entry to exit and passing through five walls. Indubitably, the bombardment completely "ruin[ed] the house."[79]

The following spring, 1864, in particular during April, Poche witnessed unusually sustained military action. He was stationed near Mansfield, close to the Texas border. On April 1, in response to intermittent skirmishing, He noted "the general opinion is that our generals will give battle in this vicinity." There was more skirmishing in the coming days and a nocturnal march, the orders coming "at the moment I was retiring," forcing Poche to spend the whole night on his feet. To make matters worse, he was irritated by a "large boil" under his arm and "inconvenienced by a choking smoke caused by the entire pine forest being on fire." It was a "miserable and terrible night."[80]

The Battle of Mansfield was fought on April 8. Poche, "very anxious to see the battle," offered his services as an aide-de-camp. The Confederate position was "on a rather high hill at the edge of a forest behind a fence," waiting for the enemy to emerge from the surrounding woods. Soon fire was upon the Confederates like a "storm tears down the trees of a forest." Men were "literally shot to pieces . . . [in] this thick wood in a continuous and terrific shower of cannon balls accompanied by grape shot." By way of "a terrific bombardment, the Yankees were routed and all their army fled hotly pursued by our men who killed them at every step, and continued the chase until nightfall."[81]

Poche stopped to visit some of the hospitals in the battle's aftermath. He found "a pitiful sight . . . crowded with the wounded, the dying and the dead, friends and enemies side by side, some calling for help, others groaning in pain so pitifully that I left with a heavy heart." There was no time to process the scene, for the Battle of Pleasant Hill, also a Confederate victory, immediately followed. Confusion reigned at Pleasant Hill. "A very thick forest," in conjunction with nightfall, produced a disorientating scene in which "Yankees fought boldly amongst themselves" after Confederate troops had withdrawn. The Confederate soldiers, likewise confused, "did not recognize one another and exchanged shots for quite a while." The post-fight battlefield was especially gruesome, littered with amputees and many "dead, dying and wounded." Furthermore, "some [were] without heads . . . others had their legs crushed, their feet torn away . . . a wounded Yankee . . . his face swollen as large as a pumpkin, [was] unable to speak, he was a truly terrible sight." Poche especially grieved for those who "had fallen in lonely and secluded spots, had not as yet been found or given any help, and were suffering a veritable martyrdom." Perhaps with all this carnage in mind, at Mass on April 22, Poche "offered [his Communion] to God in thanksgiving for his special protection on the battlefield."[82]

Poche had a special connection to the Jesuit order, visiting the priests at Grand Coteau, Louisiana, often, as he "thoroughly enjoyed the rest and the sweet tranquility which reigns among these good Jesuit fathers." There he could take "good bath[s]," so as to kill "wood ticks which were devouring me" and enjoy promenades to admire "the countless trees all in bloom, the immense country-side covered with a veritable carpet of green." Grand Coteau could make a person "forget that we are in the midst of such a cruel war, and that our heretofore beautiful country is devastated by our vandal enemies." Poche was privy to special treats there too. Once, to celebrate the feast day of Saint Ignatius of Loyola, he and the fathers had a cake, made by nuns at the nearby convent, "two feet tall, covered with white sugar, decorated in pink . . . I do not think I have had such a rich and sumptuous meal since the beginning of the war."[83]

What is most important about Poche's relationship with the Jesuits is what it says about the all-encompassing nature of Catholic Confederatization. Namely, Catholic noncombatants cared about the war and supported the Confederacy. In this way, the Grand Coteau Jesuits were like the noncombatant Catholic sister-nurses (with the obvious exception that they were never on battlefields). And so when Poche visited Grand Coteau following the victories at Mansfield and Pleasant Hill, he excitedly relayed news of the recent Confederate success. So pleased where the fathers, they shut down the school for a day, giving their students a holiday "on the strength of the good news I brought them."[84]

And so during the late fall of 1864—as Poche ate cake or nothing at all, Dooley watched baseball in prison, Garidel complained about poor coffee, and Gache sipped secret "medical remedies" away from prying eyes—Father Sheeran was imprisoned by the Union army. Sheeran's detainment and defiance of his captors gained him lasting notoriety. His experience, in particular his reasons for refusing to cooperate with the North, is comparable to Bishop Elder's refusal of a Union prayer mandate, which took place in the same year.

On October 31, Sheeran was placed in military prison in Winchester, Virginia. It was common practice for clergymen to be granted passes to move between enemy lines. This time, Sheeran was denied a pass and arrested. He did not specify precisely why he was arrested because, as he described it, there was no *actual* reason for it. He spent a week in Winchester before his November 8 transfer to Baltimore. There, Sheeran, with other men, was led up dilapidated stairs outside an old brick building and into a dark room. He and his fellow inmates were greeted with calls of "Fresh fish, fresh fish!" His first night in the Baltimore prison passed as such:

> We had hardly laid our wearied bodies down on the hard, filthy and vermin-covered floor than the former inmates of this institution, inspired as it were by the devil, commenced what appears to be their regular nocturnal exercises. They first had a quarrel, real or pretended, in which vulgarity, obscenity and profanity, such as I had never heard, were exhibited. . . . One would burst out with some verse or phrase of an obscene or vulgar song. Soon another would begin to grunt like a hog and others bark like a dog, another quack like a duck. . . . Is it needless to say that I slept none, for who could sleep?[85]

On November 17, Sheeran was informed he would be released if he took an oath of allegiance to the United States. Like Garidel, he refused unconditionally. He refused again on November 28: "To take such an oath would require on my part a sacrifice of honor and conscience which I am prepared to make for no earthly consideration." Sheeran's affair quickly became something of a cause celebre. On November 18, James McMaster, editor of the *New York Freeman's Journal and Catholic Register,* whose own anti-Lincoln polemics led to his paper being censured and him imprisoned, published an article in defense of Sheeran: "A Great and Cruel Wrong: Arrest and Imprisonment of a Confederate Catholic Chaplain."[86]

McMaster, knowing Sheeran personally, classified the man as "not only a devoted and excellent man, but one in the correctness of whose statements of fact the utmost reliance can be placed." He was a "man of *peace,* not of *war;* a man of *mercy,* not of blood." McMaster then explained the particulars of Sheeran's situation. "We have been shocked and grieved" that, despite having a pass, Sheeran "had been arrested, treated with gross indignity . . . [and] in this filthy prison, he was kept *five days;* obliged to listen to all the obscenity and blasphemies of the abandoned characters around him."

McMaster claimed there was a complex conspiratorial plot working against the chaplain. He also reprinted parts of a letter Sheeran had authored to the editor. Sheeran began in typical fashion, stopping first to castigate perceived Union barbarism: "The correspondents of the [Northern] public press have given glowing, if not very accurate accounts of General Sheridan's victories in the Valley. They have detailed minutely the number of rebels killed or prisoners taken, and of artillery captured. They have heralded to the world, even without a blush of shame for disgraced humanity, the number of barns, and of wheat and hay stacks burned, of houses plundered, of families impoverished and left without shelter or food."[87]

Also included in the dossier was a letter Sheeran had written to Union general Phillip Sheridan.[88] He began by introducing himself as a chaplain of the Confederate army, stating that during the previous three years "on all the bloody fields of Virginia, Maryland and Pennsylvania, thousands of Catholic soldiers, of both armies, have received the sacraments of the Church at my hands." He had entered the Federal lines at Harrisonburg, Virginia, whereupon he was "brought to Gen. Wright who, being satisfied I was what I professed to be, treated me very kindly, and gave me the enclosed pass." Sheeran explained that Sheridan's own adjutant general had agreed the pass was "sufficient." Sheeran demanded his release on the dual grounds of unjust imprisonment and of how Catholics North and South would suffer from one less available chaplain. "I have ministered to the spiritual wants of all who called for me," he claimed, "and I have attended the sick of *your* army, as well as of my own." Sheridan's response, if there was one, was not printed, recorded, or mentioned.[89]

Time passed. Nothing changed. Sheeran did not budge. Perhaps the Union authorities started to believe the whole case was no longer worth the hassle, especially if Sheeran could potentially become some kind of martyr or icon for the Southern struggle against "Northern tyranny." The Union army decided to set him free. But with Sheeran's release nearly finalized, the Union government tried, slyly, to get him to sign a parole promising to "deport [himself] as a good and loyal citizen of the United States."[90]

"I will do no such thing," Sheeran explained, risking returning to prison. And that is precisely what happened. His imminent release was immediately suspended. Sheeran had no qualms about stating his unequivocal Southern partisanship. "I belong to the South and am a chaplain in the Confederate army. . . . My home is in the South and there I demand to be sent." Sheeran was a citizen of the Confederate nation and he would pledge allegiance to no other. So he kept waiting in his cold, damp prison, perhaps warmed by the pride of holding uncompromisingly to his convictions. In the end, the Union government blinked. Sheeran was released unconditionally on December 30, 1864, without having to take the oath or having to sign anything.[91]

By the time of Sheeran's release, practically all the final hopes the South had entertained following Gettysburg-Vicksburg had evaporated.[92] The end of the war, and Union victory was all but certain, the remaining question being a matter of when. And so why, if the Confederacy was effectively defeated, did the war go on? There were multiple opportunities to surrender for the express purpose of preventing further bloodshed, but the Confederacy did not. Why waste human lives in impossible missions that had no hope of success? One historian offers a plausible explanation: the power of rumor.[93] Southerners believed God had predestined the Confederacy to victory. The North would soon tire of the war and let the South go. Europe would join the fight on their side; Grant was dead; Atlanta was not really lost. The undergirding belief was that the Confederacy simply *had to win*. Rumors were but one aspect of a larger group psychology, fueled by past success, in which the Confederates viewed themselves as unconquerable. Poche and Garidel's diaries are excellent sources that lend credence to this theory, demonstrating that Catholics participated in these wild fantasies as much as any other Confederates.[94]

Rumors dominated Poche's and Garidel's minds. On July 23, 1863, Poche reported that Lee's Army had captured both Washington and Philadelphia and that Johnston had soundly defeated Grant near Jacksonville, Florida. Five days later, he despaired this rumor would soon prove false. He explained he was disheartened that Confederate success could not be attained save for European intervention, which would never come; yet one month later he was rejoicing that France, Spain, and Great Britain had recognized the Confederacy. European ships and armaments were en route. Garidel reported similar news on September 22, claiming France had recognized the Confederacy a month prior. Garidel readily indulged vague speculations, once mentioning a scheme concerning Chattanooga, Charleston, and Louisiana. "We will see in the papers tomorrow," he wrote, not explaining what news he was awaiting.[95]

On July 30, Poche reported Beauregard was assaulting Washington and that Lee was in Baltimore. In November, he claimed Lee had defeated Union general George Meade and was threatening the Northern capital. In January 1864, he stated that Johnston had just defeated Grant, this time in Tennessee. He added, "I pray God that he will grant us those grand victories as they would help toward ending this cruel war and my sad separation from my beloved ones." A particularly encouraging rumor once led Poche to write, "With such glorious news we can flatter ourselves with the hope that peace will soon smile on our independent confederation."[96]

Poche seemed to have an endless appetite for hearsay. On July 1, 1864, he noted that Lee had "completely beaten" Grant and that Johnston, fighting Sherman in Georgia, had likewise put the enemy in "bad shape." "I pray to God that all these news are true," he added. "They would give us a ray of hope of an approaching peace." On July 10, Poche stated, giddily, that it had been "affirmed . . . Grant was killed . . . [and] we understand that Sherman has been beaten in Georgia by Johnston. This news has been rumored for several days and it continues without contradiction. God permit that it is true! I pray that it is from the bottom of my heart."[97]

Garidel reported Grant's death with reserve. "There is a rumor that Grant has been killed by a bomb, but that is just a rumor . . . we don't yet know what it's all about." In May 1864, he wrote, "We also see in the papers that Johnston is fighting the Yankees in Georgia. We are hammering away at them from all sides." Hammering away from all sides? Soon after, Atlanta was burned to the ground. "It seems to me that everything has been going downhill since the fall" of the city, Garidel wrote, sobered.[98]

Poche's reaction was different—anger mixed with disbelief. That a Northern paper, the *Chicago Tribune,* had reported the news only augmented his doubts. Soon it became impossible to deny facts. "It seems definite that Atlanta has fallen." Yet Poche would soon believe the city had been retaken. "Hoping that this refreshing news is true, I am waiting for its confirmation." Like nearly every rumor, it was not true. Rumors heard, believed, and ingested, then dashed, such was the usual order of business. "Madame Rumor, the unmerciful tyrant loves to torture our hearts," Poche once wrote, "and makes us drink alternately out of the invigorating cup of hope, and the bitter chalice of despair." In another moment of clarity, he reflected, "It is understood that all this news is greatly exaggerated and some of it not even true, but one loves to hear what one desires."[99]

Poche is not the only Southern Catholic whose Confederatization remained consistent throughout the war. Bishop Patrick Lynch and Bannon were so dedicated they agreed to go overseas as diplomats. Dooley remained a committed Confederate even in prison. Sheeran refused multiple times to give an oath of allegiance to the Union. He withheld even as he came close to death from malnourishment and the harsh weather. It is safe to assume that had the Union not simply let him go he would have chosen death rather than committing a treasonous act. Garidel was of like mind. The very same Southern nationalistic cohesion found among white Protestant Southerners included Southern Catholics too. Catholics supported the Confederate cause from the start of the war and remained committed to the end. These very same Confederatized Southerners were also very committed to their faith, even more devout in their Catholicism than they were ardent in their Confederatism.

CHAPTER THREE

Catholicity on the Battlefield

Chaplains and Soldiers, 1862–1864

"This night was spent to a late hour in ministering to the spiritual wants [of soldiers]," Sheeran noted in the aftermath of Second Manassas. The battle was over, but his work was just beginning. And so he had scanned the field, looking for anyone needing help. Having prayed for, and having buried, the dead, he helped others in obtaining medical assistance. Thankfully, Sheeran was not alone. "My old friend, Mr. Miller, accompanied me and displayed the very best disposition to render all the assistance in his power," Sheeran recalled. "He was a Protestant and as such cared nothing about confession or any other sacrament. Yet he went around among the wounded inquiring particularly if any of them were Catholics and, if so, came and told me."[1]

Only once their most important tasks had been completed—namely burying and praying for the dead, administering Last Rites, hearing confessions, and celebrating Mass—did chaplains, even those of the most Confederatized stripe, think of other matters. Catholic chaplains showed their spiritual allegiance in this straightforward manner, seeing to their clerical duties before all else. They were acknowledged ecumenical leaders in camp, catalysts for Bible reading, prayer meetings (especially of the Rosary), and dialogue with Protestants.

Catholic soldiers' religiosity was demonstrated in their attendance at camp prayer meetings, commitments to personal prayer and private devotions, and partaking of the sacraments. This last element most distinguished Catholic from Protestant worship, the latter centered on Bible reading and preaching. How did these men practice their faith while constantly fighting and on the move? How was it expressed? How consistent were these expressions, and what effect did proximity to death and suffering have? How does the Catholic soldier's religious experience compare to the Protestant soldier's? Finally, what is meant by the *Catholic religious experience?*

This chapter shows the specifically religious side of Catholic Confederatization. That Catholics were deeply involved in the Confederacy's politics and war does not mean their faith was secondarily important or put to the side. Rather, one could be both a devout Catholic and a devoted Confederate. And this formulation is integral in understanding the full scope of Catholics' Confederatization. A vast majority of Catholics held these spiritual and secular allegiances in tandem and without contradiction, ultimately prioritizing their faith above even the most ardent political sentiments.

Father John Bannon's story is a good place to start probing the Catholic religious experience. Bannon was reputed to be something of a spiritual master, able to speak the language of soldiers, earning their trust and so producing great fruit in his ministry. He put forth a "special effort to reach men's souls," prioritizing giving Holy Communion to soldiers, this constituting his "most important psychological and spiritual duty . . . prepar[ing] a soldier for meeting his God before an impeding battle." In the immediate preamble to battle, Bannon, armed with nothing "except for a Bible and Crucifix," blessed countless soldiers. When he saw one fall, he would administer Last Rites and, if the soldier had not been baptized, baptize him if he requested it.[2]

Bishop William Henry Elder worked tirelessly to provide dedicated chaplains like Bannon for Mississippi's Catholic soldiers. Many of Elder's priests from the Diocese of Natchez served as chaplains throughout the western theater. The first Mississippi priest to do so was Father Francis Pont of Jackson. Pont served in a hospital in Pensacola before moving onto the Corinth-Shiloh area. Father Basilio Elia also assisted in hospitals, and with the Sisters of Charity at Holly Springs. Father Julian Guillou, whom Elder called "the best missionary in the Diocese," was sent by the bishop to the Eighteenth Louisiana Regiment, in need of a French-speaking priest, upon the request of Archbishop Jean-Marie Odin.[3]

The "Good Death" was the chaplains' primary concern. Soldiers sought it both for their souls, a good spiritual death leading to heaven, and for the honor of their family names, a brave death in battle granting a lasting legacy of patriotism and heroism. Catholic priests were fully focused on the former goal, eternal salvation. "A Priest is bound to leave every thing else if necessary, to attend to the dying," Elder wrote to Father Jean Baptiste Mouton, "so that even if congregations must be neglected, the sick soldiers must be cared for." Once, as bombs were going off near him, Gache recalled thinking, "I had no fear of death for myself, but I was concerned about the others, particularly those who were not at all prepared to die. More than once I said a *Memorare* for them, begging our dear Mother to divert the shells from their direction." Such situations were terrifying but spiritually fruitful. "The big fish [hardened sinners; the lapsed], frightened by the sound of Yankee cannons, leave their deep holes and come up to where I can catch them."[4]

Conversions were essential to the chaplains' mission. "I hope," Elder wrote to veteran priest Father Ghislain Boeheme, "you will prove yourself the veteran soldier of our Lord, & teach our younger Missionaries how to fight His battles in camp, as you have done in the country." To Father Elia, Elder wrote, "The sick bed is the very place for conversions." He further asked, "Can you not do some good among the sick soldiers even when they are not Catholics? . . . [a] time of suffering is always a time of grace.—I have heard old missionaries say that they brought a great many into the Church in time of general sickness. There are great numbers of men, who have no religion—& yet wish to have some instruction before they die—& who will welcome the instructions & consolations of a zealous priest."[5]

Sheeran, like Bannon, believed "no men fight more bravely than Catholics who approach the sacraments before battle," adding there were no greater cowards, "save for the intensely worthless," than Catholics in mortal sin. Sheeran viewed his prime objective as preparing men to meet God, should they die fighting. So, too, did Gache, who, like his fellow chaplains and many soldiers both Catholic and Protestant, found a deep religious significance in the war. The battlefield became a redemptive theater, a final opportunity for sinful men to make peace with God. The ever-present threat of sudden death quickened many men's desires for repentance and reconciliation.[6]

Happening upon a mortally wounded soldier, Gache wrote, "I spoke to him about the affairs of his soul and heard his confession." When Gache encountered a Union colonel who had been hit in the chest with shot—a brutal mix of various balls and metal objects packed into a bag and fired from a cannon—he did not ask him if he was Catholic. He did not inquire about his politics. The man's soul was all that mattered. "I told him to recommend himself to God and to ask pardon for his sins," Gache wrote. The man said he had already done so but would do it again. He thanked Gache for his sympathy and presumably died shortly thereafter. Another time, Gache approached a man near death and, when he asked about the man's faith was told he was not Catholic, but "my wife and children are Catholics. I like their church very much. It is the only one

I attend." Gache asked if the man had been baptized. No, he said. Gache asked if he wanted to be baptized now. "You realize that without baptism you cannot be saved." The man requested baptism, and Gache granted this, leaving him in "a state of joy and gratitude to God," the man repeating, "Blessed be the Lord. Now I will die in peace."[7]

It was at Vicksburg where Father Bannon most brazenly demonstrated his Confederatization, joining a cannon squad enfilading Union troops. Bannon refused to stay out of the war zone. He did not take cover in the hospitals or houses behind the lines. He was on the front lines and breastworks every day. But Bannon's work on the front lines was primarily spiritual in nature, his love of artillery notwithstanding. One historian summarizes his time at Vicksburg: "Under constant danger, Bannon heard more confessions, offered more prayers, and distributed Communion more often during the forty-seven days of siege than at any time in his career. Each day of his life in a man made hell brought the graycoats closer to God."[8]

How Bannon brought Confederates closer to God is well illustrated in an exchange the chaplain had with a private named McGolfe, which Bannon recounted after the war in his memoir-essay "Experiences of a Confederate Army Chaplain." McGolfe had a reputation for illicit behavior, and Bannon had long hounded him to come to confession. "Come, man," Bannon would badger him. "I know what a soldier's confession is." Time and again, McGolfe refused. At Vicksburg the man, a rammer and sponger on an artillery crew, was severely wounded when an accident broke his arms and legs and fractured his skull. Bannon came and saw him, again imploring him to confess his sins. McGolfe refused once more. He was additionally angry about being placed next to a wounded Union soldier. "I can't make my confession with this Yankee close to me," McGolfe said. "He disturbs my mind: take him away!"[9]

Bannon told McGolfe not to mind the Union man but "attend to your own soul." For all of Bannon's solicitous fervor, it was this very same man whom McGolfe derided who led to his repentance. The Union soldier died that night and left an indelible impression on the Confederate artilleryman. "I can't help thinking of that poor Yankee," McGolfe told Bannon. "After you left him he never stopped saying his prayers. . . . I'm just sorry for the way I treated him, and if you can give me any more penance for it, do. Now, if you'll stop by me, I'd like to make my confession again." McGolfe immediately began to accuse himself in a loud voice in front of everyone. Bannon told him to speak more quietly, but McGolfe insisted. "No, I have been a bad man, and they all know it.

I have given bad example, and I want to do penance for it." Bannon heard his confession. When McGolfe finished, the chaplain said he would not demand the man complete any acts of penance, for "he had done enough." McGolfe died within the hour, reconciled to the Church and free of his sins.[10]

Gache once told Father Andrew Cornette, "The work with the soldiers continues to jog along," with, to his dismay, "only a few" attending the 7:00 A.M. Mass. The previous Sunday, however, had been a different story. The "congregation was so large that the church was more than filled." Nonetheless, Gache was horribly fatigued, "so exhausted from fasting, saying an early mass [earlier that day], and preaching." But, once again, there was something to lift his spirits, a remarkable conversion happening right before his eyes. Gache explained that he had "a very special consolation that day: the Good Lord let me see an old sinner at the Holy Table [at the altar to receive Holy Communion]. I've been on this man's coat tails for nine years—that is, ever since the first time I came to Pensacola. He was more than forty-five years away from the Sacred Banquet." He added, "You can understand that this joy compensated quite a bit for my weariness."[11]

The Good Death, important though it was, did not constitute the chaplains' entire work. Preaching was also an important facet of their ministry. Gache recounted the story of a young woman from a French family who asked him to preach in his native tongue. He agreed, but on the condition that there would be at least twenty people in attendance. She assured him this would not be a problem. "As she brought along more than thirty Frenchmen to the church that evening," Gache wrote, "I was obliged to either break my promise or give a sermon." He expressed his satisfaction that these Frenchmen were "practicing Catholics . . . all of them."[12]

When chaplains assumed the roles of itinerant preachers, they often had touchstone resting places along the way. "The only Catholic people in York-town [Virginia]," operators of a grocery store, were one such asset for Gache. Each time he passed through they would put him up in what he described as "a cubby-hole in their very modest house. . . . Here I spent the night and, like a prophet, it is here that I return every time that I pass through Yorktown." Sheeran traveled often to preach. When Stonewall Jackson once rebuked him for taking a leave of absence, he answered, "I want you to understand that as a priest of God I outrank every officer in your command. I even outrank you, and when it is a question of duty I shall go wherever called." Perhaps Sheeran should have shown more tact. Yet understood in the light of his Confederatization, it is clear that unless there was an actual need, he would not seek leave.

He truly believed his priesthood was of a higher value than anything involving military protocol. While one might think this is pure self-service, granting oneself a blank check to do as one pleases under the cover of religion, a lot of religious people—if not the vast majority—would concur with him that a clergyman is performing a higher duty than a soldier. It is ironic, and not a little humorous, that the very man reprimanding him would, as a devout, even austere Presbyterian, agree that men of God outrank men of war, even generals.[13]

The times Sheeran took leaves of absence, he often preached in other states. Such was the case in January 1864 when he was a guest of Father Leon Fillion in Charleston, Bishop Patrick Lynch's diocese. Fillion introduced Sheeran as "a Redemptorist and the chaplain of General Lee's army. . . . [H]e will preach for you today at the last Mass and I know he will tell you many good things. He has stood up on twenty battlefields and was not afraid." Sheeran described how this made him laugh, as he had not yet had been on a battlefield unafraid. To a packed congregation, Sheeran presented a discourse on mortal sin. His sermons and homilies were always of a spiritual nature, never moments to extoll the Confederacy. As he was speaking, a Union shell passed over the church roof. It narrowly missed, landing just fifty yards away. Commotion broke out. "What are you afraid of?" Sheeran asked. "Do you think God is not able to protect you from Yankee shells? Is He not able to protect you in the church as well as out of it? Keep still, there is not one bit of danger." Everyone calmed down and he was able to finish.[14]

While travel was common, Sheeran and other chaplains' primary venues were in camp among their men. In August 1862, Sheeran noted that he hoped for a few days' break from the fighting so he could have the opportunity to prepare "all the Catholic soldiers of our Brig. to meet their God." One of Sheeran's "most laborious days," in November 1864, was close to the standard for a chaplain in camp. He spent that day from "morning till late at night in hearing confessions, administering Extreme Unction, baptizing, and in washing and dressing wounds."[15]

Some people believe spiritual and political actions cannot be so easily separated. This is sometimes true, especially for avowedly secular leaders who see religion's highest value as a political tool. Within this paradigm, the sole function of religious figures is to provide psychological motivation; religion is nothing but a catalyzing placebo. Chaplains did not think this way; they possessed supernatural faith, believing in all the tenets of Catholic dogma, including the bodily Resurrection of Christ, Christ's Real Presence in the

Holy Eucharist, and a literal Heaven and Hell. The sacraments were the line of demarcation between their religion and their Confederatization, so, too, for Catholic soldiers who received the Eucharist to fulfill Christ's command that "unless you eat my body and drink my blood you have no life within you" (John 6:53) and who went to confession to be absolved of their sins. Perhaps, as Sheeran and Bannon believed, soldiers in a state of grace fought more fiercely and bravely, less afraid to die, but they partook of the sacraments not for this reason but to engage in the central activities of their faith.

Gache reported celebrating Mass in camp daily, not only on Sundays or holy days of obligation. Sheeran also celebrated Mass frequently during the week. Non-Catholic Christians often came to these Masses. When one of Sheeran's congregations was filled with "so many Protestants," he took the opportunity to preach on Catholic doctrine, making a "few remarks explanatory of the Sacrifice of the Mass." Catholics and Protestants worshiping together was common. Just as Protestants came to Mass, Catholics were present at Protestant prayer meetings. Catholics and Protestants often strove to find common ground rather than opportunities to deride one another.[16]

Nowhere was this more evident than in a shared sense of Confederate loyalty. Following victory at James Island, South Carolina, in June 1862, the *Memphis Daily Appeal* highlighted the concerted effort of "the Hebrew, the Catholic, and the Protestant of every denomination . . . found side by side with one purpose and one faith in patriotism." Nonetheless, various theological differences remained. Catholics focused on the Mass, the sacraments, and devotional prayers whereas Protestants preferred Bible reading and preaching. As the *Weekly Ottumwa* (Iowa) once noted, "Protestant and Catholic soldiers alike, according to their own belief, and in their own way, bow down and worship."[17]

Reverend Jesse Henderson's diary offers a very brief example of Protestant wartime religiosity. One day, Henderson recorded buying a Bible, which he read on "rainy and cold" days. Henderson heard preaching numerous times over the following weeks and, presumably, supplemented those sermons with ample Scripture reading. At the conclusion of a prayer meeting, he resolved to "live more humble," praying God would show him a way to "live more devoted to thy cause that I may do something for the advancement of thy kingdom." In general, Protestant Christians enthusiastically attended camp prayer meetings. Mississippi soldier B. F. Gentry explained that prayer meetings were held every night and that many in his regiment had "professed religion." Fellow Mississippian T. G. Clark wrote to his wife, "We have prayers in camp every night and we have pledged ourselves to keep it up and I think it will have a good effect." Such examples are myriad. While Catholics worshiped one way, and Protestants another, their experiences often overlapped. Theology differed, but fellowship was shared.[18]

Sheeran claimed that at a 7:00 A.M. Mass "nearly all the Protestants in camp were present." According to him, "many" Protestants hoped he would return to celebrate Mass again, and on another occasion, his sermon had such an effect that "one of the Protestant officers expressed his intention of becoming a Catholic and others requested that I should preach every Sunday afternoon." Sheeran was generally joyful in his interactions with Protestants. He once celebrated Mass in a Protestant church. "A strange sight to see an altar in a Methodist church!" Sheeran wrote happily, grateful for the opportunity.[19]

When staying with an Episcopalian family, the Southalls, Gache credited his hosts: "More gentle people you couldn't find." He was thankful they had allowed him to use their parlor to celebrate Mass. "I can't help but believe they are living in good faith and that if they had the opportunity to know us as we really are, they would become Catholics. May the Holy Sacrifice of the Mass which I offered in their home and the little pictures which I gave to the children be the source and the occasion of a great blessing for each and every one of them." Gache had given holy cards to the girls, and their mother had procured special envelopes in which to store them.[20]

Examples of ecumenical respect are plentiful. But lest some kind of perfect congruity be assumed, one need only look deeper into Gache's writings to understand the gulf separating Catholics from Protestants. Regarding Protestants, Gache oscillated between poles of frustrated antipathy and assumed good faith. He praised the religious example of generals like Lee and Jackson, and often showed a "softer side" in interactions with individuals and families like the Southalls, yet he was ever ready to allow more aggressive feelings to surface. Writing once of a Baptist minister whom he considered a friend, Gache recalled, "I take advantage of every occasion to tell him and the others of his ilk that I don't see them under any other aspect than as gentlemen." He added, "Certainly I don't consider them as ministers of the Gospel." He implied Episcopalians were insufficiently Christian: "Never before . . . [had] true worship been offered to the true God" in Virginia. He was pleased the war afforded him the opportunity, along with "a few Catholics . . . [, to] be the first people in the Old Dominion who know God truly and who worship Him according to His Holy Will."[21]

Gache claimed "great scandal" at an agreement between Catholic and Protestant chaplains to alternate leading funeral services irrespective of whether the deceased was "Catholic, Protestant, Jew or Turk." Gache was incensed at a fellow priest for an apparent betrayal of ecclesial purity, excoriating a Lynchburg cleric as "one of these priests." If anything, Gache was not *one of these priests*. "I made them understand that they were dealing with a Catholic who for many years had been inspired by the philosophy of Father Serra!" In one inter-confessional scuffle, Gache explained his modus operandi thusly: "I went to work by first dethroning a Presbyterian minister," one who had claimed seniority among chaplains and the right to have others under his charge. Gache took the case to an army official and claimed victory. "The commandant took a look at the document and immediately saw that I was right. . . . It was I," he declared, with unintended humorous petulance, "not the Reverend Presbyterian minister, who should have been 'senior chaplain.'" He then informed all parties he would not participate in the ecumenical funerals. He had entered the service of the Confederacy as a Catholic priest and therefore felt obliged only to officiate services for deceased Catholics.[22]

"Moreover," Gache continued, "there are many Protestants and Jews, who, while they were alive, not only disbelieved in Catholic prayers and ceremonies but even regarded this form of worship as an abomination. Why then . . . should we bury them with a ritual which, as long as they were alive, they rejected with indignation and horror? . . . [W]e should respect their sentiments, as well as the sentiments of their families and friends," whom Gache noted would be "horrified" by the proceedings. And, above all, "if they were not in good faith, then they don't deserve any religious service at all."[23]

Gache was preoccupied not just with dead Protestants; he readily sparred with live ones too. Once at a dinner party among a dominantly Protestant crowd, "some twenty Episcopalian ladies," he explained that "with one exception" all were cordial and welcoming. The exception was one who "declared that she was a heretic" and boasted that when in Rome she had not "asked the pope for a blessing." Gache was perplexed as to why this should concern him. The woman made a "profound curtsy" and bid him farewell with "*Bonsoir, Monsieur*." He stated that as soon as she departed, "the other ladies made it clear that they thoroughly disapproved of her provocative remarks." But his soiree was not yet over. An Episcopalian minister stopped by and soon began conversing with the Catholic chaplain. Gache claimed the minister "put on a mask of sweet innocence," one he "wore rather convincingly during the series of barbed questions and ever-so-polite objections which followed." Once again, Gache's female friends came to the rescue. The ladies "were shocked at seeing me treated with such rudeness in their home, where my status as guest should have given me immunity against this sort of outrage." Gache did not specify the theological content of his debate. He did, however, direct the Episcopalian clergyman to consult "Catholic dogma and Catholic authors."[24]

Humorous, heated, or even confusing exchanges aside, the Catholic clergy saw the Civil War as a chance to promote the faith. They took this very seriously, seldom missing opportunities to evangelize. Gache was at pains to highlight that while he was an ardent Confederate, his primary duties were to God and men, irrespective of politics. A soldier once asked him, "Do you think these dogs [Union soldiers] deserve any pity?" He replied, "I do indeed." Once the opposition had been "vanquished and can no longer do you any harm, he is no longer an enemy; he is simply an unfortunate human being who has a right to Christian charity." Withal, "I'm a Catholic priest and my work here doesn't allow me to make any distinction between Yankees and boys from the South. I see all men as redeemed by the Blood of Jesus Christ."[25]

The opportunity for Catholic priests to share their faith with non-Catholics was ever-present. Gache once had a meeting with Maj. Gen. John Bankhead Magruder, an Episcopalian, to discuss Catholic troops; what they needed and what Gache intended to do for them. They met over a bowl of peaches at lunchtime. "To what denomination do you belong?" the general asked Gache, handing him a new fruit after remarking, "You, sir, are not a good peach-picker." Gache explained that he was Catholic. "Oh, I know that," the general replied, "but to what—er, order—do you belong within the Catholic denomination?"[26]

Gache told him he was a Jesuit. "I thought so," Bankhead said. "You Jesuits are everywhere." Gache replied, "Yes, sir, doing all sorts of good works." To which Bankhead replied, "Oh yes, that's exactly what I understand." Gache was certainly pleased that the example of not just Catholics but Catholics of his order had come to the attention of a Protestant general—a rank of men, it should be remembered, whose military stature often granted them freedom from Gache's censure. Nonetheless, Gache could not resist indulging one of his favorite pastimes. "'Tis curious how much more esteem educated and intelligent men have for Catholicism than they seem to have for the Protestant sects," he wrote. "This is particularly evident where there are two chaplains, one Catholic and the other Protestant in the same camp—the Catholic receives all the attention and respect and the poor Protestant is forgotten. This in my opinion is a sign that a great harvest is ripening in America: *Oremus enim Dominum messis, ut mittat operarios in messem suam.*"[27]

In Williamsburg, at the house of his Episcopalian women friends, one evening Gache had been, as he saw it, attacked by a member of the hosting party and a local minister. Williamsburg was located in a state Gache claimed had not received any proper Christian worship until Catholic arrivals. All this notwithstanding, Gache envisioned a profoundly Catholic Williamsburg just waiting to take root and flourish. "I am very fond of the people of Williamsburg, and it seems unfortunate that there is not a single Catholic home here around which a priest might build a parish. If there were, I feel sure that it would not be long before one could have a sizeable congregation."[28]

For Gache, the material for sizeable congregations was usually right around corner. Such was the case when he happened on a "marvelous old lady" who quickly informed him she had the "highest esteem and the utmost respect for priests." She explained, in considerable detail, that when she was young she had been warned against Catholics and, especially, Catholic practices. However, coming into adulthood, she had read some books and now believed Catholicism had been misrepresented. She had become a strong partisan of Catholic churches and made it a habit to say her prayers there. "Right now I believe most of the doctrines that Catholics hold and the Protestants reject," she told Gache. "I believe in miracles, in the Communion of Saints, and I also believe in confession." The priest was dumbstruck by the encounter. "Well, now, Mrs. Stuart," he finally managed, "you're more of a Catholic than any other Protestant I've ever met. Let's hope that one day you'll come all the way over and have done with it."[29]

Chaplains were, almost to a man, devout and dogmatically solid Catholics. What has been recounted about Sheeran, Gache, and Bannon could stand in for most of the Southern Catholic chaplaincy. Regarding soldiers, it is best to say their religious practices were a mixed bag. Historian George Rable has noted that while the Civil War is the most religious war in American history, the unchurched, lukewarm, and apathetic, taken as a whole, outnumbered practicing believers.[30] Some Catholic soldiers fall into this category. John Dooley once recorded that some men would read the Bible piously on the eve of battle—and sing hymns on Sunday—but wouldn't "go anywhere near a prayer meeting" and that many were "very indifferent to religion." Following Mass one day, Sheeran complained about the "cold indifference of the Catholics of the battalion." Gache once commented to a fellow priest at Spring Hill College, "it is better not to talk about religious practice in this regiment. It is too discouraging."[31]

This being true, there were large numbers of practicing Catholic soldiers committed to living out their faith. The first proof of this is looking at Catholic soldiers en masse. Consider, for example, times such as when additional accommodations had to be made to house an overflow of Mass attendees, which was not uncommon. The chaplains are an especially good source for soldiers' religiosity, as these men were the primary recipients of the chaplains' ministry. When it was noted that Father Bannon heard the confessions of thirty men in three hours, one's first inclination is to appreciate his endurance. The fact is also a statement about soldiers' piety, as are Sheeran's many "laborious days," ministering from early in the morning until nightfall. For Gache, there was no limit to the settings in which he would hear confessions. "As I didn't have a tent to myself," he explained, "I persuaded my penitents to join me in an evening stroll along the James." A quarter mile from camp was "a huge tree trunk that the tide had washed up on shore. It was bathed in a magnificent moonlight. Here, I thought to myself, is my confessional, and so here it was that each man, sitting beside me looking as if he were carrying on the most ordinary conversation, settled his affairs with God."[32]

Bannon, Sheeran, and Gache were taxed to their limits precisely because Catholic soldiers practiced their faith. They wanted Mass and the sacraments. If a vast majority of Catholic soldiers were lapsed, there would be no long days. There would be no moonlight walks by the river to impromptu confessionals in the wilderness. While it is true the Southern chaplaincy was understaffed, requiring a greater concentration of men to encroach on a priest's time, chaplains noted when a turnout of soldiers was large by normal standards. This was often the case. In early April 1862, Gache, who had previously claimed he did not want to discuss soldiers' religion, wrote that since the beginning of Lent, "things have improved. Now each morning I have a good number at mass. Every evening right after the seven o'clock roll-call, I conduct a service consisting of rosary, catechetical instruction, and night prayers, which is attended by about thirty or forty persons." He added, "The number of confessions and Communions has picked up. . . . I would like to have as many as three hundred Easter Communions, and I'm hoping that there will even be more."[33]

On Easter Sunday 1863, Sheeran mentioned a "heavy snow" falling all morning: "One cannot see 50 yards ahead." He believed this might cause a poor turnout for Mass. The opposite was true:

To my surprise I found a large concourse of boys around my tent. To see so many of our brave soldiers knee-deep in the snow, cheerfully awaiting the Holy Sacrifice of the Mass, was perhaps one of the most consoling sights of my life, and never did I pray more fervently for my congregation than on this occasion. But if it was edifying to see them standing in the snow before Mass commenced, how much more to see them on their bended knees and with uncovered heads defying as it were the angry elements during the offering of the Holy Sacrifice. . . . A greater number of those present received Holy Communion, after which we recited the rosary of our Blessed Mother as part of our thanksgiving.[34]

An ample number of deathbed conversions further shows the prevalence of religion among men who, like Private McGolfe, appeared to be wholly worldly, even antireligious. One cannot, of course, know the reason for, or level of sincerity in, these acts. While some may have been done for authentically devout reasons, others may have sprung from superstition, habit, or the fear of death. Even in these cases, there is some practice of faith present. A last-minute conversion by a soldier who does so simply because he is afraid to die is still an act of faith. This is why the Catholic Church differentiates between perfect and imperfect contrition. The first is better: sorrow for sin out of love for God. The second less noble: sorrow for sin out of a fear of Hell, essentially out of love for self. Both are sufficient to receive absolution. Both are acts of faith, of turning to God for forgiveness. So while historians cannot know which deathbed conversions and battlefield confessions were "perfect" and which "imperfect," this is ultimately unimportant. The presence of so many of these events testifies to soldiers' religiosity. "I'm still very pleased with my soldiers . . . every day some come to confession and to communion," Gache once recalled. "I assure you they do so with a good intention and not just because they are afraid."[35]

Regarding soldiers and religion, another factor is important as well. Many practiced their faith wholly in private, before God and no one else, something impossible to analyze, as the very private nature of the matter makes it inaccessible. Dooley was this type of Catholic. He had just commemorated his first live action, at the Battle of Cedar Mountain, by eating some bread and washing it down with "make believe coffee." He then set off to bed. "I felt strange enough, I assure you, lying down this my first night in camp," Dooley wrote. "So, kneeling for a few moments I said some brief prayers and lay me down in peace and quietness." He added, "My Guardian Angel was watching by my side [and] though I little suspected it then, bore me through many a dreadful peril even to this hour." When Dooley noticed another soldier observing him he added a key phrase. "I deferred saying my prayers until I lay down. . . . I had that portion of the Scriptures on my side when our Lord counsels his followers to pray in secret."[36]

When one reads Dooley's journal, there are clear indications that he was a devoutly religious man. He prayed the rosary. He was a fixture at camp prayer meetings, presumably many of them Protestant-led. Dooley claimed that in March 1862 the Devil was responsible for preventing men from hearing the Word of God, and he consistently longed for a greater spirituality among the men. If one misses these points amid a profusion of reflections on politics and war, it is easy to assume Dooley was more Confederate than Catholic. His intention to pray in secret is key; he kept the majority of his spiritual life hidden from others. He cultivated the interior life just as fervently as they did, if not more so, as he prepared for battle. Only when one considers one of his final journal entries do the full extent and depth of his faith become clear. It was a short step from this letter (discussed in this book's conclusion) to Dooley beginning studying for the priesthood, which he commenced shortly after the war's conclusion.[37]

In addition to private prayer and public worship at Mass, Catholic soldiers practiced devotions together. Sheeran reported walking back to his tent after confessions one day, "hear[ing] the sturdy voices of many of our Catholic soldiers united in reciting the rosary of our dear Lady in an adjacent tent. I cannot describe to you the effect this had on my mind." Elder claimed, "Almost all our Catholic soldiers approach the Sacraments and carry with them their prayer book, crucifix and medal." Medals were common, even among non-Catholics. A priest reported that soldiers, Catholic and Protestant alike, showed a great "eagerness to obtain a Medal of our Immaculate Mother, a chaplet. . . . [O]nly when furnished with a medal [do] they return to their regiments." Some of the Protestants who requested medals of the Blessed Virgin Mary were presumably like a Protestant minister Dooley once described, who "looked upon devotion to the Blessed Virgin as the most beautiful feature in the Catholic religion."[38]

While it is true Poche spilled a lot of ink on his rumor obsession, references to his faith outstrip any other topic. His record is evidence that often the Catholic soldiers who were serious about their faith were *very* serious about it, fully devoted and prioritizing it above all else. Shortly after joining the Confederate army, he wrote, "Since I have separated from my sweet little wife, I have never had such pleasant reminiscences of her, as I did this morning when I knelt during the holy sacrifice, and read the same prayers which we, every Sunday, read together in our old parish church." Poche's faith was foundational to his military service. It is natural to assume that churchgoing of any kind is difficult during a war. Certainly it is. Nevertheless, Poche found time to attend Mass on Sundays as well as during the week.[39]

In July 1864, Poche attended Mass at least eleven times, including six during the week. He made frequent use of the Sacrament of Confession and once offered his Communion "especially for the benediction of an early peace." Poche, like Bannon and Gache, believed entering battle in a state of grace was a necessity. "In these times of danger, one should do everything possible to be in God's good Graces." He was theologically minded, too; his journal contains various expositions and opinions concerning doctrine. On August 9, 1863, Poche recalled hearing a "great sermon" on Confession: "The subject is one upon which the Catholic Church is universally attacked, and which needs a great tact to defend." He had a deep devotion to Jesus in Holy Communion. He said that having received "His Body and Blood," he would enter "supreme moments, when my consciousness is in perfect accord with my Divine Saviour." Another time, Poche wrote that he had "the good fortune of taking part in the holy Sacrifice in receiving the body of the Divine Saviour in the Holy Eucharist," adding, "it is in these moments of happiness and of rapture of divine joy that the Christian feels in the bottom of his heart the truth of the Catholic Church."[40]

Garidel's diary was similarly stuffed with references to an active, lively, and daily practiced faith. Garidel was a man of many devotions. The rosary held such a prominent place in his daily prayer life that he once referred to it as "my only consolation in the world." Naturally, he had a deep devotion to the Blessed Virgin Mary. He consistently recommended to her the protection of his loved ones—"to place my dear Lolo and my dear children under the protection of the Blessed Virgin, which I do every day"—sought her intercession for his own health and protection on the battlefield, and attended Month of Mary rites at the Richmond cathedral during May. Garidel once noted hearing a sermon on the first chapter of Luke's Gospel, which he especially enjoyed because "Mary was the subject of his [the priest's] magnificent sermon."[41]

Garidel's Marian devotion extended to scouring the Richmond cityscape in order to buy a picture of her. This search proved unfruitful. Garidel seemed to share Gache's sentiments about the largely non-Catholic character of Virginia, certainly of the capital city. "I went down to the end of Main Street . . . to a very high hill. . . . Filled with awe, I was moved to say my rosary on top of this hill thinking that perhaps I was the first human being to address a prayer to the Blessed Virgin in such a Protestant place."[42]

Some days Garidel virtually lived inside a church, as when on the Feast of the Annunciation he rose at 6:00 A.M. to attend 7:00 Mass, returned later in the day to adore the Blessed Sacrament, and then at 7:30 in the evening recited the rosary, in communion with the other congregants, before hearing a sermon by the visiting bishop of Charleston "on sacrifice in all religions and particularly in the Catholic religion, where the Son of God sacrificed himself." But the night was not yet through. Following Lynch's sermon, they "had the Benediction of the Blessed Sacrament."[43]

Garidel made prolific use of the sacraments throughout his stay, particularly confession, and practiced the Forty Hours' Devotion along with attending Stations of the Cross services during Lent. He was something of an evangelizer too. One of his friends had been away from the sacraments for decades. Garidel, having resolved to go to confession, told this friend about his plans before leaving. Finding John McGill, the bishop of Richmond at the Cathedral, he asked for confession. The bishop obliged, "direct[ing] me to his confessional." Later that day, Garidel's friend informed him that being so long away from confession "had been tormenting him." He added, "You have convinced me that I too must go to confession. I will go with you this afternoon." Garidel explained that he had just been but would accompany his friend. He later noted, "We went to the church, and there he took confession, something he hadn't done in thirty years, since his first Communion. I was only too pleased that I convinced him to do so, and he thanked me for making him so happy."[44]

Garidel was an avid lover of Jesus Christ in the Blessed Sacrament and Holy Eucharist. He would make a special note when a sermon or homily touched on the doctrine of the Real Presence, listing one such "superb" discourse concerning Christ's dictate that "unless you eat the flesh of the Son of man and drink his blood, you have no life in you." To attend Mass on a more than weekly basis, as Poche and Garidel and many other Catholics did, was to receive Holy Communion regularly. And so Garidel attended as often as he could, spent hours in Eucharistic adoration, even participated in processions of the Blessed Sacrament, describing one such time thusly: "All the orphans were marching, some dressed in their first Communion costumes, some with crowns of flowers on their heads and carrying beautiful bouquets. Two at the head of the procession were throwing flowers in the path of the Blessed Sacrament as it passed. At the head of it all, a Sister of Charity was singing the *Pange Lingua*."[45]

Catholic chaplains and soldiers were deeply committed to the Confederacy. The vast majority volunteered to fight or serve, remained faithful to their new nation throughout the war, and bitterly detested their enemy while assured that their own cause was just—politically and in the eyes of God. The same Confederatized Catholics were also devout in their faith. Sheeran, Bannon, and Gache were priests before all else. For every cannon Bannon fired, he likely baptized, absolved, and gave Communion to a hundred, if not a thousand, men. For every lapsed Catholic soldier, there were those like Dooley, Garidel, and Poche—men who prayed the rosary publicly and prayed in private ten times more; devotees who not only met their Sunday obligation but went to Mass three, four, five times a week.

These men's dual religious and political allegiances were neither paradoxical nor in opposition to one another. One could be a devoted Confederate and a devout Catholic with easy symbiosis, diving headlong into the political and military maelstrom of the day without compromising or forgetting his religion. For some, like Gache, there was a certain mirth in carrying out one's religious practices in the midst of such a costly war. "Don't think, however, dear Father, that all of these privations and hardships make life disagreeable or make me regret my assignment," he once wrote to Cornette. "Not at all. By God's grace my life up till now has been utterly free from tedium, and I am more content with my lot today than I have ever been before. I have never been more certain that this is where God wants me to be and that I am doing His will."[46]

CHAPTER FOUR

The Ambiguities of Peace

The Bishops during the War

During the summer of 1864 in Union-occupied Natchez, Mississippi, Federal authorities asked Bishop William Henry Elder to read a prayer supportive of Abraham Lincoln during Mass. He declined. Undeterred, the Union army tried gentle coercion. Other churches had complied, might not he also? He would not. Following subsequent refusals, Elder was imprisoned in nearby Vidalia, Louisiana. After a brief exile, he would be quickly released, not to be bothered with the matter anymore. He returned to Natchez a bona fide Confederate hero, the cleric who had defied Lincoln and the Yankees. One of the most famous "Catholic moments" of the Civil War, North or South, came not from a man fighting on a battlefield but from a noncombatant.

While noncombatants often get less recognition than soldiers, their impact on wartime events can be just as significant. This chapter, which carries the bishops' secession story into the war years, demonstrates how the already Confederatized Southern episcopate maintained its Confederate allegiance throughout the conflict. Much of the bishops' wartime focus centered on home front issues and peace advocacy. They labored to rebuild dioceses, assisted brother bishops in need, and provided the sacraments and religious instruction for their congregants. Yet for many bishops, the hope for peace was tied to a desire that it be advantageous for the Confederacy. They worked for a unique double victory that would fit with their duality of their devout Catholic, devoted Confederate Confederatization paradigm. If a favorable, pro-Confederate independence peace settlement could be brokered, then bishops would, along with other Southerners of like mind, achieve a "double-victory": a political win for the Confederate nation and a Christian triumph, securing victory without further bloodshed. Pope Pius IX's involvement in these intentions shows the international character of the Catholic-Confederate war narrative, and Bishop Elder's refusal of a prayer request for Lincoln shows how visible, and societally important, was Catholic Confederatization.

As mentioned, the bishops' secession crisis peace initiatives carried over into the war. In this spirit, Bishop Spalding summed up what he saw as the Church's fundamental mission regarding earthly conflict. "The Catholic Church seeks to save souls, and rises, in her sublime mission, far above the passions of the hour. Deus Providebit pro Suis!" As Spalding's diocese was "cut in two by this unhappy war," he wished to "attend to souls without entering into the angry political discussion." He acted on his own advice. While writing these lines, he was in Cincinnati with the local archbishop, staunch unionist John Baptist Purcell, holding a retreat. According to Spalding, "much good was accomplished" during the visit, which consisted largely of preaching, hearing confessions, and administering the Sacrament of Confirmation. Spalding noted that forty-eight people were confirmed and twenty-five made their First Holy Communions. In the midst of war, two bishops on opposite sides of the conflict came together to provide spiritual nourishment. Each put his partisanship to the side, prioritizing religion over politics.[1]

Sometimes religious prioritization meant inter-episcopal charity. Bishop Augustin Verot's December 1861 letter to Bishop Patrick Lynch, offering condolences and detailing forthcoming financial assistance, was the first of many such actions Southern prelates undertook to help their brother bishop. On January 18, 1862, Archbishop Jean-Marie Odin wrote that he was "truly grieved when I received the sad intelligence of the great conflagration which desolated your city and of the loss you have sustained." He told Lynch that he was praying for him and that he had instructed all his parish priests to take up special collections for Charleston. On February 1, Verot informed Lynch that he had sent him seven hundred dollars, for "you personally & the church." Elder wrote to Lynch asking for conformation that money he had sent to Charleston had arrived. If it had, he intended to send more.[2]

Odin further extended Lynch an invitation to come to New Orleans, "at a future day, when peace will be restored to our confederacy," for the purpose of making a personal appeal to help rebuild the Charleston cathedral. From the war's outset, Southern bishops viewed the Confederate nation as their own, with this new country quickly becoming the sole repository for their national allegiance. When peace would eventually be restored, it would come to "our Confederacy," sovereign within the family of nations.[3]

On February 26, 1862, Spalding gave a funeral sermon for deceased soldiers in the Louisville Cathedral, filled to capacity with a gathering of least three thousand people. Catholics, he said, should place God and the faith above all else. The spirit of the Catholic Church had always been "pacific, conservative, and forgiving. Her mission was to preach peace and good will." Peace, while it had intrinsic worth, was not an end in itself. It had to serve a higher purpose, namely to "direct the attention of men to heaven where all will be peace and eternal repose." The Church "takes the view of eternity rather than that of time, and of heaven rather than that of earth . . . wherever souls are to be saved, or afflictions bodily or mental to be alleviated, there she is always to be found discharging her heaven-born office of charity."[4]

This "view of eternity" is why chaplains worked so hard to get dying men to confess their sins, why Catholic soldiers received the sacraments before entering battle, and why bishops and priests stressed the importance of the eternal over the temporal. The ultimate goal was salvation. Spalding focused on spiritual matters so that men might pour their energies into God and their faith rather than into war and politics. His reflection on peace is telling. While many spoke of peace as "honorable" or "just," code for *pro-Confederate*, he was speaking solely in Christian terms.

"When death comes to the soldier," Spalding continued, "whether from disease or on the battle-field, she [the Church] weeps like a mother over the fallen, [and] without distinctions of persons, does everything in her power for their eternal repose by prayer and sacrifice, and bids all to rise above the passions and animosities of the hour in the awful presence of death." The bishop also touched on the horrors of the battlefield and explained why Catholics pray for the dead. He concluded by calling the war "unholy." In the face of extreme carnage, many made this point, and it is why today some historians argue the conflict cannot be seen as a "just war" in the traditional Christian sense.[5] Ironically, clergymen of all denominations, in giving their blessings to the war effort, fanned the flames of already escalating passions. Supposed divine sanction of a cause frequently exacerbated violent impulses.[6]

The year 1862 was filled with these violent impulses prodigiously loosed. Any predictions of a short war were no longer tenable. One headline from the June 7 *Catholic Mirror* surely spoke for millions: "When Will the War End?"

Spalding attempted to provide an answer. The bishop of Louisville—busy in the fall of 1862 taking up a collection for the pope himself in the midst of civil strife, the Italian *Risorgimento*—seconded Verot's prior analysis, claiming personal sin had caused the war.[7] "God is evidently scourging us for our sins," he wrote. "God help and preserve us!" he added on All Saints Day, for "He alone can help us, & we daily beseech the Immaculate Mother. . . . She will help us, & by her powerful intercession restore peace and happiness to the Country." In a final entry for the year, Spalding once more placed his hopes for peace with the Mother of God. "My confidence in our good & sweet Mother restoring peace is greatly increased," he wrote. "She is our Patroness & will take care of us."[8]

Other bishops echoed Spalding's intentions. In February 1863, a week before Ash Wednesday, Lynch addressed the Charleston faithful, reiterating many of the sentiments Spalding had expressed a year earlier in the Louisville Cathedral. He encouraged Catholics to tend to their faith first, regardless of external pressures, for neither war nor circumstance of time could change the Church's mission. It was not possible for a "condition of society [to arise] in which the necessities of her children are unknown to her, or beyond her maternal solicitude."[9]

Lynch, on the precipice of the season of prayer, fasting, and almsgiving, told his congregants, "The extraordinary circumstance in which the country is placed requires this year a corresponding modification of the Disciplinary Enactments of the Church, as to the observance of Lent." The usual order of fasting would be lessened. "During this season, by the ancient laws and spirit of the Catholic world the use of Flesh meat was entirely forbidden, and every day, Sundays excepted, was a fast day on one meal, generally to be taken only after sunset." No meat every day; one meal a day, but only after sunset. This was not the isolated practice of desert hermits but the standard for everyday Catholics. Because of the war, meat consumption would be permitted every day except Ash Wednesday, all Fridays, and Holy Saturday. Soldiers were added to the usual list of those exempted from the fast—children, the elderly, and pregnant mothers. Lynch called for an increased devotion to prayer and almsgiving. The Church "exhorts us and expects us to make as it were some compensation, by more abundant charity, according to our means, to the poor . . . and by fervent and unceasing prayer to God for a speedy and honorable termination of the war, and the establishment of a happy peace."[10]

Lynch often left traces of political inferences in his addresses. One can read between the lines of "honorable termination" to understand *pro-Confederate* is implied. Yet, on the whole, this particular address was primarily spiritual in nature. Lynch, like Elder in his November 1860 circular, asked his congregation to do something about attaining peace—that its members pray for it. Food scarcity had changed the rules of fasting, but Lynch still expected his parishioners to put their faith first, to pray more fervently and tend to the poor with greater care and frequency, and to make "some compensation" in a time when the usual penances were not possible.[11]

As the war progressed through its climaxes in the summer of 1863, the Southern clergy tried to remain focused on peace. When Bishop Elder noted that his vicar general, Father Mathurin Grignon, preached on the topic, this was but one example of an intention replicated countless times throughout Southern churches, Protestant congregations included. On another occasion, Grignon preached on the "efficacy of the Holy Sacrifice to obtain peace," echoing a point Elder had once made, that had there been more saints in America the war might have been avoided. Grignon believed that if Catholics would properly dispose themselves to receive the Holy Eucharist, transformative effects would come about in their lives. From these individual metamorphoses, society could be transmuted from strife into tranquility.[12]

At this same time, in the immediate aftermath of Gettysburg and Vicksburg, the Catholic Church in America suffered an unexpected blow. The bishops' collective focus shifted from peace to sorrow. The archbishop of Baltimore died suddenly, on July 8. The "meek" Bishop Peter Richard Kenrick was deeply disturbed by the war, and perhaps the recent events proved too much for his nerves. The Washington, DC, *Evening Star* wrote that the bishop's death "is mourned by the entire Christian community of Baltimore." The Raleigh, North Carolina, *Semi-Weekly Standard* remembered him as of the most prominent theologians in the country, a true classicist whose "translations from the original of the four Evangelists and the Acts of the Apostles with annotations of his own, will be read with instruction by both Protestant and Catholic to the end of time."[13]

The Confederacy might have lost a secret ally in Kenrick, who, according to one historian, possibly recommended a plan to US secretary of war Edwin Stanton whereby the North would let the South go for the sake of peace. If true, Kenrick was essentially proposing to the Northern government Confederate victory as a peace plan. Because he was archbishop of Baltimore, his opinion carried the most weight within the episcopate. Whether his views mattered to the US government is another matter.[14]

With Kenrick dead, the prime American see became vacant, one that directly oversaw numerous Southern dioceses. The Southern bishops took the news hard.

"Dear friend," Bishop John McGill wrote to Lynch, "I doubt not that you have heard the sad news of the death of our saint and venerable Metropolitan, Abp. Kenrick." McGill was confident Kenrick was spiritually ready to die but wondered, "What will be done to provide him with a successor?" Lynch responded in kind. He, too, was "deeply sad" to hear of "our Saintly Abp." passing, but as for a successor he believed that it would not be a Southerner.[15]

Lynch added that he was not the man for the job: "Nothing short of a mandate from Rome would induce me to accept." His recommendations were Newark's Bishop James Roosevelt Bayley, who would assume the post in 1872, and Wheeling's Richard Vincent Whelan. Whelan thought Elder was best suited for the position. Yet it was the man who was the most affected by Kenrick's death—and, unexpectedly for Lynch, a Southerner, a Southern sympathizer in a nominally Union state—who was eventually appointed to the post: Louisville's Martin John Spalding. Upon hearing of Kenrick's death, Spalding wrote in his journal, "Death of good and holy Archp Kenrick of Baltimore, found dead in bed—I feel like an orphan—he was my father in Christ."[16]

Lynch's recommendation of two Northern prelates to fill the most important seat in America is evidence of the bishops' cross-sectional spiritual unity. The same can be said for Whelan's endorsement of Elder. The bishops recognized that the prime American see needed simply the best man for the job, irrespective of politics. They chose Spalding, who, according to one historian, was the most able Civil War bishop, North or South.[17] Any political considerations were conciliatory. Spalding did favor one side, but he was not a rabid partisan like Lynch, Quinlan, or the archbishop of New York, John Hughes. He was, furthermore, a good candidate to maintain North-South ecclesiastical unity, because in moving from one border state to another he was used to living within a diverse mix of political viewpoints. These pragmatic factors, in conjunction with his ability, made him a natural choice.

On October 5, 1863, Verot wrote to Lynch: "I wish to communicate to you a project I have of inviting all the faithful of Georgia & Florida to pray more particularly for peace in accordance with the intentions & desires of our Holy Father." He wanted to invite people to receive Holy Communion during the Octave of the Immaculate Conception and to offer prayers for peace. "It seems to me that if all the Catholics of the Nation in a state of grace unite to ask peace of Almighty God, heaven would not refuse of that favor." His inspiration was Pope Pius IX's recent letter to Archbishops Odin and Hughes, of monumental importance to the Southern episcopate. Pius asked that Odin and Hughes put

aside politics and work for reconciliation. The pope even declared his willingness to personally mediate a settlement between the North and the South.[18]

"Amongst the various and most oppressive cares which weigh on us in these
turbulent and oppressive times, we are greatly afflicted by the truly lamentable
state in which the Christian people of the United States of America are placed
by the destructive civil war broken out amongst them," Pius IX began. He expressed being "overwhelmed with the deepest sorrow" when considering "the
slaughter, ruin, innumerable and ever-to-be-deplored calamities by which the
people themselves are most miserably harassed and dilacerated." His concern
was that of a father, he explained, and as such he placed ultimate hope in God
the Father, "that He would deliver them from so many and so great evils."[19]

"We cannot refrain from inculcating, again and again, on the minds of the
people themselves and their chief rulers mutual charity and peace," the pope
continued, "by the virtue of the office of our apostolic ministry, embrac[ing],
with the deepest sentiments of charity, all the nations of the Christian world,
and though unworthy, administer here on earth the viceregent work of Him
who is Author of Peace and the Lover of Charity." It would be Hughes and
Odin's task "to exhort, with your eminent piety and Episcopal zeal, your clergy
and faithful to offer up their prayers . . . to restore forthwith the desired tranquility and peace by which the happiness of both the Christian and the civil
republic is principally maintained."[20]

The *Wilmington Journal* claimed Pius's intervention was inherently pro-
Southern, advocacy for peace "irrespective of terms." If not exactly "pro-Southern," it certainly was compatible with Southern hopes. Did not the pope's call
for immediate peace prioritize the cessation of fighting above all else? If peace
was all that mattered, what difference would it make if this resulted in two separate Americas? That the CSA would remain a separate nation would achieve the
foundational goal of the Confederacy's revolution. The Confederacy additionally hoped Pius might somehow discourage Catholics from joining the Union
ranks and even influence the Catholic monarchs of Europe. Furthermore, the
letter encouraged the Confederacy to seek help at the Vatican, inspiring the diplomatic missions of Father Bannon and Bishop Lynch. It is easy to understand
why these bishops were ecstatic. A great double victory was now a possibility;
a peace for the higher Christian purpose of ending a brutal war and restoring
fraternal harmony, and, at the same time, one that would serve their nation's
independence.[21]

Like Verot, other Southern bishops responded enthusiastically to the papal appeal. The archbishop of New Orleans published a pastoral letter in the *Freeman's Journal* on September 26, using language both Verot and Spalding had previously employed concerning sin and chastisement. Southern Catholics, and Southerners in general, needed to repent. "War is but one of the scourges of iniquity," Odin wrote. "God outraged by sin uses men to wreak on men His merited vengeance; He arms them one against the other and punishes them by making them instruments of His wrath and of His justice, through mutual hostility." Southerners were their own worst enemy, for "the more God blessed and favored us, the more we seemed to forget Him." Odin argued that God's blessings only increased the people's pride. Success whetted appetites for more worldly goods. "In a community professing to be Christian," he concluded, "let us acknowledge that we have belied our title of Christians by our aversion to the cause of Christ, by our preference of sensual ease and enjoyment, by our worship of gold and vice."[22]

The Southern press celebrated the Catholic episcopate's peace initiatives. "A Clerical Move in the Right Direction," Raleigh's *Semi-Weekly Standard* declared, specially mentioning Odin's institution of a Forty Hours' Devotion for "blessed PEACE." The paper further noted: "We commend this pacific movement to our clergy as one in the right direction, and far more likely to produce good results than a tour to Europe." Three weeks later, the same paper added, "Surely the united prayers of the faithful throughout Europe and America will prevail over the evil passions of godless fanatics, and draw down on our unhappy and devastated land the blessings of a speedy and honorable peace, crowned with liberty and independence." The *Memphis Daily Appeal* wrote, "The Catholic hierarchy of the South are warm supporters of the Southern cause" and "zealous advocates of the justice upon which this war of defense is conducted."[23]

The *Richmond Enquirer* featured Pius IX's recommendation of a twenty-day devotion specifically for "peace in America," and the article quickly was reprinted throughout the South. The "very learned and exemplary Dr. McGill," bishop of Richmond, was expected to take a leading role in fulfilling the pope's wishes. He reminded his congregants that "he expected them to pray [for] such a peace as honorable and patriotic men could accept and which did not involve any sacrifice of their rights and liberties." Southerners should rest assured that, taken together, the bishops' patriotism was beyond reproach. None would settle for a dishonorable peace, least of all McGill, for there was "no sounder Confederate than the Bishop." Perhaps the pope's peace initiatives could serve a secondary goal too. "Surely here is a platform and an occasion on which all Christendom could lay aside its internal differences, and send up to the throne of the Eternal Father, from the altars of Catholic temples and the pulpits of Protestant Churches, one bleeding volume of solemn, earnest, and faithful prayer," that God might "'abate the pride, assuage the malice, and cofound the devices' of our enemies.'"[24]

On November 26, Lynch offered a detailed response to Verot's October 5 letter. In his "Pastoral Prayers for Peace," he called for the immediate implementation of the pope's wishes.

> Beloved Brethren: Deeply moved by the calamities of these times, and in agreement with our Venerable Brethren of the Episcopate, we invite you to join with the Faithful in other Dioceses in earnest and preserving prayers to the Father of Mercy and the giver of every good gift, to obtain from Him, in whose hand are the hearts of men, a cessation of war which at present afflicts our country, and the speedy establishment of a just and honorable peace. War is a consequence and a punishment of the sins of man. However just in its origin any special war may be, however necessary for the protection of important rights unjustly assailed, it is unavoidably attended by many evils and much suffering. . . . So deeply must the Christian heart lament the anguish and evils of warfare, that even in giving thanks to Heaven for victories obtained, we must pray that they may lead, under God's blessing, to a just and more blessed peace.[25]

Lynch singled out the war's effects on families as particularly disastrous. Many wives had been made widows, many parents had buried their children, and the decrepit morality of the soldier's life had left many marriages in peril. War was a consequence of sin, a "potent means whereby sinful nations become the instruments of their own chastisement." Lynch's language concerning the Confederacy is important. Catholic Confederatization was not simply Catholic involvement in the Confederacy but full ascent to the Southern national ideal, complete immersion in the cause. When Lynch stated that war was afflicting "our country," he meant the Southern nation. The just and honorable peace that he was hoping for, the one that would give birth to an even "more blessed peace," was to come upon an independent Southern nation. In his eyes, just and honorable peace by which the South had to return to the Union would be anything but.[26]

In addition, Lynch's spiritually themed political address is a good example of a Christian-based Southern nationalism. Lynch wanted the Confederacy to gain independence and begin its own national story. He proved this most convincingly when agreeing to serve as a Confederate diplomat. But how did he believe the Southern nation would gain its independence? It would do so through prayer and by faith, with Catholics, in concert with all Southern Christians, uniting their petitions before God. While commanders and political leaders had a role to play, people must first acknowledge their sinfulness and repent. "No time can be more appropriate for such petitions than the approaching Patronal Festival of Our Church, when the Immaculate Virgin Mother, at whose entreaty Our Lord wrought His first miracle, may plead with her Divine Son in our behalf," Lynch declared, adding, "[with] no mode more powerful than that of united prayer, which He has specially promised to hear."[27]

It is well known that Southerners of all denominations prayed for God's favor upon their arms. One cannot overlook how much they prayed for providential favor in granting peace. Confederate Catholics didn't especially care how they won the war; winning was all that mattered. Praying for victory on the battlefield or a favorable peace settlement served the Confederate telos the same. Lynch provided his congregation with a spiritual blueprint for this work. He desired that Verot's idea for a Novena to the Blessed Virgin Mary be undertaken, and that the rosary be recited as well. Lynch decreed that a special Votive Mass for peace be celebrated on December 12 and that each day following Mass the Litany of Loreto and a *Memorare* be recited. "We trust the faithful will be [ready] to approach Holy Communion with worthy dispositions on the Pastoral Festival itself, December 18, and will, on that happy day, pray with all fervor that God grant us a firm and just peace," Lynch wrote. Verot echoed these hopes: "May God . . . grant us the peace for which we have prayed fervently & will continue to pray until we are heard."[28] The bishops' calls for peace joined a chorus of similar appellations throughout the South.[29]

Although the bishops stayed abreast of military events, significant focus was dedicated to pastoral care. This was often extended to Northern soldiers, especially prisoners of war. Bishop McGill preached to nine hundred Union prisoners detained in Richmond's Libby Prison, these men coming from all walks of life: "editors, lawyers, merchants, mechanics, doctors, artists, actors, etc etc." Lynch visited Libby Prison as well, delivering an "impressive discourse" to Federal officers. "He was listened to with marked attention, and at the close was heartily thanked by the prisoners for affording them the opportunity of hearing him preach," Richmond's *Daily Dispatch* noted. Even the distraction of food on the table did not "draw off many from the divine influence which the reverend father was exercising over them." Throughout Lynch's career, his oratory ability and physical presence were frequently noted.[30]

Preaching in prisons and serving soldiers was common, but bishops had to take care of their congregants back home too. Elder's wartime record provides a good microcosm of the bishops' domestic work, which can be grouped into the following categories: theological instruction, local education, dialogue with Protestant Christians, interactions with African Americans, and hospital ministry. Elder faced a host of quotidian duties on the home front, including overseeing local Catholic education. He once mentioned having to examine a large school in catechetics, grammar, spelling, history, reading, geography, and Latin. While the students improved in every subject, they "failed entirely" in geography. When a pupil at the Catholic school, a Protestant named Preston Thomas, was injured falling out of a tree, it was Elder's duty to send someone to check on him.[31]

While Elder played many roles in addition to bishop, including parochial school headmaster and welcoming committee, his lasting impact on the home front came from his commitment to evangelization. His primary concern was the human soul. Such was the case related to the death of Mrs. Kenny, a lapsed Catholic with a Protestant husband and Protestant daughters who were away from home at the time of her fatal illness. Elder recorded her story as "a remarkable one." "Very bitter against the Church," Mrs. Kenny was being cared for by one of her nieces, "a practical Catholic," who had sent for Elder in her aunt's final hours.[32]

Elder asked the woman, in the presence of her doctor and the doctor's sister, if she wished to receive the Catholic sacraments. She said she did. "It must have been [the] especial prayers of her Mother in heaven," Elder recorded in his journal, "that obtained for her to receive the Sacrts, just when she did.—What a happy thing is a good religious education. It kept the faith alive under all those cold embers of 25 years. . . . Blessed are the mysterious ways of God!" Mrs. Kenny died that day. Three days later, her husband, furious upon learning of his wife's reconciliation to the Catholic Church, confronted Elder. Mr. Kenny came to see the bishop again the following day; he had changed his position on the matter. He was no longer upset and actually wanted his wife to receive a Catholic funeral. Some theological questions ensued, Elder explaining "why people wish to die in the Cath. Church . . . because only there . . . the helps & consolations

wh.[ich] God has appointed [reside]," he wrote of his impromptu apologia, "&
taught in His Holy Scrp. The Sacrts—Penance—Eucharist—Extreme Unction—
Communion of Saints."[33]

Elder was indefatigable in his service to the sick and the wounded. His routine following battles was simply to go to the hospitals, to see who needed help.
In May 1863, he reported visiting "all the hospitals" in the Natchez area. With
many lodged in private houses, he went to "all I c[oul]d. find." Following the
fighting at Vicksburg, Elder was again in the hospitals, where he noted anoint-
ing a man shot through the head, one of the many examples of last-minute sacramental administrations. In his hospital ministry, Elder was doing work similar to the battlefield chaplains but with less sustained interaction. Chaplains had
plenty of time to develop personal relationships with soldiers, to form lasting
bonds of friendship, to mutually support one another through the duration of
their service. Bishops did not have this luxury. One man in charge of an entire
state and this daunting task exacerbated by the reality of nineteenth-century
travel, a bishop had to move quickly from one post to another, seldom staying
anywhere for too long, save for the diocesan headquarters.[34]

Elder's ministry to both slaves and freedmen was likewise extensive. Having
once described African Americans as his spiritual brothers and sisters, "every
one of them immortal, made to the image & likeness of God, redeemed by the
Precious Blood of the Son of God," he backed up this sentiment via his wartime
record, visiting black men and women at home and in hospitals, sending religious items on request and performing baptisms, all for the goal of bequeathing
what was, in his estimation, the most precious of gifts: the Catholic faith; and
the Catholic faith in its entirety, not some edited and truncated version high-
lighting the virtues of obedience to authority and little else.[35]

September 1863 was a typically busy month for Elder. On the fourth, he visited African Americans in hospitals, baptizing a young man into the faith. Later
that day, he baptized seven more people (three infants, four adults). An elderly
man, ninety-two years old, called for Elder and asked that he pray with him. Elder did. Shortly afterward, the man entered the Church and received the scapu-
lar. The next day, Elder baptized fourteen infants and two youths at the "colored
camp." On September 8, the Feast of the Nativity of the Blessed Virgin Mary,
Elder baptized ten more African American children. On September 12, he "prepared five for death" before returning again six days later; for four consecutive
days at the end of the month he went to the African American camp. Throughout the war, he visited African American soldiers, dispensing the sacraments,

especially baptism, and often just giving of his time. Elder went to see his African American congregants with similar frequency even when they were interred at the smallpox hospital.[36]

Elder held paternalistic views toward African Americans, but he was not a hypocrite when it came to living his own evangelical prescriptions. He implemented his call for "putting the sickle into the abundant field" of souls, giving African Americans unfettered access to the fullness of the faith, the sacraments, all the gifts of the Church. When an African American man named Alonzo asked Elder for religious items, the bishop sent him a rosary. Elder made house calls to his black congregants, too, visiting a woman named Eliza three times in five days in March 1863. When Alonzo was afflicted with an unspecified hemorrhage, Elder went to see him immediately following Mass. Elder sometimes held theological instruction for African Americans following the Benediction of the Blessed Sacrament, teaching fundamental Catholic doctrine.[37]

Regarding historiographical opinion of Elder's views on African Americans, Benedictine priest and scholar Cyprian Davis, author of *The History of Black Catholics in the United States,* writes: "For a truly pastoral bishop like Elder, the needs of the slaves were evident. Still, even he saw them as basically inferior to whites in regard to character and intellect, although, as he clearly pointed out, grace could make up for these deficiencies and make them saints." Davis writes that Elder's concern for African Americans was "from all indications genuine" and that the bishop of Natchez viewed former slaves as "refugees in a land that had been a prison more than a home."[38]

Elder wanted to give African Americans the faith solely for their spiritual benefit. Nonetheless, he was not free of the paternalistic racism endemic to white southern culture. The fundamental tragedy of Elder's relationship with African Americans is that of the Southern bishops writ large. Although all of the bishops did some good things for slaves, and later for freedmen, and although almost all viewed blacks and whites as equals before God, they still endorsed the slavery system. Such diplopia was not unique to the nineteenth century but extended back to the early Church Fathers. The effects of granting slaves spiritual freedom while denying them temporal freedom were the same in the nineteenth century as they had been in the third or fourth. Southern Catholics' endorsement of slavery left as chattel slavery those men and women whom the bishops claimed were spiritual equals, an unspeakable degradation and a blight upon the bishops' record.[39]

That Catholic bishops were authentic in spiritual matters does not excuse their position on slavery. Having genuine religious motives and holding racist views are not mutually exclusive, after all. And the bishops are certainly guilty of helping perpetuate the peculiar institution. In sum, the Southern bishops were good Catholic bishops although flawed, sinful men. They could, as bishops, see through the eyes of faith, while remaining equipped with the prejudiced views typical of Civil War Southern society, in which they were fully immersed.

If one thing can be stated assuredly, it is that Elder was looking for souls. The more people who entered the Catholic Church the better, and no number of converts could meet a quota. Helping non-Catholics become Catholics and Catholics become more fervent in their faith was the ultimate goal of Elder's priesthood. He rarely missed an opportunity. Once, at a farmhouse turned hospital, he gave a makeshift sermon to two Protestants inquiring about the faith. "I exhorted them to at least make an offering to God to that they wd. search for the truth & embrace it—& also to make an act of Contrition." In August 1863, he went to see Union general Ulysses S. Grant concerning the building of a convent. Grant was not in, but his son was there. He had "very sore eyes." Elder told him to wash them in holy water and to say the Litany of Jesus every day.[40]

Elder consistently exhorted his people on the home front to make their spirituality a priority. The first entry in his Civil War diary, November 1, 1862, All Saints Day, notes a sermon he preached at Mass on the divine origins of the Church, the communion of the Saints, Apostolic succession, the martyrs, and the popes and doctors of the Church, all for the purpose of showing "she is still the same Church—wishing to makes Saints now—'tis her whole business—and we are material—just like the other Saints—to be perfected by the same means if we will use them."[41] Elder preached often on redemptive suffering, a theme that must have resonated in war-ravaged Mississippi. The Blessed Virgin Mary's sufferings during Christ's Passion were a good example of how Mississippi Catholics should bear their own crosses. No better example of heroic suffering was available than Christ himself. It was "man's vocation to follow in the footsteps of Christ," to unite the struggles of the war to Calvary. On Easter Sunday, Elder connected his previous sermons on suffering to the Resurrection, arguing the latter was unattainable without the former.[42]

Although Elder might have preferred to focus on the home front, he was unafraid to enter the political arena when necessary. And within this realm, the bishop of Natchez would find the defining moment of his Civil War, perhaps of his entire life, when, on June 4, 1864, he learned that no one would be allowed out of Union-occupied Natchez without taking an oath of allegiance to the United States. Such mandates were commonplace throughout the war. As has already been discussed, Henri Garidel left occupied New Orleans for Richmond precisely for this reason and Father James Sheeran's detainment in Federal prison lasted as long as it did because he refused to take the oath.[43]

Elder was presented with Special Order No. 31 on June 25, three weeks after he initially heard of the travel restriction. Union general Bernard G. Farrar addressed it to him, commanding "all Pastors of Churches to read a prayer expressive of a proper spirit towards the President of the U. States." Elder need not worry, his vicar general assured him because he, Grignon, had communicated to Farrar the bishop's application, sent to authorities in Washington earlier in the year, to receive exemptions from such directives. There was reason to believe this would be sufficient. However, Sheeran, too, had been told that his pass was sufficient for travel behind Union lines. That Elder was not the first Southern prelate to make such a petition helped his case. Bishop Spalding had written a letter to Kentucky governor Beriah Magoffin in 1862, protesting a law that required marriage-officiating ministers to pledge an oath of allegiance to the United States. That Magoffin had rejected Spalding's petition did not help Elder's case. Spalding eventually took the oath, under protest.[44]

Responses to the oath varied. There was a class of hyper-Confederatized Southerners who believed taking an oath to the Union was worse than desertion. Sheeran and Garidel were both of this mind-set. Felix Pierre Poche once assured a man that certain people were "good Confederates" simply because "many among them have refused to take the Yankee oath." Some Southerners who took it did so under false pretenses. Sheeran once mentioned a squad of Confederate prisoners who consented only for the purpose of being paroled so as to betray their pledged neutrality and rejoin the South. Many simply signed it and kept their word, although their motive was self-interest, not repentant patriotism. In December 1863, Abraham Lincoln had promised full pardon and the restoration of all political rights to men who took an oath of allegiance to the United States and agreed to accept the abolition of slavery. Andrew Johnson seconded this deal in May 1865, with the addendum that property rights would be restored to loyal ex-Confederates.[45]

Elder, who would rebuff the prayer demand through the end of his ordeal, took a balanced approach. Judging solely by his refusal to read the prayer, and grant the Union the implied support, Elder seemed to hold views similar to

Sheeran's and Garidel's. At the same time, Elder instructed his priests not to make any pulpit statements about secession, so as not to scandalize, or open to potential violence, those immigrants who had made the oath. He did not want political divisions among his parishioners distracting them from more important religious matters.[46]

In a Sunday sermon on July 3, 1864, Elder said that in light of the Union occupation of Natchez and the subsequent allegiance demands of the occupier, "an Oath is a solemn calling on God to bear witness to the truth of what you say, & to your fidelity in keeping your promise." He added—in condemnation of the kind of machinations Sheeran described—that "to take an Oath which a person does not intend to keep in its fair & honest sense, is a mortal sin of perjury,—& no excuse of inconvenience nor of compulsion can authorize a person to insult Almighty God by calling on His divine Majesty to bear witness that he intends to do, what in truth he does not intend to do."[47]

Elder had previously explained his position on church-state matters to the highest authority in the United States of America. In an April 1864 letter to President Lincoln, he explained, "My resistance [to prayers for the Union] is based simply on the broad ground that our Church Service is a matter to be regulated exclusively by the authorities of the Church." "I have never attempted to influence the political opinions or conduct of the people under my care," he wrote, adding that neither had his clergy. "They have devoted themselves to rendering spiritual services to all who desired them at their hands, without distinction of politics of section or of color." Even if Elder was as disinterested in secular allegiance questions as he claimed, and really just wanted to be left alone to minister to his congregation, there was everything at stake, politically, in the Union prayer request. Acceding to it might be seen as an endorsement of the Union. Refusing it might paint Elder as a true Southern patriot. Even if he did not covet such status, his rejection would only augment the already favorable opinion of him amongst his parishioners.[48]

Farrar did not believe Elder's letter to Lincoln had put any controversies to rest. As such, the Union officer invited Elder and Grignon to a "long interview in his private room" on July 6. Elder described Farrar as "very polite." He presented his argument that it was "unreasonable" to require clergy to hold special prayers for the president. It was a violation of the separation of church and state, political meddling into ecclesiastical affairs. Farrar "always fell back to the position that the other Churches had done it, & he must therefore require us to do it." Elder proposed writing a letter explaining his position and asked that Farrar publish it in a spirit of fairness and transparency. Farrar gave him permission to write the letter, but he promised only to consider the request. In the meantime, he expected the bishop of Natchez to read the prayer for President Lincoln. Elder again refused.[49]

On July 13, Elder detailed his position to Farrar. He acknowledged receipt of Special Order No. 31, putting parentheses around the word *order* to make clear his belief in its ambiguous nature. The bishop then expressed gratitude to the Union army for the "politeness" of the occupiers and their treatment of civilians, in particular orphans, who had been well provided for materially. He then added, sarcastically, "It is true that the presence of the [Union] Army was the very cause of their needing this assistance . . . but this does not cancel our obligations of gratitude." He explained that during the daily recitation of the Litany of the Saints, "express supplications for all Christian rulers:—for peace and unity among all Christian people" were made. As such, any requirement concerning praying for political leaders had already been met. This prayer was for "all Christian rulers" worldwide, not specifically for those in the South. Elder was willing to pray for political leaders, and he did so, but only outside of Mass, not during it as the order demanded.[50]

Elder then listed two reasons why he refused to comply. First, religious authorities should direct religious worship, and this privilege was to be wholly free of any interference from secular authorities. Secondly, in "Divine Worship, being directed to God, it is not proper to introduce anything into it for the purpose of exhibiting our sentiments in temporal things. This [Special Order No. 31] appears to be the addressing of our devotions to men instead of God." Elder's rationale for refusing the prayer request certainly is Catholic—very Augustinian even, drawing clear lines between the City of God and City of Man—but it is likewise an American one in the mold of the Jeffersonian-Dansbury Baptist ideal concerning the separation of church and state.[51]

Elder further argued against "adaption to the spirit of the age." To compose entirely new prayers, "appropriate to the times, and expressive of a proper spirit towards the chief magistrate of the United States," would be to engage in precisely that. The Mass, as the Catholic faith in sum, was about the worship of God and the saving of men's souls, not politics. He closed his letter with a catchphrase of Augustinian thinking: "Render to Caesar the things that are Caesar's and to God the things that are God's."[52]

On July 13, Brig. Gen. Mason Brayman replaced Farrar prior to Elder's next interview with Federal authorities. Brayman conceded that he "did not approve of men being compelled to read prayers against their conscience," but if he found Elder was a "rebel" he would be "treated as such." On July 16, Elder received a note bluntly informing him "military orders must be obeyed & not discussed." Elder rebuffed the prayer request for a final time, believing that to capitulate would "be for me to do a grievous injury to religion. . . . I had nothing else to do but oppose . . . & leave the consequences to God."[53]

On July 18, as speculation built over why he had refused the request multiple times, Elder noted in his diary that it had nothing to do with politics. His reasoning is consistent with his persona as a whole. Elder was being asked to put politics above the faith, to violate the sacred liturgy of the Mass with political propaganda. He was not going to do that. "Some Catholics & many more Protestants were under the impression that my refusal to read the Prayer arises from a preference which I give to the Southern Confederacy—I wanted them to understand that it was not so—but simply from an unwillingness to acknowledge the right in any secular power to direct our religious worship."[54]

Elder's protection-of-sacred-space rationale fit the way Catholic worship was generally understood, even by those outside of the Church. The Maysville, Kentucky, *Dollar Weekly Bulletin* published an article titled "A Catholic View of Political Preaching," lamenting the politicization of religious services—"Churches are built for the worship of God"—and upholding the Catholic Mass as an apolitical template. The *Memphis Daily Appeal* claimed the growing numbers and influence of the Catholic Church was owed to the apolitical Mass, unlike services held in the "abolitionized" Northern churches. The Tunkhannock, Pennsylvania, *Democrat* seconded this contention. "For the past three or four years, since the protestant clergy have generally been preaching war and bloodshed, Catholicism has been rapidly spreading." The reason was simple: "The Catholic clergy do not preach politics. Suppose the Protestant war clergy follow their example, and see what effect it will have?"[55]

On July 25, Elder received Special Order No. 11, which informed him that he was under arrest and must report to Vidalia, Louisiana (right across the river from Natchez), within twenty-four hours. The next day, scores of people, Catholic and Protestant, stopped by to give Elder their well wishes, moving him to write, "God forgive me for not doing my duty better by such a people!" Elder was not being hyperbolic in noting the large crowd. An article in the *Cincinnati Enquirer*, subsequently reprinted in Richmond's *Daily Dispatch*, presented a private letter "written by a gentleman from Natchez."[56] This man described "the greatest excitement" on the day of the bishop's departure. Elder's defiance of Federal authorities had quickly become a symbol of citywide defiance against the occupation. "I never witnessed such a sight as when the orphans came to bid their father good-bye," the man wrote. "I was surprised to see all the ladies, old and young, waiting for the Bishop, to take a last farewell." When Elder boarded the boat that would take him across the Mississippi, "they all fell on their knees, and, for the last time, the poor Bishop gave them his blessing." This man only wished others could see this picture he was having difficulty capturing. "I cannot describe it. . . . [T]he Bishop was the only person, during all the time, that seemed in good spirits."[57]

The *Alexandria Gazette* seconded this account, noting that Elder's departure was "most affecting—a large crowd of men, women and children kneeling on the wharf to receive his parting benediction." So, too, the *Wilmington Journal,* which reprinted an eyewitness account from the *Jacksonian Mississippian* titled "The Outrage upon Bishop Elder." Elder's conduct during the whole affair had won him "the admiration of the entire community." The observer added, "I feel proud of this course. Some thirty young ladies met him at the river to bid him good-bye and knelt before him in the dust to receive his blessing and adieu. It was a most affecting scene. He is in fine spirit; says others have suffered, why should not he."[58]

Elder arrived in Vidalia and was placed in a "very small room" but one, nonetheless, that he reported sleeping in comfortably. At first he was informed that he would be given soldier's rations but was soon told circumstances had changed. By General Brayman's order, "the Bishop must provide for himself." Elder immediately filed a protest with Secretary of War Stanton. The paperwork was forwarded to the Spalding, new archbishop of Baltimore. Spalding promised to do all he could to help but advised Elder to cooperate with Federal authorities. Bishop R. V. Whelan of West Virginia—who had believed Elder was the top candidate to replace the deceased Kenrick as archbishop of Baltimore, who held an arguable quantity of Southern sympathies—disagreed with Spalding's advice that Elder should acquiesce.[59]

Whelan argued that the matter was a case of religious liberty. No man should be compelled to read prayers against his conscience. "I would simultaneously appeal to Catholics & Christians of all denominations who value liberty of conscience to unite against men who dare to lay their hands on the Ark of God." The situation was an offense against not only Catholics but Protestant Christians and Americans of good conscience everywhere. It was an affront to basic religious liberty and the freedom to worship without state interference.[60]

Other Catholic clergymen felt the same. One such priest was a Father Hennessy from Detroit, who railed against Abraham Lincoln and Northern conscription. Especially odious for him were Northern attempts to conscript priests. The draft was already "worse than the cholera or the plague . . . they only destroy the body; this tortures the soul. It drags its victims from their agonized families. Talk not of the tortures and barbarities of the middle ages. None of them ever equaled this in cruelty." Now it was being imposed upon the priesthood too. "In all the countries of Christendom . . . the priesthood are exempt from conscription," Hennessy wrote, "but here there is no exception. How long will it be before they lay their hands upon the church and the sacred vessels? Soon they will reach the point where they have no respect for God himself."[61]

Whether Whelan was incensed at the Federal treatment of Elder or Hennessey enraged by Union designs to impress clergy, the rationale in each situation was the same: these actions were the unlawful overstepping of secular authorities into sacred space. That is how historian Father James Pillar framed the issue when writing of Elder's prayer refusal one hundred years after the fact.[62] Others historians have taken a different lesson from the affair. David Gleeson believes Elder an "ardent Confederate," the prayer incident but one more example of his deeply held Southern partisanship. Randall Miller concurs, stating that the affair only confirmed how completely Elder had absorbed the Southern culture and its way of life.[63]

This book takes yet another view on the matter. It is most accurate to place Elder in a middle ground regarding the prayer request, as in his relationship to African Americans. Just as Elder was both genuine in his spiritual ministry to African Americans and the holder of racist prejudices, he also refused the prayer mandate because, he claimed, he wanted to keep the worldly out of sacred space. Against this assertion however, he remained the Confederatized partisan he had been throughout the war. Elder was not some knight fighting for the religious liberty of all Americans. Politically, he was a devoted Confederate, deeply absorbed in the Confederate nation and its cause.

This true, Elder's response to Lincoln's prayer entreaty cannot be facilely classified as just another piece of evidence for Elder's rabid Confederatization. It certainly was about Confederate loyalty, possibly the most public expression of Confederatization anywhere, but this is not the entire story. Perhaps paradoxically, politics was not the fundamental impetus behind a very political expression of Confederate fealty. The Confederatized Elder acted primarily from sincerely held religious beliefs, which in turn produced highly visible, public, and political effects.

Ultimately, the Union threats of an open-ended jail sentence and with-held rations proved empty. On July 30, Elder was transferred to the house of a Catholic family in Vidalia; the McDowells happily received him, assisted at the Masses celebrated in their home, and "did everything they could think of to make me comfortable. And I was very comfortable—in body." Elder's captivity was brief. Roughly two weeks after he began his exile, the Union forces capitulated. On August 11, Brayman published a letter on August 11 declaring that Special Order NO. 31 was "suspended, and he [Elder] may return to his home and duties . . . [to conduct] divine worship at liberty." But that was not all. Brayman implicitly conceded that maybe Elder had been right all along, that forcing anyone to pray against their conscience was wrong. "All solemn appeals to the Supreme Being, not proceeding from honest hearts and willing minds, are necessarily offensive to Him," as well as "subversive of sound morality." Elder was released unconditionally the following day. He would not be bothered with the matter again.[64]

The Elder affair made headlines North and South, and was given ample coverage even in out-of-the-way papers such as the *Manitowoc (Wisconsin) Pilot*, Griffin, Georgia's *Daily Chattanooga Rebel,* and Ebensburg, Pennsylvania's *Democrat and Sentinel.* The *Democrat and Sentinel* launched a multilayered jeremiad against Abraham Lincoln, delivered in a mocking tone, condemning what the paper claimed was nonexistent religious freedom in the North. It was true that Elder had been removed from his post for refusing to pray for Lincoln. Did not the bishop of Natchez realize how all this could have been avoided? "All that the clergy have to do is to preach Abraham and him re-elected, and they are perfectly safe! Yes! 'We thank God for the freedom of the Pulpit,'" the paper continued, "that we are *free* to make the pulpit the vehicle of political speeches. We thank Him that instead of being narrowed down to the doctrines of the Prince of Peace, we can now preach murder and bloodshed." All religious freedom meant in the North was the right to thank God for "election returns, and the success of the shoddy."[65]

Even a paper far outside the Union and the Confederacy, Idaho City's *Idaho World,* picked up on the news and ran a reprint from New York's *Metropolitan Record.* Faulting "the old spirit of intolerant Puritanism," the *Record* claimed the Elder incident was evidence that "the war upon the Catholic Church has commenced at last in earnest." The article reported the particulars of the situation, the closing of Catholic and Protestant Mississippi churches, the ensuing spiritual deprivations inflicted upon Mississippi Christians, and, of course, the seizure of the "saintly and beloved prelate . . . torn from his people and sentenced to banishment from the sphere of his episcopal duties." Lincoln was then compared to Queen Elizabeth, Victor Emmanuel, and the Russian Czar. "We are glad the Government has thrown off the mask and revealed itself in all its hideous deformity," the article stated. "If there be one solitary Catholic who, knowing of this high-handed outrage on a Bishop of his Church, clings to the Government that perpetrated it—we pity him from our very soul."[66]

Elder returned to a hero's welcome in Natchez. He went immediately to the Cathedral, where "both bells were rung," to offer his thanksgiving. "What a greeting those good people gave me," he wrote. "The Sisters came crowding in more noisy than the others." A theme of Elder's preaching on the Feast of the Assumption of the Blessed Virgin Mary, August 15, was an appeal to the "experience of the week to show that the B.V. hears our prayers," for, Elder claimed, the true reason for his release and return was "the mercy of God, obtained by the intercession of Our Holy Mother."[67]

CHAPTER FIVE

Healing

Catholic Sister-Nurses during the War

"Men go to war to kill one another, and you, sisters, you go to repair the harm they have done. . . . Men kill the body and very often the soul, and you go to re-store life, or at least by your care to assist in preserving it." Saint Vincent de Paul spoke these words to sister-nurses on the eve of war in seventeenth-century Europe. This exact sentiment could have been expressed two centuries later in America concerning the sisters who tended to Civil War soldiers. This succor came in significant quantity, too, as at least 617 sisters from 21 different com-munities ministered during the war. The largest order, numbering more than two hundred and serving in over thirty geographic areas, was the Daughters of Charity, which St. Elizabeth Ann Seton founded in Emmitsburg, Maryland, in 1809.[1]

The sister-nurses had a tradition of medical care dating back centuries, and their medical practice was as up to date as possible. They gained widespread acclaim for balancing medical professionalism with spirituality. Sister-nurses were medics possessed of superior "bedside manner," symbols of good med-icine and sincere Christianity woven together. Thus, many wounded men re-quested to be put under the sisters' care. Moreover, the sisters demonstrated a willingness to serve wherever needed, which won them additional respect.[2]

The sister-nurses were not simply compassionate women; they were traveling medics ever ready to be deployed where needed. And their importance was all the more pronounced because of their singularity, as they comprised all trained nurses available at the beginning of the war. In conjunction with their medical duties, they also worked as administrators, housekeepers, and cooks and filled countless other roles as needs arose. In the postbellum era, many of the orders cared for the myriad orphans and destitute children made so by the war.[3]

In focusing exclusively on Catholic sisters who served during the war as sister-nurses, this chapter shows the diverse expression of Catholic Confederatization. Taken as a whole, the sister-nurses were neither politicized nor open supporters of the Confederate cause. They were devout Catholics while remaining largely disinterested Confederates, but Confederates they were indeed. While they treated men from both sides without discrimination, they were nominally part of the larger Confederate apparatus. This testifies to the nearly complete Southern Catholic involvement in the Confederate nation, even when that involvement was their unique "participation without politicization" Confederatization. Although noncombatants, the sisters were active participants on the battlefield, their work was every bit as important as that carried out by the men who fought and to whom they ministered.

Sister-nurses were the most single-minded of all Southern Catholics in the realm of spiritual allegiance. Providing spiritual succor and physical healing mattered above all else. When a Northern surgeon noted their political indifference, adding that they gave exceptional medical care to men on both sides, it was both a typical analysis and a fair summary of their entire Civil War story. Sister-nurses were the most prolific Catholic converters of the war, desiring to introduce Christianity to the secular and the fullness of Christianity to Protestants.[4]

Those who lived with, worked alongside, and were cared for by the sister-nurses tended to portray them as nothing short of living saints. While they were people, not angels, it is safe to say they were remarkable people, as worthy of hagiography as anyone can be. Their wartime narrative demonstrates that studies of Civil War women need not be restricted to the home front and that one can find in them examples of nineteenth-century women going against the current of expectations. It was a widely held belief, and a near unchallengeable societal norm, that a woman's place was in the domestic sphere. In more ways than one, sister-nurses were stark exceptions to this rule. As scholar, and sister, Frances Jerome Woods writes,

> The sisters were not stifled by the restrictions that Southern society placed upon women. They challenged the laws prohibiting the education of slaves. . . . Through their vows, the religious women . . . were liberated to express their love of God and neighbor and to give witness to gospel values. They had

no fear of losing material goods, for what they had was at the service of their neighbor. Through their vow of celibacy, the sisters were free to defy the norms that marriage was the proper state of life for women [and] that women should be dependent upon their husbands.[5]

Many heaped ample praise on Catholic nuns for their dedication to spiritual and physical healing, and this is not restricted to Catholic testimonials of the time or to Catholic scholars writing later on. According to Lt. Col. Daniel Shipman Troy, of the Sixtieth Alabama Regiment, "One of the things that impressed me was that the Sisters made no distinction whatever between the most polished gentlemen and the greatest rapscallion in the lot; the measure of their attention was solely the human suffering to be relieved." He added, "A miserable wretch in pain was a person of more consequence to the Sisters than the best of us when comparatively comfortable." Mary Livermore of the Sanitary Commission, a Universalist, claimed, "the world has known no nobler and no more heroic women than those found in the ranks of the Catholic Sisterhoods."[6]

A newspaper correspondent observing the happenings at a Confederate hospital in Virginia could not restrict his glowing praise for the sisters' management of the infirmary. With the exception of the medical department, "this hospital is under the sole superintendence of the Sisters of Charity," the correspondent noted. Furthermore, "their kindness and attention is worthy of all the praises so worthily merited by their works"—this because they were "modest, unpretending, and with a singleness of purpose in doing good, these good sisters dedicate their whole existence in ameliorating the suffering of the soldiers, and act as ministering agents to their wants." The *Daily Chattanooga Rebel* once explained that Sisters of Charity ran all the hospitals in Mobile and New Orleans. They carried out their functions so well, and were so highly respected by the general public, that "they would be welcome to assume charge of the public charities in all the Southern cities."[7]

Bishop Augustin Verot once told Bishop Patrick Lynch, "The Yankees seem to be willing to do any thing for the Sisters who have been kind to their wounded soldiers in Charleston." The Reverend George W. Pepper, a US Army Protestant chaplain, said, "God bless the Sisters of Charity in their heroic mission! I had almost said their heroic martyrdom! And I might have said it, for I do think that in walking those long lines of sick beds, in giving themselves to all the ghastly duties of the hospital, they were doing a harder task than was allotted to many who mounted the scaffold or dared the stake."[8]

John McGill, the bishop of Richmond, was constantly trying to place sister-nurses in hospitals. This was as pressing a goal for the Confederatized prelate as encouraging men to enlist in the army. Bishop John Martin Spalding of Louisville heaped effusive praise on the sisters: "The good Sisters of Charity & of the Holy Cross have been laboring for nearly a year in four Hospitals of this city, with great relief & consolation to the sick & wounded & with great fruit of souls." He highlighted the sisters' success in bringing converts into the Church, especially through baptism.[9]

Often the cleanest, most efficient, and most medically up-to-date hospitals were staffed by Catholic nuns. Episcopalian nurse Kate Cumming noted this in her diary, writing that whenever Daughters of Charity were present "as usual with them, every thing is *parfait*." On another occasion, she praised the sister-nurses' commitment while berating Southern women who would not help at hospitals unless a relative was present. "I wonder if the Sisters of Charity have brothers . . . in the hospitals where they go? It seems strange that they can do with honor what is wrong for other Christian women to do." The sisters' reputation stood the test of time. In an article largely about Southern Protestants, written more than a half century after the war, one historian singled out the Sisters of Charity's work in "nurs[ing] many sick and wounded soldiers"; another scholar records similar approbation of the sisters and their ministry.[10]

Religious life shaped the sisters and underpinned their work.[11] But how did nuns become sister-nurses? Sister Lauretta Maher's "Reminiscences of the Civil War" is a good place to start. Maher, born in 1844, entered the Sisters of Charity novitiate in Nazareth, Kentucky, in July 1860. Near the outbreak of the war, she noted that little was heard of it within the walls of her convent, "that peaceful abode," where only the passing mark of a visitor brought any news at all. As rumors of war evolved into full-fledged fighting, the sisters were pressed into action. Maher and her fellow younger sisters entered special medical classes led by an older nun, Victoria Buckman, who taught what in "modern parlance is called 'First Aid.'" In the fall of 1861, Bishop Spalding officially appointed the Sisters of Charity to posts as sister-nurses. Many sisters immediately set off for the hospitals. Those who stayed behind were eager to be deployed.[12]

The sisters' eagerness was of a different variety than that of the chaplains' and soldiers', who were likewise anxious to join the conflict. Chaplains' and soldiers' willingness was rooted in a deep Confederate partisanship. They wanted to fight for a cause they endorsed and often infused with religious meaning. The sisters' primary goal was to provide indiscriminate spiritual and medical aid.

Chaplains, soldiers, and bishops saw a conflict saturated with religious meaning: God favored the South; the Confederacy would finally realize Winthrop's City on a Hill vision; the Confederacy's providential blessing was matched by a heavenly rejection of the North and its values. The list is practically endless, and the vast majority of Southern Catholics subscribed to these sentiments.

That sister-nurses did not see the war in this light, that they did not view the South as divinely blessed nor the North as wicked or barbarous, is not just a fact but a remarkable one. These women managed to somehow step outside their societal circumstances. They perceived their service as a spiritual endeavor, their only secular considerations coming in the realm of medicine, not politics. Their sole mission was to help heal the men whom they treated while simultaneously sharing their Catholic faith.

This distinction is important. Confederatized Catholics supported the Southern cause passionately in speeches and sermons and backed up their rhetoric by fighting and dying. What makes the sister-nurses' apoliticization fascinating is that it was not simply pacifism. They were not noncombatants who stayed at home. They were noncombatants on the battlefield, as close to the action and the danger as soldiers were. Their service, while devoid of fighting, killing, and dying, occurred alongside these things. As witnesses to the Catholic faith and medical professionals, they conducted their duties in the very epicenters of harm.

In January 1862, Sister Maher received the call to hospital duty. "Like the Apostles," she wrote, "we left our peaceful home without scrip or staff or money in our purses." The Confederate government paid all of her expenses and those of her traveling companion, Sister Mary Joseph Hollihan. Sister Hollihan, an older nun, and according to Maher a "timid, retiring religious," left the arrangements of the trip to the younger woman. Maher evidently handled this "burden upon [her] inexperienced shoulders" because soon both sisters had reported for duty at the hospital.[13]

Maher was assigned to the typhoid ward. She soon got sick herself, stricken with erysipelas, before recovering and returning to work. Her first major assignment was at the Battle of Shiloh in April 1862. Maher notes that the lack of medical attention left many wounded men lying on the battlefield for three days after the fight. Thanks to "a body of charitable citizens of Louisville" who chartered a boat, along with helpful doctors, soldiers, and nurses, many men were rescued and removed to a Louisville hospital. With the men en route,

Maher, along with her fellow sister-nurses, sanitized beds in preparation for the incoming patients.[14]

When the men arrived, the scene was harrowing. Medicine had to be supplied all around and quickly. The wounded called out for help, but in the chaos of the moment, with all men grouped together it was challenging to discern who required immediate attention. Some of the wounded were on the verge of bleeding to death. "Heads, hands, and hearts were all taxed to their utmost," Maher wrote, referring to the attending sister-nurses, who were "striving to alleviate the suffering of the poor men irrespective of the cause they served."[15]

This attitude, attending to the dying with only the soul in mind, found consistently in the sisters' work, finds a parallel in the chaplains' work with dying men on the battlefield. The key difference is that the sisters did not have overtly political sides, no moments such as when Father Louis-Hippolyte Gache felt relief having confirmed that a dying man was not an abolitionist. While Father James Sheeran and Sister Maher might have each been wholly Christian in their intention to help dying men, Sheeran might have later on rattled off a list of reasons the Southern cause was just and why the North alone was to blame for the war, as he often did.

As in the case of Father John Bannon, a chaplain who just heard the confessions of a group of soldiers, might later on join a different group in firing cannons at the enemy—although this was indeed *very* rare, further demonstrating just how fanatically Confederatized Bannon was. The lone manifestation of the sisters' brand of Confederate involvement was the carrying out of their medical duties, direct participation within the Confederate military sphere in helping Southern soldiers recover and return to action. Part of this recovery process was in the emotional realm. As Father Francis Burlando recorded in a letter after the war, the sisters' bedside manner was no small thing: "Men [for] whom the horrors of war has as it were brutified [them] felt themselves moved at the sight of a Sister of Charity in the performance of her duty. The remembrance of a mother, a wife, a sister was presented to their mind with all the charm of virtue, and their eyes, which the cruelties of war seemed to have dried forever, flowed again with tears of tenderness."[16]

Burlando explained that war-hardened men dropped coarse language in the presence of the sisters and suffered their afflictions in silence; so silent one would mistake a military hospital for a cloister. Of course, his analysis must be taken with a grain of salt. The tone is so full of undiluted praise and hyperbolic expressions, it seems too good to be true, and yet, Burlando's portrayal matches much of what Catholics and non-Catholics alike wrote about the sister-nurses. Wounded men readily declared an immense gratitude to the sisters for their help, and many were so impressed by their examples that they expressed a desire to become Catholics themselves.[17]

If the sister-nurses' wartime duties were not stressful enough, they were often greatly understaffed. A Richmond hospital had 700 patients yet only seven sisters. A Louisiana hospital had 350 and only six sisters. These were typical cases, and so it was commonplace for one sister to shoulder the workload of what normally would be spread out among three or four. The sister-nurses were pressed to the limits of their capabilities. For those working at the hospitals, there was hardly a moment of rest, making the sisters' tranquility and Christian joy all the more noteworthy. Not only were sister-nurses just as busy as soldiers, chaplains, and bishops, they were perhaps more taxed than all of these men.[18]

Soldiers were amazed at the sisters' courage under fire. This appears a further reason so many men decided to become Catholics after having spent time in their presence. Consistent charity and good medical care went a long way, but what historian George Rable noted about chaplains, that those who marched and endured with men won innumerable respect, was true for the sister-nurses too. Once when a soldier inquired as to why the sisters did not cringe under the incessant shelling near the hospitals, one nun replied in the style of Bannon on the front lines: "Fear not for us, good friend. God is watching over us, and even if we were to die, have we not an eternity of happiness as our reward?"[19]

The sisters' bravery must have been even more impressive against the backdrop of their political neutrality. It appears their faith alone gave them courage in the middle of a war zone. There was nothing added to this bravery, no blind, intense devotion to the Southern cause that for many men served as an opiate of sorts with which they tempered their fear. The sister-nurses had no political encouragements, no civil religion to help them along. While these women were often exemplars of bravery, duty executed, and skilled medics indeed—especially judged relative to the state of the field at mid-nineteenth century—their dedication to their faith was the preeminent aspect of their Civil War story.

Gache called the Daughters of Charity "saintly" and wrote that he believed the nuns' presence among non-Catholics was among the best evangelical tools the Church possessed, their mere ubiety dispelling biases against Catholicism. A Protestant soldier, reflecting on his interactions with sister-nurses, wrote, "I am not of your church, and have always been taught to believe it to be nothing but evil; however, actions speak louder than words, and I am free to admit that if Christianity does exist on earth, it has some of its closest followers among the Ladies of your Order." Another Protestant soldier once "wept aloud" when learning that the sister who had been caring for him was a Catholic, but his prejudices soon vanished and he resolved to take as many books about Catholicism back to the battlefield with him as he could for the purpose of learning about the faith. Burlando wrote, "Protestants ask themselves with astonishment, and in admiration, if these women really are Catholics . . . [for they] would wish to belong only to the religion of these true Daughters of Charity, instead to the Catholic religion."[20]

Considering the short amount of time they spent with men, it is remarkable that sister-nurses had so profound an effect on soldiers. These men really only came in contact with the sisters when they were wounded and in hospitals, having more frequent interactions with Catholics while in camp and on the march, with chaplains and fellow soldiers. From these battlefield contacts came conversions, too, but what might have taken a chaplain an extended period of time to accomplish—Bannon convincing McGolfe to finally come to confession, for example (and in this case it was the dying Union soldier who ultimately persuaded the Confederate artilleryman)—the sister-nurses seemed to achieve in a single hospital visit.

Soldiers asked for instruction on the "White Bonnet religion," and one asked to be baptized, but only if a sister would do it. Bannon recounted the story of a soldier who wanted to join the sisters' religion but did not believe that it could be the same Catholicism he had grown up abhorring. When Bannon gave the soldier some doctrinal instruction, he protested: "Oh, come now, you don't expect me to believe that!" For the man to be convinced and say, "Very well, all right, I believe it . . . what's next?" it took only a sister to confirm that she believed the doctrine, and that she and the priest were of the same faith.[21]

Gache recounted a similar story. As chaplain, he had asked some men that had been treated by sister-nurses if they wished to become Catholics. "Oh no," one replied, "I don't like that church a bit! I've never seen a Catholic, but I've heard a lot about them. The sisters' church is the church for me!" The men didn't believe Gache when he told them the sisters' church was the Catholic Church. He asked the sisters if it were so. When they responded in the affirmative, one of the soldiers replied, "Well, I declare. I'd never have suspected it. I've heard so many things. . . . I thought Catholics were the worst people on earth." The sisters hoped this long-standing opinion might change; the men agreed that it would and later on became Catholics.[22]

In the very same letter from which this anecdote is drawn, Gache could not restrain his effusive praise for the sisters' ministry. He immediately followed that story with another one, claiming to a colleague that it was one "about the sisters that you might find interesting." A company of Texans, five men, were brewing coffee beneath the stars one night "on a rustic hearth which they had improvised 'neath a noble oak, with the intention of using this stimulant to repulse the advances of Morpheus." General banter quickly turned to the subject of religion, just as the "Brazilian brew was slowly absorbing calories propelled from the blazing pine chips beneath."[23]

As all five men were Protestants, "it wasn't long before someone added a dash of anti-Catholic seasoning." But then, one of these five cried out for the discussion to end immediately. "Stop friends, stop! I don't know what Catholics are, what they believe, nor what they do," this man explained, "but since I was attended, in my sickness, by the Daughters of Charity at Richmond, I swore never to allow anyone to speak against their church in my presence. Please do not oblige me to go further to fulfill my oath." Gache noted, humorously, that the "young theologians, who expected to hear anything but a warning like that, stopped short and changed the subject." Burlando wrote that the sisters extended their ministry "to the two belligerent factions . . . this policy of charity which occupied itself in ministering to the body having only in view the salvation of souls." Early in the war, Archbishop Kenrick wrote to New York archbishop John Hughes, "The Surgeon General is desirous of having the services of Sisters for the hospitals."[24]

The sister-nurses, like the chaplains who gave men absolution before death on the battlefield, brought many to the faith in hospitals by way of last-minute conversions or reversions to Catholicism. Such stories are plentiful. A few are provided here as examples. Sister Maher, working in the hospital after the wounded men from Shiloh had been brought in, was treating a Northern soldier from an Illinois regiment when she noticed a medal of the Blessed Virgin Mary draped around his neck.[25]

"Are you a Catholic?" she asked. No, he replied, explaining that the medal was a gift from his girlfriend. He promised her he would wear it, and while he was not initially a Catholic, he resolved to become one after returning home from the war. Sister Maher and the soldier kept up a dialogue, and she found him, a daily reader of a catechism, knowledgeable concerning Catholic doctrine. When later he became faint, the soldier told Sister Maher he wished to be baptized into the faith; he was, and soon after writing to tell his girlfriend of his conversion, he died.[26]

One of the sisters' prime spiritual successes was in leading men back to the Church by putting them into contact with priests, who then heard the men's confessions; baptized them; and gave them other sacraments, such as the Holy Eucharist and Confirmation. This further speaks to the sisters' humility. It appears that the sister-nurses simply desired that lapsed Catholics return to their faith and that non-Catholics become Catholic. They did not care who got the credit, yet it was they, ministering to wounded and dying soldiers in the hospital, who did the true spiritual spadework. It was they who often cracked years of bitterness against Catholicism or gave men even the most rudimentary knowledge of religion that they had never been given before. They did the hard work changing hearts. Once this conversion experience was set in motion, the sisters took a backseat, to put the men into the hands of priests who would reconcile them to, or bring them into, the Church.

One sister-nurse wrote that it was a great "consolation for the Sisters to snatch these poor souls from the evil One" by way of conversions. She recounted a man who received baptism the day he died and how she encouraged him "to raise his heart often" to God in his final moments before "calmly expire[ing]." A Sister Regina, ministering in a New Orleans hospital, claimed that the infirmary was daily flooded with soldiers, many of whom had never been baptized or had any religion at all. Yet some of these men found faith, and "many souls who have long been estranged from God, are reconciled and slumber in the sleep of peace." When one soldier, a twenty-year-old named William Let, came under the care of sisters, they quickly learned that he knew nothing of religion at all. As they cared for him in hospital, they shared the faith with him. A sister, recommending him to the care of "Our Immaculate Mother[,] . . . felt convinced that he would not be lost."[27]

Gache concluded that the sister-nurses, by way of their Christian example, in the end proved to be the Civil War's most evangelically effective Catholics:

> In their capacity as nurses in the military hospitals, the Daughters of Charity, scarce though they may be, do a great deal of good for the church. They are in daily contact with a multitude of persons: doctors, army officers, government agents, and particularly with the ordinary soldiers. Most of these men either

know the church not at all or know it through the sermons and scurrilous pamphlets of Protestant ministers. But because of their esteem, their respect and their admiration for the sisters, those who were once wary of us become less wary or, sometimes, even favorably disposed. Let us hope that this good impression made by the sisters will not be easily forgotten, and that it will be a source of salvation for many. When I consider how little I have been able to accomplish, it's consoling to think of all that these sisters have done.[28]

Bannon concurred: "Four years [of] civil war has done more to advance the cause of Catholicity in the States, both North and South, than the hundred years that preceded . . . [and] the principal cause of this advance has been the charity shown by the Religious Sisters who tended the sick and wounded." He added that "thousands of men, who either knew nothing of the Catholic Church, or only such lies concerning it . . . were brought into intimate contact with it its most energetic work, in its most winning character." The chaplain believed those who had entered the Church had been brought *in Fidem Sororum* ("in the faith of the sisters") rather than *in Fidem Ecclesiae* ("in the faith of the Church").[29]

The sister-nurses who treated wounded soldiers in the hospitals were exclusively committed to the men's souls and their physical recuperation. Their good medical practice, political neutrality (in reality, a political disinterestedness), and Christian example won many converts to the faith. The sister-nurses are an integral component of the Southern Catholic Civil War narrative. While not politicized, they were highly active during the war. They show just how thorough Catholic involvement in the Confederacy was; this true, it should not be surprising that Confederatization extended beyond America's borders and played an important role in the Civil War's international theater too.

William Henry Elder, bishop of Natchez. A Confederate partisan, Elder showed remarkable balance between religious and political allegiances while prioritizing the spiritual over the secular. All this was brought under a microscope during the affair of Elder's Lincoln prayer request, arguably the most famous Catholic moment of the war, North or South. (Courtesy of the Collection of Joan and Thomas H. Gandy via St. Mary Basilica Rectory, Natchez, Mississippi)

William Henry Elder, bishop of Natchez. (Courtesy of the Collection of Joan and Thomas H. Gandy via St. Mary Basilica Rectory, Natchez, Mississippi)

Patrick Neeson Lynch, bishop of Charleston. Perhaps the most Confederatized Southern bishop, Lynch supported the Southern cause from the outset, attacking the North in inter-episcopal correspondence and openly celebrating Confederate victories. Lynch served an official, state-sponsored diplomatic mission late in the war, trying to win the sympathy, if not outright support of European powers and the papacy. (Courtesy of the Catholic Diocese of Charleston Archives)

Patrick Neeson Lynch, bishop of Charleston. (Courtesy of the Catholic Diocese of Charleston Archives)

Augustin Verot, bishop of St Augustine (1870–76), bishop of Savannah (1861–70), vicar apostolic of Florida (1857–70). Verot's 1861 tract on slavery was an early example of overt Catholic Confederatization and evidence of the bishops' willingness to comment on issues not directly related to their episcopal duties. (Courtesy of the Diocese of St. Augustine)

Jean-Marie Odin, archbishop of New Orleans. Odin's 1862 *ad limina* visit, a strictly ecclesiastical voyage, catalyzed Catholic-Confederate diplomacy, inspired Pope Pius IX's joint peace letter to him and archbishop of New York John Hughes, calling for North-South Catholic cooperation in bringing the war to and end, along with Jefferson Davis's overtures to Pius and the Confederate government's employment of Catholic clergy envoys Lynch and Bannon. (Courtesy of the University of Notre Dame Archives)

Archbishop Jean-Marie Odin of New Orleans. (Courtesy of the Office of Archives and Records, Archdiocese of New Orleans)

Father John Bannon, Confederate chaplain and diplomat. Bannon left his St. Louis parish under disguise to serve in the Confederate army as a chaplain, passing the first year in this post on a volunteer basis. In 1863, following two years as a chaplain, and having been regularized the previous year, he again volunteered his services, this time as a Confederate envoy to Europe. Bannon was in Lynch's party for the 1864 meeting with Pope Pius IX, and his work in Ireland, according to some, constituted the Confederate States of America's most successful diplomatic efforts. (Courtesy of the Irish Jesuit Archives, Dublin)

Sister Euphemia Blenkinsop directed the Sisters of Charity in the South during the Civil War. (Courtesy of the Daughters of Charity Province of St. Louise, St. Louis, Missouri)

Sister Bernard Boyle, DC, served at the Hospital of Saint Vincent DePaul in Norfolk, Virginia, during the war. (Courtesy of the Daughters of Charity Province of St. Louise, St. Louis, Missouri)

Sister Juliana Chatard, DC, served at various hospitals in the Richmond environs during the war. (Courtesy of the Daughters of Charity Province of St. Louise, St. Louis, Missouri)

Richmond General Hospital, 1861, sketch by R. M. Shurtleff. Here, the Daughters of Charity are tending to wounded Federal officers. (Courtesy of the Daughters of Charity Province of St. Louise, St. Louis, Missouri)

Pope Pius IX (1846–78). Pius's fierce opposition to the Italian Republicans during the *Risorgimento* perhaps contributed to his warm feelings toward Jefferson Davis and the Confederacy. Pius gave the Confederacy its most potent sign of foreign recognition when he addressed Davis as "Illustrious President" and claimed that it was "obvious" the North and South were "two nations" rather one country with a rebellious faction. (Courtesy of the Library of Congress)

Jefferson Davis, president of the Confederate States of America. Although he was an Episcopalian, the Confederate president held and maintained a connection to the Catholic Church his entire life, from his boyhood education by Dominican friars in Tennessee, through the interchanges with Pius IX during the war and his enlistment of priest-diplomats, to the postwar era, when he enrolled his daughter in a Catholic school in Montréal. (Courtesy of the Library of Congress)

General Pierre G. T. Beauregard. The French Creole Catholic general was as known for his social savoir faire as much as for his military ability. He played instrumental roles in the Confederate victories at Fort Sumter and First Manassas. (Courtesy of the Library of Congress)

Stephen R. Mallory. A US senator from Florida between 1851 and 1861 and a Catholic born in Trinidad, Mallory served as CSA secretary of the navy for the war's duration. In January 1863, Mallory, at the bequest of Bishop John Quinlan, ensured Bannon was appointed to an official chaplaincy within the CSA service and received the back pay owed him. (Courtesy of the Library of Congress)

CHAPTER SIX

Across the Sea

Catholicism and Confederate Diplomacy

"Reposing special confidence and trust in your Integrity, Prudence and Ability, I do appoint you the said P. N. Lynch, of South Carolina, to be Special Commissioner of the Confederate States of America to *The States of the Church*; authorizing you herby to do and perform all such matters and things as to the said place or office doth appertain." With these words, Jefferson Davis made a Catholic bishop a diplomatic agent, investing him with the full confidence and material support of the Confederate government.[1]

International diplomacy was a critical component of the Confederacy's war plan. In many ways, the difference between independence and reunification rested on the question of foreign assistance. Within this crucial sphere, many questions abound. Why, after having failed to gain the aid of France and England, did the Confederacy turn to the Roman Catholic Church? Pope Pius IX cared only for peace in America, irrespective of political outcome. But the pope's avowed neutrality did not stop Jefferson Davis from trying to win his support. Davis commissioned Bishop Patrick Lynch a Confederate diplomat and supported Father John Bannon's European mission for that very purpose.

Confederate leaders saw the Southern nation as a natural friend of the Church. Bannon was more than happy to play up this supposed consonance. In Ireland, he repeatedly claimed the South was a longtime friend of foreigners and that it was decidedly the more Catholic part of America, especially in comparison to a North he derided as the land of witch-hunters, covenant arsonists, and Puritan heretics. It is true Pius had some sympathy for the Confederate cause. Was this because he saw in the Northern United States the same liberal-egalitarian values of the Italian Republicans whom he bitterly opposed during the *Risorgimento?* Was it because he thought the Confederate South was a more Christian society than its adversary? The answer to the first question is a fairly certain yes. But on the second point, if the pope did in fact see something more Catholic in South-ern culture, why did formal recognition never come?[2]

Why did neither France nor Britain extend diplomatic recognition when both seemed close to doing so? Both nations appeared content to witness the disintegration of the United States. Why not help speed the process along? Many Europeans saw in Southerners something of the nationalistic self-determination that had swept across the continent in 1820, 1830, and 1848. Why did formal recognition never come? Slavery is a primary factor. European liberals and con-servatives alike opposed it, and the Church had denounced it—in various forms, most specifically pertaining to the slave trade itself—for hundreds of years be-fore the American Civil War.[3]

The South had slavery as its economic and societal cornerstone. This is why the Emancipation Proclamation is so important. That it sprang not from purely humanitarian motives but was a multipronged piece of political machination is beside the point. Before the proclamation, Europe, and the papacy, could consider supporting the North or the South somewhat apart from the question of slavery. Lincoln changed the entire nature of the conflict. Slavery moved to front and center, and no European nation wanted to be an ally of explicit human bondage. This was a main reason for Confederate diplomacy's failure. It is like-wise crucial to understanding why the pope would not support the Confederacy and why Lynch's mission was doomed from the start. Even so, when diplomat James Mason's mission ended in 1863, and with it the South's diplomatic talks with Britain, the Confederacy turned to the Catholic Church.[4]

This Catholic facet of Confederate diplomacy is this chapter's prime focus, challenging assumptions that once attempts at secular recognition failed, the Confederacy abandoned Europe. The key phrase here is *the Confederacy aban-doned Europe.* There is no desire to contest the consensus that after failure with Britain, Confederate diplomacy was essentially broken beyond repair. This is true. On this score, the author agrees with many historians of Confederate foreign relations. What is to be challenged, however, is the notion that the Confederacy did not put significant stock into any further diplomacy once the British channel went dry. The Confederate government believed the Vatican was a viable diplomatic avenue, and this has been underplayed, if not outright ignored, in studies of Confederate diplomacy. The missions to the pope were not without purpose, not without a real hope from the standpoint of those who commissioned and undertook them. Furthermore, Catholic-Confederate diplomacy brings the Confederatization thesis full circle, revealing its climax in Catholic wartime internationalism. Bannon's and Lynch's missions prove Catholic involvement in the Confederacy was exhaustive and consistent, even extending overseas to a crucial theater of the war.[5]

"King Cotton" was the South's unofficial economic motto and foreign policy strategy. While the position had roots in what one historian termed the Southern people's "susceptib[ility] to logic and philosophical matter," it was more practical than metaphysical. Europeans were heavily dependent on the South's staple export. If the South just turned off the faucet, recognition would quickly follow. From the war's outset, the foundations of Southern diplomacy rested on this assumption. Although British textile workers were initially in favor of intervention to break the blockade and restore the cotton supply, the idea of King Cotton was full of problems. It engendered a false confidence in Southern leaders that "cotton for recognition" was foolproof, thus relegating actual diplomatic work to the side. This attitude extended to Jefferson Davis, who believed Southern goods would automatically "furnish attractive exchanges." In a list including sugar, rice, tobacco, and timber, cotton was indexed first. Davis's presumptions led him to choose envoys more for personal reasons than actual diplomatic ability.[6]

The first Confederate representatives to Europe were fire-eater William Lowndes Yancey, former US assistant secretary of state Ambrose Dudley Mann, and Louisiana lawyer and planter Pierre Rost (chosen mainly because he spoke French). The three, appointed in March 1861, received commissions to Great Britain, France, Russia, and Belgium. They were directed to explain why the South had seceded and to make clear that the Confederacy was a "well-organized Government instituted by the free will of their citizens." The nucleus of Southern foreign policy was, according to Secretary of State Robert Toombs, "peace and commerce." Initial forays were unsuccessful. Yancey was prone to droning on about "southern rights" while emphasizing over and again that the South had separated solely out of peaceful intentions. In light of the events at Fort Sumter, this last point must have struck the British as odd.[7]

A few minor victories arrived in the early summer of 1861. On May 14, world hegemon Great Britain, prizing the stability of the Atlantic market and viewing Lincoln's government as inept and vacillating, officially declared neutrality in the American Civil War. France followed suit on June 10. Yancey and Mann wrote that formal recognition was soon forthcoming. All that remained was for the Confederate military to do its part, to make it apparent that the United States could not defeat the South on the battlefield.[8]

Rome matched the major European powers' neutrality, primarily because at the start of the American Civil War the pope had little time for even passing consideration of the conflict.[9] Nonetheless, Seward wrote to US diplomat Rufus King claiming the pope was on the North's side because "he is a friend of peace, to good order, and to the cause of human nature, which is now, as it always has been, our cause." Seward nonetheless conceded Pius was above all a "friend of peace [and] human nature." Both North and South would come to see this outweighed all else. US diplomat John Stockton was correct when relaying Giacomo Cardinal Antonelli's assurances that "Catholics of the United States, as Catholics, as a church, would take no part in the matter [the war]," for "the government of his Holiness concerns itself mainly in spiritual matters." The Confederacy faced neutrality on all fronts, and many in Europe believed the American separation would prove permanent. In France, opinion was split only over the war's cause, not whether the Confederacy would reintegrate. Liberal newspapers like *Siècle, Temps,* and *Courrier du Dimanche* listed slavery as the catalyst. Conservative newspapers like *Patrie, Pays,* and *Constitutionnel* cited "northern aggression."[10]

Media and public opinion notwithstanding, it was the *Trent* affair that provided the best chance for a permanent rupture. On November 8, 1861, Union captain Charles Wilkes, in command of the USS *San Jacinto,* stopped a British mail boat, the RMS *Trent,* in the Caribbean. Wilkes removed Confederate agents from the ship before letting it resume course. Great Britain viewed the action as an affront to its neutrality and national honor, and throughout Europe the deed was widely condemned as a violation of international law. Most importantly for the Confederacy, there was now a real chance Britain would declare war on the United States. "There is a probability that our recognition by Her Britannic Majesty's Government will not be much longer delayed," Mann wrote from London on December 2. Britain would punish "the so-called United States for the flagrant violation of the integrity of her flag upon the high seas. Her 'voice' will now be found in her 'sword.'" Britain ordered the United States to formally apologize and to release the Confederate prisoners, threatening military action if the nation refused to comply.[11]

Eventually, the crisis was averted, and the Confederacy lost a massive opportunity. The *San Jacinto* released the agents, and the threat of British intervention passed quietly. Just as Lincoln's government had skillfully navigated the events at Fort Sumter, painting the Confederacy as the aggressor by getting it to fire the first shots of the war, back-channel diplomacy cooled British anger and disarmed a dangerous situation. The *Trent* crisis dissipated without much explanation and would become one more example of the Union fortuitously stepping through a minefield of potential disasters.[12]

As the *Trent* crisis was ongoing, the Catholic Church in America made its first diplomatic move. Catholics in the Union, by way of New York archbishop John Hughes's European mission, seized the initiative. Hughes and Northern journalist-politician Thurlow Weed set off for Europe in November 1861. Hughes was headed to France, Weed to Britain. Hughes met with Napoleon and Empress Eugenie on Christmas Eve. The archbishop asked the emperor to take on a mediation role in the *Trent* crisis. Napoleon refused. Hughes also encouraged the French to acquire their cotton from Algeria, so as to fully cut ties with the South. Napoleon didn't warm to any suggestions, forcing the archbishop to redirect his efforts. He aimed the remainder of his trip at "creat[ing] good will among the higher class of French society and . . . mold[ing] public opinion against the recognition of the Confederacy." Hughes, working against a majority opinion that saw parallels between the 1848 uprisings and Confederate secession, confessed there was little European support for the United States. Nonetheless, he judged his trip to be as successful as it could have been. The United States agreed.[13]

Southern Catholics entered the diplomatic arena with the mission of Jean-Marie Odin, the archbishop of New Orleans, in 1862. The trip was not officially diplomatic but an *ad limina* visit incumbent on all bishops worldwide. Nevertheless, Odin campaigned for peace and therefore served as an unofficial Confederate representative. This worked to great effect; following his trip Pius IX issued the joint letter to him and Hughes calling for immediate peace. As discussed, the pope's letter inspired numerous peace pastorals and became the initial contact point between Davis's government and Pius's court.[14]

The missed opportunity of the *Trent* affair compelled a shift in Confederate diplomacy; the focus became securing relief from the blockade. Yet it was wartime events in America, not diplomatic strategy of any kind, that gave the South another shot at European recognition. The Confederacy had incredible success following Lee's assumption of command in 1862. Europe took notice, with the British moving closer to initiating peace talks. Napoleon also put forth a proposal for a six-month armistice, and among the European powers there was also talk of a joint mediation plan—directed by France, Russia, and Great Britain—including a stipulation to grant the Confederacy official recognition outright if the Union refused to join the proceedings.[15]

Then the Battle of Sharpsburg/Antietam was fought. Confederate failure caused immediate doubts for the British about possible intervention. More importantly, the war took on a new meaning with Lincoln's announcement of the Emancipation Proclamation. Fiercely antislavery Europe would have a much harder time justifying backing the South. Lincoln's timing was impeccable. In a speech to an antislavery delegation, he had claimed that "no other step would be so potent to prevent foreign intervention." He was right. Although the proclamation was certainly politically motivated—coming after the South's first military loss in months, and after the president had vetoed earlier wartime emancipatory decrees on two occasions—the Union could now claim the moral high ground, couching the war as a human rights crusade.[16] Whatever the contradictions present, it was a stroke of diplomatic genius, further evidence of Lincoln's deft tactical ability.[17]

The European press was merciless toward the US president. *Pays* pointed out what it saw to be the fundamental hypocrisy of the proclamation, Lincoln "wish[ing] to abolish slavery where he is not able to achieve it [the CSA] and to save it where he would be able to abolish it [the USA]." The *Courrier des deux Charentes* wrote that according to Lincoln "no person will have slaves, except ourselves and our friends."[18] London's *Spectator* claimed the proclamation meant a person "cannot own [another person] unless he is loyal to the United States." Another British paper stated, "Lincoln offers freedom to the negroes over whom he has no control, and keeps in slavery those other negroes within his power. Thus he associates his Government with slavery by making slaveholding the reward to the planters of rejoining the Old Union." Some thought Lincoln was inviting, even inciting, "acts of plunder, of incendiarism, and of revenge."[19] Bishop Martin John Spalding was among this group.[20]

Race war and insurrection did not come. But the meaning of the war was fundamentally changed. The proclamation made it highly unlikely, if not impossible, for the Confederacy to gain official help from the pope, temporal head of the Church, whose views on slavery were well summed up in a 1862 pastoral letter by the bishop of Orléans, Félix Dupanloup.

I say to myself, My God died upon the cross for all mankind, and yet there are still men crucified. He died to deliver all from bondage, and there are men . . . millions of men who are still in slavery . . . in Christian countries eighteen hundred years after the Crucifixion. *What I do know is that the horrors of civil war have been let lose [sic] by this fearful question, and that the peace of the world is threatened, and is already disturbed* . . . they [slaves] have lost not only the right of primogeniture, but all rights, and because they are sometimes allowed a plate of lentils, proclamation is made that they are happy. . . . Immortal souls! Ah! the Church knows the price of souls. . . . Is it not yet time, after eighteen centuries of Christianity, for us all to begin to practice the ever enduring law, "Do not to another that which you would not he should do to you; and that which your brothers should do for you, do ye fore them?"[21]

The Confederate failure to gain recognition in 1862 proved fatal, the diplomatic version of the twin defeats at Gettysburg and Vicksburg. King Cotton diplomacy was unsuccessful. Later missions failed too. On September 21, 1863, James Mason ended his mission and the Confederacy's relationship with Britain, having been relieved of his duties in August. US diplomat Henry Adams rightly diagnosed the situation when he asked, "Why should Mr. Davis aid our diplomacy by himself directing all our causes of alarm towards France, a nation whose power we have no real cause to fear, and away from England, with whom we have been on the very verge of war?" It was at this point that the Confederate government turned to the Catholic Church.[22]

On September 5, 1863, Judah P. Benjamin wrote Confederate agent Henry Hotze concerning Father Bannon: "The Chaplain of the gallant Missourians" had "at my solicitation . . . consented to proceed to Ireland and there endeavor to enlighten his fellow-countrymen as to the true nature of our struggle." Bannon's eagerness to become an emissary demonstrates the steady growth of his Confederatization. He had volunteered for the chaplaincy; now he would serve his country in the diplomatic arena. Benjamin claimed the North was enticing prospective immigrants with railroad jobs only to "get them as recruits for the Federal Army." Bannon's mission was to convince Irishmen to stop emigrating to the North and to flip sympathies. It was not sufficient just to stymie Union recruitment; the Confederates desired overt Irish support. Bannon was to travel to Ireland after stopping over in "Rome for the purpose of obtaining from the head of the Catholic Church such sanction of his purpose as may be deemed necessary to secure him a welcome among the Catholic clergy and laity of Ireland." Benjamin told Hotze to pass along further diplomatic instructions directly to Bannon. Hotze was to assist the priest in his travels, pay his expenses, and provide him with any "information in your power."[23]

The Confederacy's recruitment and support of Bannon (the same can be said for Lynch and his mission) demonstrates its dedication to a Catholic foreign policy. The CSA fully invested from both the diplomatic and financial sides and, in assigning Bannon the ambitious goal of essentially winning Ireland for the South, showed its confidence in a Catholic priest being able to accomplish such a daunting task. Bannon successfully ran the blockade in October 1863. He traveled from Wilmington, North Carolina, to Bermuda before heading across the ocean to Great Britain. During the course of the trip he discussed Catholic doctrine with a non-Catholic crewman from Virginia, a teenager named John Banister Tabb. Tabb later recalled this as a seminal moment in his own conversion to Catholicism and decision to become a priest.[24]

When Bannon met with Pope Pius IX in Rome, he became the first official Confederate representative to do so. Pius took an immediate liking to him. Bannon was a tall and strong man with a full black beard, whom the pope referred to as "*cette homme magnifique*." When, later in the war, he asked Bannon who had given him permission to wear his beard, the priest responded that he was "only a poor Confederate chaplain" who grew it while with his soldiers. "My son," Pius said, "you may wear your beard." During his initial meeting with the pope, Bannon delivered a letter from Jefferson Davis, who informed Pius that the joint papal letter to Archbishops Odin and Hughes the previous year had come to his attention and that he was pleased to have the pontiff "exhort the people and the rulers to the exercise of mutual charity and the love of peace." Davis's letter implicitly expressed a Confederate-papal unity, especially concerning the desired peaceful solution, while playing up the degree of separation between this supposed camp and the United States.[25]

No such camps existed. Pius IX might have favored the South in some ways, and he may have even taken a personal liking to Davis, respecting him as a political leader—it seems obvious that he did—but the idea that the pope was a Southern partisan was a one-directional product of Confederate propaganda. Davis's letter was, naturally, politically and diplomatically motivated. Peace was a secondary concern to, or even a tool for, Confederate success, aimed at securing a peace guaranteeing Southern independence. The Confederate president claimed it was his "duty to your Holiness in my own name and in that of the people of the Confederate States to give this expression of our sincere and cordial appreciation of the Christian love and charity by which your Holiness is actuated, and to assure you that this people . . . have been earnestly desirous that the wicked war shall cease." Davis pointed out, "We desire no evil to our enemies, nor do we covet any of their possessions," as the South was fighting a defensive war against a cruel invader.[26]

He claimed the war was being fought for the sole purpose that "they [the Union] shall cease to devastate our land and inflict useless and cruel slaughter upon our people." The Confederacy desired only to live in peace and to enjoy political and spiritual freedom. The letter, while not wholly insincere nor fully misleading (it was true that the South was, in effect, trying to be "left alone"), was above all a piece of political machination aimed at creating simplistic dichotomies that would gain the Confederacy Rome's sympathy if not outright support.[27]

As Bannon readied to leave Rome, another Confederate agent, Mann, of the original mission to Europe, met with the pope. Davis had named Mann "Special Envoy to the Holy See," telling him that he placed "trust and confidence in your prudence, integrity, and ability." Mann was instructed to convey the Confederate people's personal thanks for his involvement in peace initiatives, which both Benjamin and Davis claimed were the South's main objective. Mann, like Bannon, was handed a copy of the presidential letter to give to the pope. His three letters to Benjamin, reports on the Vatican meetings held between November 14 and December 9, 1863, brimmed with confidence, suggesting papal recognition was imminent.[28]

Mann's first audience with the pope was a "remarkable conference." The pope began by explaining why he had written his letter to Odin and Hughes and said he did not believe his desire for a quick end to the war would be fulfilled. Mann seized the opportunity to inform Pius that he had been appointed for this very reason, to work for immediate peace. He then handed him Davis's letter. Although this would be at least the second time the pope had read the letter, Mann observed that when hearing it read aloud Pius IX was "absorbed in Christian contemplation . . . a sweeter expression of pious affection, of tender benignity, never adorned the face of mortal man." When the pope read the passage in which Davis said he offered the same prayers for peace to God with "the same feelings which animated your Holiness," Mann mentioned that Pius looked upward "toward that throne upon which ever sits the Prince of Peace, indicating that his heart was pleading for our deliverance from that ceaseless and merciless war which is prosecuted against us."[29]

Mann reported that Pius had told him Lincoln had been working, via the US diplomatic corps, to create the impression in Europe that ending slavery was the war's ultimate aim. Perhaps, Pius suggested, the South could initiate a program of gradual emancipation, to contribute to this urgent humanitarian question? Mann replied that the Confederacy, as well as the United States, had "no control whatever" on the issue of slavery. He then listed the usual Southern apologies about why slavery must be left to the states, that "true philanthropy" was opposed to the way Lincoln wished to free the slaves—"convert[ing] the well cared-for civilized negro into a semi-barbarian"—and that slaves preferred their bondage in the South compared to freedom elsewhere.[30]

Mann, like Yancey blinded by myopic self-assurance, opined, "[His] Holiness received these remarks with an approving expression." Pius further told him he wished to do anything in his power to end "this most terrible war which is harming the good of all the earth." Mann, like Bannon would argue in Ireland, also told the pope the real problem was Union deception regarding immigrants, especially the Irish, promising them jobs while in reality bringing them over to join the Northern war effort. Mann explained that at hearing this, the pope "expressed his utter astonishment" and promised to write Davis a letter that might be published for the general public's reading.[31]

Mann characterized the meeting as "among the most remarkable conferences ever a foreign representative had with a potentate of the earth." "And such a potentate!" he wrote, "a potentate who wields the consciences of 175,000,000 of the civilized race . . . the viceregent of Almighty God in his sublunary sphere." Mann's enthusiasm had nothing to do with his own religious beliefs; he was not a Catholic and told the pope so. Mann authentically believed real diplomatic assistance could come from Rome, even that it was assuredly forthcoming. Great Britain and France did not matter anymore, because "when contrasted with the sneaking subterfuges to which some of the Governments of Western Europe have had recourse in order to evade intercourse with our Commissioners," the papal court displayed a "strikingly majestic" conduct. Mann hoped the pope would issue to those "175,000,000 consciences" some edict that might help the South. Perhaps a formal declaration supporting the Confederacy would stem the tide of Catholic immigrants flowing into the Union ranks. Maybe it would cause Catholics already fighting for the Union to have doubts. Mann believed all this was on the horizon.[32]

The most important thing is that Mann did in fact believe, and this belief did not end with him. The Confederacy, from Davis on down, put real stock in the pope and the Roman Catholic Church. The fundamental reason these hopes were frustrated was not that the pope had no power to offer. A papal endorsement might indeed have had an effect on the war, the degree of which is impossible to know. There was no authentic hope because Pius was solidly focused on his spiritual obligation to shepherd all Catholics without distinction, and, combined with the South's insistence on defending slavery, this would eventually render Catholic-Confederate diplomacy null and void.

Mann wrote to Benjamin again on November 21, a week following his initial conference. He reminded Benjamin of the pope's promise to write Davis but conceded that he did not know when the letter would be completed; "weeks, perhaps months." It came much more quickly. Dated December 3, 1863, the letter was addressed to the "Illustrious and Honorable, Sir, Jefferson Davis, President of the Confederate States of America." It was brief and to the point. Pius began by explaining he was greatly pleased, finding "certainly no small pleasure," to learn from Davis's letter, as well as from his envoys, that the Confederate president had so well received the pope's own letter to Archbishops Odin and Hughes. It was, furthermore, "very gratifying . . . that you and your people are animated by the same desire for peace and tranquility which we had so earnestly inculcated in our aforesaid letter to the venerable brethren above-named." Pius only prayed that other leaders would, like Davis and himself, "embrace the counsels of peace and tranquility." That was it. There was neither official recognition of the Confederacy nor any plan to do so in the future; there was no taking sides. Pius focused on the one thing that defined and underpinned his entire involvement in the American Civil War: a call for peace.[33]

Some Southern newspapers drew the correct conclusions from the papal-presidential exchanges. Raleigh's *Daily Confederate* highlighted Davis's framing of the war as a defensive struggle against oppressive foreign invasion but conceded the pope desired nothing more than peace. In this vein, Richmond's *Daily Dispatch* correctly summarized the pope's outlook later in the war: "Being Vicar on Earth of that God who is Pastor of Peace, he yearns to see these wraths appeased and peace restored . . . his most earnest wish that all nations may be united in the bonds of charity, peace and love." Mann took a different view. In a December 9 letter to Benjamin, he wrote that because Pius had saluted Davis as "president . . . we are acknowledged by as high an authority as this world contains to be an independent power of the earth." This was "positive recognition of our Government." Benjamin viewed the salutation as a sign of respect, nothing more. This does not mean the pope did not believe Davis was the president of an independent nation; by all accounts he did. One does not address someone as president simply to fulfill basic rules of etiquette; one does not call someone president unless that person is, in fact, a president.[34]

While the pope may have seen the Confederacy as a sovereign entity, he was not going to press the point. He was not going to stand with it against the

Union; he was not going to attempt to garner support for the South among European Catholic monarchies; he was not going to declare that American Catholics should see the justice of the Southern cause. Mann may have argued correctly that the pope viewed the Confederacy as an independent nation and that he believed Davis was a legitimate president. Mann may have been right that Pius was *implying* some kind of recognition. But Benjamin was right diplomatically speaking: Pius's view on Confederate independence was, fundamentally, a personal matter, one from which the Confederate nation would not reap any tangible benefits.

Benjamin understood this reality, but others did not. The majority of the Southern press matched Mann's enthusiasm. The *Alexandria Gazette* agreed with Mann that the papal presidential salutation meant "Pope Pius IX, as sovereign of Rome and as the head of the Roman Catholic Church, acknowledges the Independence of the Southern Confederacy." Charlotte's *Western Democrat* featured the "important correspondence" to its readership in the Carolinas, while the *Staunton Spectator* was one among many small, local papers relaying the news to rural parts of the South, drawing attention to the fact that "the Pope's reply is addressed to the illustrious Honorouble Jefferson Davis, President Confederate States of America."[35]

Perhaps no Southern newspaper was more enthralled than the *Memphis Daily Appeal*; it claimed, this correspondence "cannot fail to be followed by moral effects of great importance and value to the Confederate cause." That the Holy See's temporal reach was relatively limited was of little importance because "its spiritual and moral power is so great that the proudest potentates of the earth are solicitous to secure its power." The *Daily Appeal* reminded its readership that the "great majority of Christendom acknowledge the Pope as their ecclesiastical head, and regard him as the successor of PETER, and the representative upon earth of the Divine head of the Church." This mattered for Confederate independence, as "such a source to the Christian world in behalf of peace and justice" could not fail to produce the desired effects. Because the pope was a Confederate partisan, "no tool of Seward can hereafter stir up the foreign Catholics of New York to a bloody war, nor refrain from using the influence of his office in favor of peace and good will among men."[36]

The pope "alone, of European potentates," the *Daily Appeal* continued, "has addressed the chief of the Confederate States as 'President.'" Just as Mann eviscerated the "sneaking subterfuges" of secular governments compared to the papacy, the *Daily Appeal* stated that Southerners, Catholics and Protestants alike, "cannot but regard with profound respect and gratitude this truly Christian and manly conduct of the head of the Catholic Church, which is only the more conspicuous and brilliant from its contrast with the callous and inhuman indifference by the other rulers of Europe to this most bloody and barbarous war." A week later, the paper published a follow-up article claiming the pope's support would doom the North: the South's "practical inauguration of official intercourse with Rome will produce an estrangement of the moral support of the Catholic world, which the Yankees, by a system of unscrupulous falsehood and deception, managed to conciliate heretofore." Davis interpreted the papal salutation along the same lines. Soon afterward, he appointed Bishop Lynch as an official Confederate agent to the pope, to hopefully build off of this assumed sign of recognition.[37]

Bannon concurred. In Ireland, his main propaganda tool was a poster titled "Address to the Catholic Clergy and People of Ireland." It included three letters: the first from the pope to Odin and Hughes, the second from Davis to the pope, and the third, the pope's response to Davis. Bannon additionally posted "two broad sheets . . . on the gates and doors of Roman Catholic churches in Dublin." Both were discourses on the American Civil War—the first, letters from Pope Pius IX and the second, "Letters of John Mitchell, William Smith O'Brien, John Martin." Bannon told Irishmen the letters between the pope and Davis meant Pius IX viewed the South as a "remnant of Christian civilization," while the North was but an "amalgamation of German and Yankee infidels." Who were the Yankees? They were the descendants of Cromwell, Puritan "witch hunters" who took pleasure in burning convents and devastating private property. In the North, a country overrun by Know-Nothingism, being Catholic was "worse than being black." In contrast, Southerners were "the natural ally of the foreigner and the Catholic," the rich and deep history of Louisiana and Florida attesting to the South's intrinsic Catholicity.[38]

It was common that southerners played up the supposed immorality, inhumanity, and irreligiosity of Northerners, which served their assumption of victimhood in the face of barbarian invaders. Bannon's employment of these arguments was drawn from a deep well of similar rhetoric in the South, especially useful for Confederate agents in overtly Catholic countries where depictions of anti-Catholic bigotry hit home. The *New Orleans Daily Crescent* referred to Northerners as "wicked anti-Popery and abolition miscreants." The *Spirit of the Age,* in Raleigh, launched a broadside against New Englanders in particular, claiming that a once tight-knit Puritan community had disintegrated in the avaricious pursuit of monetary gain. Civil liberties had been exchanged for civil license, religious toleration was nonexistent, and all that remained was "infidelity, Beecherism, Parkerism, Cheeverism, and war on Catholics." The *Memphis Daily Appeal* wrote that the "Irish and Catholic element in the Northern armies is an unpleasant feature to an actively anti-Irish and no Popery population."[39]

The *Daily Appeal* did view Northern Irishmen's Catholicism as a saving grace. While all Yankees were "thieves and miscreants," Northern Irishmen "are true gentlemen, and thoroughly disciplined soldiers. It is only that they as Catholics refuse to pick and steal and maraud after the bad example set them by some of their Yankee associates." This "bad example" was, according to the Southern press, to be found everywhere. The *Daily Appeal* reprinted a letter from Woodstock Mills that had originally appeared in the *Savannah News* under the title "Yankee Doings in Lower Georgia." Therein was recounted a recent Northern raid on Southern churches, "particularly the Catholic church," where Union soldiers "stole the chalice, and destroyed everything they could lay their hands on." When a woman asked them if they were not ashamed of such conduct, the soldiers said no, because "they were rebel churches."[40]

Northern troops were accused of committing arson against Catholic churches, stripping altars, and stealing the vestments of priests, once even throwing these "into the mud and completely destroy[ing] them." Union soldiers from Maine were accused of marching up to a church in Jacksonville and "after glutting their beastly minds by desecrating the house of God, cutting and defacing the sacred symbols of religion, set fire to the building, destroying everything." The *Memphis Daily Appeal* once wrote, "The Yankee country has, for many years, been conspicuous for intolerance towards the Catholics," noting the burning of a convent near Boston, the destruction of a church in Newark, New Jersey, anti-Catholic riots in Philadelphia, and "a hundred other examples of mob persecution." In contrast, "in all these Confederate States there never was a church wrecked, nor a Catholic clergyman even insulted."[41]

"The Yankees, despising all religions, seem to have an intense hatred for the Roman Catholic faith," the *Richmond Enquirer* once claimed. The paper listed the "seeking and burning" of two Catholic churches in Florida and Mississippi and the plunder of another one in Baton Rouge. In Baton Rouge there was the added atrocity of Eucharistic desecration. "The Blessed host was scattered on the ground, while these monsters called out for the Catholics to 'come and look at your God'!" Another soldier seized a benediction veil, claiming, "This will be a nice blanket for my horse when I get one!" The remonstrations of Louisiana Catholics against Northern anti-Catholic attacks usually fell on deaf ears, the *Enquirer* explained, citing a time when Catholics protested to Adm. David Farragut. He dismissed it with, "Good enough for the damned secesh rebels." The *Enquirer* explained that appeals were being made to Northern bishops and Union Catholics so as to "prevent its becoming a war against the Catholic religion at the same time that it is a war against the States and people of the South!"[42]

In addition to featuring numerous similar episodes of Northern anti-Catholicism for his Irish audience, Bannon commonly painted Irishmen who fought for the North as disrespecting the efforts of John Mitchel and the '48 movement. Bannon drew on this tradition to argue that the South, like Ireland, was fighting for home rule and was therefore the true heir to the Revolutionary glory of 1776. Bannon claimed the Confederacy was fighting a defensive war against Northern aggressors, invaders who, in addition to their misguided warmongering, wanted to use Irishmen as cannon fodder. Bannon explained the South just wanted to be left alone, in peace, and now the pope was on its side, too, both parties wanting the war to end so as to return to antebellum normalcy—the one difference being that the Confederacy would now be an independent nation, as was its natural right.[43]

Bannon was well received in Ireland. Thousands of copies of his curricular were distributed, and he was invited all over the country to preach and explain the Confederate position. An Irishman who heard Bannon said, "We who were all praying for the North at the opening of the war would willingly fight for the South if we could get there." Irish clergymen complained to Lincoln to stop "using up the Irish in the war like dogs." John Martin, who along with Mitchel formed the "Moses and Aaron" of the Young Ireland '48 movement, wrote, "I am heart and soul a partisan of the Confederates in this war. These sentiments are the sentiments of the great majority of the people of Ireland," adding, "the South has the right of self-government as clearly as the Belgians, Italians, Poles, or the Irish."[44]

At the conclusion of Bannon's mission, in March of 1864, an Irishman said, "The people [now] sympathize with the South, the priesthood [has] advocated the Southern cause[,] . . . and should the Federal and Confederate recruiting officers be allowed to enter the field of competition for recruits within a month from now the Southern cause would attract four-fifths of the material." Bannon seemed to have convinced many Irishmen that the North wanted to use its citizens expendably on the front lines, thus accomplishing his mission from the Confederate government. Judah Benjamin had specified to CSA agent James Mason that Bannon would assist in "communicating directly with the [Irish] people, and spreading among them such information and intelligence as may be best adapted to persuade them of the folly and wickedness of volunteering their aid in the savage warfare waged against us." This, Bannon had certainly done.[45]

While Bannon was discouraging enlistments into the Union army in Ireland, the Confederate press was supporting this work at home. In October 1864, the *Wilmington Journal* ran a piece titled "To Emigrants from Ireland." "On your arrival in the port of New York you may expect to be immediately solicited to enlist in the Federal army for the restoration of the Union, and for the pretended liberation of the Negro," the article warned. Irishmen should "read; and learn from the letter of our Holy Father Pope Pius IX, that the war of the North against the South is the direst, most destructive, and most dismal of all the evils that could befall a people of a nation."[46]

The *Journal*'s contention regarding "the pretended liberation" of slaves, that the North was only using emancipation as a tool in its larger projects, and possessed no sincere concern for equality or human rights, was a popular argument in the South. This extended into specifically Catholic quarters, too, and not simply within the borders of the Confederate states. The *Wheeling (West Virginia) Register* once published an article claiming the National Protestant League's mission statement was presenting "a bold, vigorous, and continuous protest, by word and act, against Infidelity and Roman Catholicism." Furthermore, the New School Presbyterian Assembly "recommended that the right of suffrage be conferred upon the negroes in order that their vote might 'counteract that of the Roman Catholics.'" The *Idaho World* once ran the headline "The National Protestant League—Negro Suffrage the Ally to Exterminate Catholicity."[47]

The *Memphis Daily Appeal* went a few steps further in its alarmist tone. In an article titled "A Hint to the Catholics," the paper claimed that nothing less than Catholics' religious and political liberties were at stake. Would the North, should it be successful in destroying "the slaveholding interest, [along] with the liberties of the South," then turn its aim on Catholics? "No man of sense can doubt it." The *Daily Appeal* urged "every true Catholic to sustain the southern cause as his own cause," because "it is hardly surer that God Almighty reigns in the universe than that Puritan domination will be the ultimate ruin of the religious liberties of the Catholic people."[48]

Many Irishmen appear to have been convinced by Bannon's arguments. But how have scholars assessed the efficacy of his work so many years later? Historian Phillip Thomas Tucker seems to have solid ground for his conclusion that Bannon was the most able Confederate agent in all of Europe—especially based on the words of Henry Hotze, who said, "Bannon's accomplishments represent the most important diplomatic success achieved by the Confederacy in Ireland." Historian Leo Francis Stock concurs, showing that Irish emigration to the United States dropped precipitously following Bannon's mission: 54 percent in one year.[49] Stopping Irish emigration to the North was the whole point of Bannon's mission. Judged by this metric it was a success, although not all historians agree.[50] In September 1864, the *Wilmington Journal* published an article that arrived at the same conclusions Stock and Tucker would highlight years later: "Whether due to the exertions of the Catholic clergy [or other factors] . . . certain it is that the Irish emigration to the Northern States has greatly fallen off, if it has not wholly ceased for the present."[51]

As Bannon was completing his mission, the bishop of Charleston was preparing for his. In March 1864, Lynch responded to Benjamin's inquiry about his willingness to become a Confederate agent. "After mature reflection," he explained, "I believe it is my duty to accede to the desire of the Government, and to accept the position." But, he added, should the Confederate government find a more suitable agent to go in his place, "it will give me personally much pleasure to be relieved of a duty which I feel to be very responsible, and for which no previous training has prepared me."[52]

Lynch, the most Confederatized of bishops, claimed he only undertook this task because it was asked of him. In truth, the man who gleefully wrote about South Carolina independence as Fort Sumter was being shelled, held public thanksgiving in his cathedral following the victory, and never missed a moment to defend the Southern cause in debates with other bishops must have been very pleased to be chosen for this mission. Lynch, like Bannon, did his part for the Confederacy at home. Now he would contribute overseas. He was given three weeks to get his affairs in order before reporting to Richmond. Lynch appointed Father Leon Fillion as vicar general of Charleston, citing his "piety and ecclesiastical quality." Before leaving for the Confederate capital, he heard from Bishop Augustin Verot. Verot said he thought clergy should do what they could, but "I do not see what good your mission to the Holy Father can do toward putting an end to the war." Curiously, Verot wrote that he believed a delegation sent to the French emperor Maximillian "offering him an alliance offensive & defensive with the Confederacy would do more good."[53]

Perhaps Verot had a romantic notion that such a delegation sent "in the name of humanity, civilization & liberty" would somehow convince the French, who had little to gain for themselves, to join the war. Maybe he was just desperate, evidenced by his writing to Lynch that he believed the war could not end without some foreign intervention. If such intervention really were the final missing piece, then any country would do, including a nation that, while demonstrating some degree of pro-Confederate sentiment, had shown no willingness to act unilaterally.[54]

On March 25, Lynch wrote to Benjamin again, stating that he hoped to bring an aide with him, one who could write French and Italian, and that he would carry five bales of cotton as a source of currency. He confirmed that he would be in Richmond on the agreed date, April 5, and speculated that he might arrive a day early. Less than a week before his departure, Lynch received a letter from Gen. P. G. T. Beauregard, wishing him luck and safety on his mission. On April 4, Benjamin wrote to Lynch with information regarding his upcoming duties as "Commissioner to represent the Confederacy near the States of the Church." Benjamin informed Lynch that the recent exchange between Davis and the pope was the reason for his mission. Benjamin credited the pope's "earnest desire to for the restoration of peace on this continent." No one, Benjamin assured the bishop, was better suited to serve a diplomatic mission to the Vatican than he was.[55]

Because all of Europe had refused to admit the Confederacy to the "family of nations," Benjamin cautioned Lynch not to impetuously push for papal recognition. "To make a formal demand for our recognition by His Holiness," Benjamin wrote, "would therefore seem to be ungracious and inconsistent with the friendly feelings which prompt this mission." But lest Lynch think the mission was solely of a fraternal nature, Benjamin made clear "the honor and interest of our own country are, however, paramount to all other considerations." In addition, the bishop was to do his best to mold public opinion at Paris, Madrid, and Vienna and to amplify the goodwill Pius's court had already shown Davis. Lynch was also reported to be in possession of an "Official Manifesto of the Confederates," a joint note addressed to the pope and the French foreign minister, stipulating Confederate war aims and stating that "all they [the CSA] ask is immunity from interference with their internal peace and prosperity, and to be left in the undisturbed enjoyment of their inalienable rights of life, liberty and the pursuit of happiness."[56]

Benjamin's directions were opportunistic and pragmatic; the interests of the Confederacy superseded all else. Benjamin recognized that while the pope's letter to Davis was no sign of recognition, it was nevertheless an indication of friendship. Trying to force recognition could offend the pope. Perhaps Benjamin had in mind Yancey's failure in the original Confederate mission when the agent's bravado regarding King Cotton diplomacy and Southern rights was off-putting to Europeans. It would therefore be Lynch's "delicate task to keep in view the great advantage which would accrue to our cause by the formal recognition of the Government by the Sovereign Pontiff, and the establishment with him of the usual diplomatic intercourse." Even the cynical Benjamin, who did not share Mann's or Davis's enthusiasm about the papal exchanges, believed that there was some, even if miniscule, hope of papal diplomatic assistance.[57]

Lynch was instructed to be watchful. Benjamin commanded that, if an occasion presented itself, "the President expects that you will not fail to avail yourself of the opportunity." In sum, when it was to "the indirect than the direct effects of your mission that we are disposed to look for fruitful results," he believed the most favorable outcome would be Lynch increasing the goodwill of the papacy toward the South and maybe causing that to affect some of the European powers, to nudge them closer to Southern sympathy. And still, if outright recognition, the ultimate goal, was possible, Lynch was expected to seize the opportunity without delay.[58]

Lynch received his commission from Davis on April 4. The president told his cabinet Lynch had been invested with "full and all manner of power and authority, for and in the name of the Confederate States, to meet and confer with . . . [a] person or persons duly authorized by the Sovereign Pontiff of the States of the Church." News of Lynch's mission was widely reported throughout America, North and South. Like many Northern papers, the *Burlington (Iowa) Hawkeye* painted Lynch as a Confederate zealot: in "all the wide region controlled by the Rebels, we have never yet heard of one Catholic priest who was not on their [the CSA's] side." The Confederate government would pay Lynch a monthly salary of one thousand dollars, with allowance to draw an additional five hundred dollars for miscellaneous expenses. Lynch was given permission to hire a secretary, who would be paid three hundred dollars a month. He took two men with him: Conrad Wise Chapman, a solider and artist; and seminarian Daniel J. Quigley. The former spoke Italian, the latter was on his way to the American College in Rome.[59]

Lynch left Richmond on April 6. He reached Wilmington, North Carolina, two days later, boarding the steamship *Minnie,* in the mouth of Cape Fear, for his departure to Bermuda. Lynch and his party reached Bermuda on April 14, greeted with great fanfare. "He was waited upon by a large concourse of people, with whom he conversed freely," the *Alexandria Gazette* reported. "He speaks with great confidence of the Southern cause, and is hopeful of the ultimate success of the Confederacy." From Bermuda, it was on to Halifax, Nova Scotia, where, the *Yorkville (South Carolina) Enquirer* reported, Lynch was "met with a very cordial reception and finds the people quite warm-hearted towards the Southerners." During his brief stay, Lynch was a guest of Archbishop Thomas Louis Connelly and given a public dinner.[60]

Lynch then proceeded to Ireland, where he was again a guest of the local bishop, this time the archbishop of Dublin, Paul Cullen. Cullen asked if Lynch would "be so kind as to preach for us in the metropolitan Church on next Sunday, feast of the H.[oly] Trinity." Cullen also told Lynch to "come to my house and I will have a room prepared for you" when he returned from preaching in other parts of the country. Lynch's goal was similar to Bannon's: dissuade Irishmen from immigrating to the United States. Lynch's and Bannon's paths actually crossed in Ireland. The two decided to henceforth carry out their work together, with Bannon accompanying Lynch on the remainder of his journey.[61]

From Ireland, the bishop and the chaplain traveled to London—dining with Nicholas Cardinal Wiseman, the first Catholic archbishop of Westminster since the reestablishment of the Church hierarchy in England and Wales in 1850—and then on to Paris, where Lynch met with Confederate agent John Slidell and the archbishop of Paris, Georges Darboy. Lynch also secured an audience with the French foreign minister, Éduoard Drouyn de Lhuys. Drouyn, referring to Napoleon's 1862 armistice plan, told Lynch he believed the Confederacy was having some measure of wartime success and "that long ago, the French government was disposed to intervene, and propose terms of peace, [but], unwilling to act alone, it had proposed a concert of action in the matter to the English government. But the proposal was not accepted." Drouyn explained that the French preferred a policy of neutrality and that slavery, which France had abolished in its colonies in 1848, was the biggest stumbling block to recognition.[62]

A report about Lynch from the *Richmond Enquirer*'s Paris correspondent is telling of a larger problem for the Confederates concerning timing; throughout the war, whether in the diplomatic arena or on the battlefield, they never seemed to be able to capitalize on opportunities, the *Trent* crisis but one example. Contrary to what Drouyn had told Lynch, it seemed slavery was not the prime issue, but rather the Confederacy's severely delayed diplomacy was. "We have had Bishop Lynch, of Charleston, here for a few days, a man who has impressed all who have seen him most favorably," the correspondent began. But Lynch was not "destined to be more successful, diplomatically, than his forerunners." The "only drawback to the fertility of Mr. Benjamin's invention is the length of time he requires in getting up his imitation of Mr. Seward. It is more than two years since Archbishop Hughes came over on a mission from the North, and now comes Bishop Lynch as a sort of corollary from the South."[63]

Lynch finally arrived in Rome in the summer of 1864, some three months after receiving his initial commission. Rather than stay with Bishop William G. McCloskey, his friend and the rector of the American College at Rome—and in doing so perhaps cause hard feelings among some of the seminarians, a mixed class of Northerners and Southerners—Lynch took an apartment on the Via Condotti. Regardless, McCloskey missed Lynch at the time of his arrival; he was on vacation in Naples, hoping to avoid the "terrible furnace" of the Roman summer. On June 28, Lynch had his first meeting with Cardinal Antonelli, Pius's secretary of state, a man whom the bishop credited as being as well informed about American events as any European and someone who never wavered from a position of neutrality, if not subtle Northern sympathy. Lynch, and by extension the Confederacy, was dealt a crushing blow almost immediately. He was informed that the pope would see him only in his ecclesiastical capacity, as a bishop of the Catholic Church, not as a Confederate agent.[64]

It was a full circle of cruel irony: a strictly ecclesiastical visit—Odin's 1862 *ad limina*—had birthed an unintended but potentially golden political opportunity for the Confederacy. Davis was ecstatic; it seemed the pope had noticed the Southern struggle. Pius's joint letter to the archbishops of New Orleans and New York appeared the perfect prescription for a fast-failing Confederacy, containing the promise of a peace that would end fratricidal bloodshed along with securing Confederate independence. With this in mind, Davis quickly sent envoys to the Vatican. And then, when another Southern prelate was in Rome primarily as a Confederate agent, not on ecclesiastical business, he was treated the way Odin should have been in 1862. The Vatican's immediate designation of Lynch solely as a bishop, not a Confederate emissary, practically ended all diplomatic hopes before the first meeting even began.

When the pope finally met with Lynch, on July 4, in a party that included Father Bannon, he asked him about the condition of the Charleston diocese while Lynch conveyed Davis's "respect, veneration, and good will." If Lynch tried slyly to bring the conversation around to his mission, it was to no avail. The pope actually spoke of politics first, but only to announce with finality his unwillingness to grant the Confederacy any official help.[65]

It is most clear that you are two nations. . . . When some foreign power will have to be called in as umpire, then, perhaps, by a miracle, for it would be a miracle if the North should consent, that I might be called in as an umpire, I wish it to be understood before hand that I could not say anything directed to confirm and strengthen slavery. I hold that Christianity has benefitted society as to the position of women and as to the position of the slaves. The first has been elevated and made equal to men, and has her appropriate sphere of action. I am happy to believe that [sister-nurses on] both sides have done and are doing an immense good in the hospitals. The condition of the Slave was likewise improved, until in the course of time it cease to exist. As to your slaves, I see clearly that it would be absurd to attempt, as it were to cut the Gordian Knott, by an act of Emancipation. But still something might be done looking to an improvement in their position or state, and to a gradual preparation for their freedom at a future opportune time. I have already said this much to several Americans from the South and they seemed to agree with me.[66]

The pope's claim that the North and South were "two nations" had as much political capital as his salutation of Davis as "Illustrious President." The Roman Catholic Church was not going to do anything official to help either side. There would be neither a formal declaration of recognition nor any political weight brought to bear on European countries to do the same. This greatly benefited the Union, for it, unlike the Confederacy, did not need external help and would most likely only be harmed by a foreign power's intervention.

Although Lynch's audiences with the pope proved unfruitful, this did not deter the Confederatized Southern press from claiming the pontiff was, and had always been, on its side. The *Wilmington Journal*'s July 28 article "Interesting from Rome" claimed that since Pius "exhibits much courage in championing the cause of Poland, neglected as she is, and consigned to the most cruel fate, by the nations of Europe" he was a natural friend of the Confederacy too. For the South, like Poland, was also being unjustly denied its right to national self-determination by tyrannical oppression (the Russian czar Poland's own Lincoln, et cetera). Other Southern papers made the Poland-Confederacy connection as well. "It is the natural, necessary protest and revolt of, not a class or order, but an ancient and glorious nation . . . it is the aristocratic and high-bred national pride of Poland revolting against the coarse brute power of Russian imperialism," the *Richmond Enquirer* wrote in March 1863. "At bottom, the cause of Poland is the same cause for which the Confederates are now fighting."[67]

The *Wilmington Journal* further stated that the pope had always possessed sympathy for the Southern cause. In the Confederacy he saw "the blood of an innocent and comparatively weak people, wantonly shed with the most wicked designs, by a ferocious enemy as proud of his strength as was Golia." The "frankness with which the present Pontiff has signaled his sympathy with the Confederate cause, has been very beneficial to us," the *Journal* added, especially in "influencing the minds of adherents of the Catholic faith." Writing about Lynch's audiences with the pope nearly two months after the fact, the *Richmond Enquirer* conceded that the bishop-diplomat had been received solely in "the character of a dignitary of the Church" but that, nonetheless, "the Holy See entertains a profound sympathy for the Confederate States."[68]

Lynch had a few additional audiences with Antonelli and the pope, but they came to naught. The United States knew it too. US diplomat Rufus King wrote a series of letters to Seward in this vein. On July 30, he mentioned that Lynch, "a supporter if not an accredited agent, of the so called Confederate Government," had been in Rome for a few weeks. He explained that Lynch had not met with official papal recognition nor was he likely to. On August 16, King reported that Cardinal Antonelli had told him Lynch had been received in his "clerical capacity" alone. Six days later, King informed Seward that Antonelli had read the US Constitution and "could plainly perceive that the so-called Confederate States had sought an unconstitutional remedy for their alleged wrongs." Whether Antonelli plainly perceived the injustice of the Confederate cause is, of course, speculative, but King correctly predicted that there would be no change in the papal court's neutrality. On October 25, King reported that Lynch, about to leave Rome and, having met with no diplomatic success, declared his mission "a failure."[69]

The *New York Herald* agreed with the US diplomats. Concerning Lynch's mission the paper wrote, "Whatever efforts he may have made to obtain the aid of the European Powers in favor of the confederacy, it is plain that they have all been futile and abortive." Assuring their readership that they were presenting the "whole story in a nutshell," the paper explained that the pope's response to Davis had signaled the end of Confederate diplomacy. "No negotiations have brought about intervention or anything like it. The Pope's reply, as well as those of the other Powers, put a finishing blow to the rebel hopes in Europe," the *Herald* concluded, "and beyond the mere cant expression of sympathy with this or that ride, they will not attempt any direct interference with our affairs."[70]

Before leaving Rome, Lynch made a last-ditch effort to gain papal support by drawing up a pamphlet on slavery, in response to Pius's request that "something might be done looking to an improvement in their [the slaves'] position or state, and to a gradual preparation for their freedom at a future opportune time." Lynch began "A Few Words on Domestic Slavery in the Confederate States"—a pamphlet partitioned into twenty-four subsections—by explaining that he did not intend to start a discussion about, nor provide a defense of, slavery. He was simply submitting a "statement of facts." He promised to be neither the passerby who "yearning for horrors to be discovered . . . was sure to be satisfied by some wag who loves to mystify strangers" nor someone "feted by the hospitable planters and who saw every thing *couleur de rose.*" Lynch claimed he was qualified to assess the situation because of his Southern background and clerical station, the latter comprising twenty-four years of ministry to Southern slaves, and that his viewpoint would be echoed by "every Catholic clergyman, who has similarly laboured there for even half the time."[71]

Lynch explained that he was like a medical doctor, a diagnostician, carefully gathering evidence in order to empirically test possible hypotheses. Other would-be diagnosticians, particularly Northern ones, had gotten it woefully wrong. These philanthropists and puritans, "in their horror of Slavery and their blind zeal against it," had become theorists proposing to banish sickness by "slaying doctors and burning all hospitals." They had taken an obvious fact, that freedom was superior to the lack thereof, and allowed themselves to be carried away by reformist passions. As long as their singular goal—abolition—might be accomplished, no amount of destruction, terror, or strife resulting from this work could be counted as anything other than necessary. Quixotic Northern reformers were like a Prussian ambassador to Great Britain who, having been in the country for three weeks, was sure he could pen a thorough report on the government. At three months, he realized some subjects could not be easily summed up and would require further study. After three years in the country, he gave up, confessing total incompetence to state anything of value. "How many positive writers against slavery have not given even three weeks to an examination of the subject?" Lynch asked. And so he set out to give a definitive, balanced, and unbiased accounting.[72]

However honest Lynch's intentions may have been, the final work served only to further confirm his severe racism and prejudices and to cement his status in the realm of the most hyper-Confederatized Southerners. Lynch painted a classically paternalistic image of the master-slave relationship, the analysis undifferentiated from the typical Confederate Southerner. Lynch, like the majority

of Southern Catholics, was indeed that: a typical Confederate Southerner. Per
Lynch, slaves not only knew slavery was good for them—superior to "brutal-
ized and barbarous" Africa, where tribal chieftains slew captives en masse to
watch blood flow into graves as a "last tribute to [a] deceased King"—they loved
their bondage and their masters even more. If that was not true, why had there
not been widespread Stono Rebellion– or Nat Turner–style revolts in the South?
Why did slaves pay no attention to the Emancipation Proclamation? Why did
Southern white men leave wives and children at home on plantations, "a few
hundred scattered among thousands of slaves and almost unprotected . . . and
yet no soldier dreams that his family is more exposed, than when he was at home
to protect it"? Slaves just wanted to be left to their work, "pursuing, as their fathers had, the easy cultivation of the fields, under the guidance and discipline of
their masters." Being "transferred from a land of the most degraded heathenism,
to countries where they could receive the light of Christianity," slaves had es-
caped harsh conditions for something more sublime.[73]

Lynch's long pamphlet was, from start to finish, in line with contemporary
Southern Catholic views on slavery as well as those of Southern society writ
large. Like Verot in his 1861 tract, Lynch argued slave marriages and families
had to be respected—blaming Protestants for corrupting marriage among the
enslaved and the free alike: "The general Protestantism of the country . . . which
does not accept the full Catholic sense of the words of our Saviour, 'What God
has joined, let no man put asunder.'"[74] Workloads and punishments had to
be reasonable and humane, and he spoke at length on the mutual obligations
within the master-slave relationship; the slave owing his master "the produce
of his reasonable life long labour under the owner's direction," and the master
returning to the slave "reasonable support according to his condition, from
infancy to death"; meaning food, clothing, medical care, and shelter.[75]

Unsurprisingly, Lynch was at his most Catholic when discussing slave religion. In these reflections, Lynch, no fan of slave religion, showed himself to
be, like Gache and like a plurality of Southern Catholics, viscerally opposed
to Protestantism above all.[76] Lynch blamed Protestants for everything he believed was wrong with slave religion, especially the focus on emotionalism
over reverent piety, and the prevalence of antinomianism.[77]

But what of Catholic slaves? Per Lynch, Catholic slaves were of a much
higher caliber than non-Catholic slaves. This was true especially in the realm of
sexual morality: "Among our Catholic negroes we sometimes find exemplary
instances of that to them most difficult virtue,—purity. I have heard men of
distinction, even Protestant judges, on the bench, bear ready testimony to the

superiority and exalted character of Catholic negroes over the others." Lynch
further stated, "It is only through their instruction in the Catholic faith, and
their elevation to something of Catholic virtue in their lives, that the negroes
can be raised from their present state of moral turpitude, and their character
be really improved." Considering these sentiments, it is little wonder the sole
possible alternative to the extant system Lynch imagined was placing all slaves
under the control of the Jesuit order, a mission system like Father Junipero
Serra's in California transplanted to the South, "the negroes would yield readily to this religious, almost theocratic rule . . . [and eventually] they [Jesuits and
slaves] would work harmoniously together."[78]

Lynch argued slaves had not yet shaken the remnants of "barbarism and heathenism" and were therefore in need of their white masters' "guidance." Therefore any alternatives to the system—immediate and unconditional abolition,
a "preparatory apprenticeship," carving out sections of America as a type of
"Black Republic," or repatriation to Africa—were too expensive, too compli-
cated, or just too utopian to work. Per Lynch, slavery as practiced in the Southern states was not simply humane or mutually beneficial. In Panglossian fashion, he saw it as the best of all possible worlds. Because of something he termed
"the Antagonism of races," nothing but this best possible system was acceptable
(Jesuit oversight excepted); he essentially meant things were best left alone, as
any disturbance to the social order might result in a Haitian Revolution–type
event creating untold amounts of bloodshed for all parties involved. But this
was irrational and circular reasoning, holding that it was fine to allow an egre-
gious evil, slavery, to continue on undisturbed because one feared the potential
of another evil, vigilante carnage, arising.[79]

Lynch's pamphlet was well received by some in the European press. *La Civ-
ilta Cattolica* commented that the work was a statement of the "true condition
of slavery in the American South . . . set forth in this letter written by an impar-
tial person, superbly well-informed and of broad and just views." Hotze said
no one was better suited than Lynch to handle the topic; the British *Army and
Navy Gazette* called the French edition "by far the best which has appeared on
the subject of slavery." Others were less enamored. Montalembert wrote in *Le
Correspondent:*

> I refuse to acknowledge the priestly character of the author. If the writer of this
> shameful book really were a priest, and if it has suffered for him to live, as he says,
> among American planters for 24 years, to proclaim the utility and legitimacy

of black slavery, to see in their very servitude the only possible barrier to their licentiousness, the sole fact of such perversion of moral feeling and priestly conscience would constitute the severest argument against the social and religious regime of the slave countries.[80]

Lynch's goal was to take the one roadblock to papal recognition and dismantle any objections from the Vatican. Once he had successfully done so, the pope would accept Lynch's views and perhaps even extend diplomatic recognition to the Confederacy. This did not happen. The reason was not so much Lynch's "failure," as Rufus King put it, but rather the steadfast spiritual allegiance of Pope Pius IX, a loyalty to Catholics everywhere, one engendering political neutrality. Pius IX would not give his support to any side in what he saw as a destructive and fratricidal war, especially not to the participant whose foundations were supported by chattel slavery.

The Confederacy believed in its Catholic diplomats, who in turn believed in the Confederate nation. That Catholic-Confederate diplomacy was ultimately a failure should not dissuade scholars from further study, especially when it is understood, first, how important the diplomatic arena was to the Civil War and, second, that the Confederacy placed significant hope in the Catholic Church. This involvement in Confederate diplomacy—from Bannon's trip to Ireland through the exchanges between Davis and the pope, up to Lynch's mission— was set against the unchanging fact that Pius IX was staunchly committed to putting God and the Church first. As Loretta Clare Feiertag has properly diagnosed, "Both factions turned to Rome, because of the moral influence which opinion expressed there might have everywhere and because of their importance, dignity, influence and highly representative character of the diplomatic corps at the papal court. Both factions attempted to place upon correspondence emanating from the Pope a political significance in harmony with their views." But Pius and his court were "concerned primarily with spiritual matters."[81]

1865

The End of the War Everywhere

"Above all I hope that the present year brings me to the day when I will be reunited with my beloved never again to be separated," Felix Poche wrote on New Year's Day 1865. Just getting out of the war alive was the most any Confederate soldier could hope for. Father James Sheeran's reflection on January 3, having just been released from his celebrated captivity, mirrored Dooley's after Sharpsburg/Antietam. Riding his horse southbound through the Shenandoah Valley, the journey ahead long and the weather cold, he recalled his voyage down the same road two years prior. The failure of the Maryland campaign notwithstanding, Sheeran remembered "magnificent mansions, well-cultivated farms, splendid barns . . . orchards loaded with autumn fruit." Now, all this was gone: "Houses, barns, stables, haystacks, orchards, fences and every other improvement burned to the ground." A heavy snow began to fall, "accompanied by a strong wind which blew it directly in my face." As Sheeran suffered through intense pain in his legs, he took particular note of the people he saw. They "seemed afraid to appear out of their homes."[1]

It is true that with the ushering in of a new year, something else was coming to an end too. From the outset of the war, the Confederacy, deficient in men and munitions, needed help to gain its independence. It lost its best chance at European recognition when the *Trent* crisis passed without consequence. France and Britain were out of the picture two years later and the work of the priest-diplomats Lynch and Bannon ultimately amounted to nothing. The stunning victories of the Confederacy's annus mirabilis of 1862 were soon neutralized by the failure at Sharpsburg/Antietam. Lincoln's subsequent issue of the Emancipation Proclamation made the war a crusade to end slavery. Gettysburg made for two failed Southern invasions; another one was not feasible. Following Vicksburg, the Union controlled all of the Mississippi River and the western theater. The slight hope the North might tire of the war vanished with Lincoln's reelection. Throughout 1864, Grant kept pressing down on Lee farther and farther into Virginia, and by year's end, Sherman's devastation of the lower South had been completed.[2]

These realities did not, however, prevent Confederatized Catholics from hoping against hope. They were going to see this experiment through to the end, even if that meant trying to stay their nation's imminent execution with the most far-fetched rationale. Anti-Northern and especially anti-Lincoln conspiracy theories flowed freely; not all originated in the Southern states. An unnamed Catholic priest from Orange, New Jersey, penned a letter that appeared in the Dublin, Ireland, *Nation*, titled "A Catholic Priest on the Yankee Presidential Election." This was duly reprinted in Richmond's *Daily Dispatch* in January 1865.[3]

The New Jersey priest argued that during the previous year it had become evident McClellan was going to win and make peace with the Confederacy. Lincoln "set his agents to work, and there was not a city, town, hamlet or village in the Northern and Western States but were bribed with thousands and thousands of greenbacks to secure his re-election." The priest further stated, "By getting re-elected, he considered that this would prove to all Europe that the Federals endorsed him and his administration, whereas the contrary is the fact." He made no mention of the monumental role Union victory in Atlanta played in the election; he only wrote that "all of us know full well how the constitutional rights of the North and South have been trampled upon and invaded by the Know-Nothings and Abolitionists of the North. And all Europe can surely and clearly see, after four years of hard fighting against overwhelming numbers, that the Southerners have *earned* and have *established* their independence."[4]

The same day Sheeran was riding down the snow-covered Shenandoah Valley, Henri Garidel entertained a rumor that Hood had beaten Thomas in Tennessee. This was not just false but completely backward. Thomas's victory over Hood at the Battle of Nashville in December 1864 had destroyed the CSA's Army of Tennessee. Garidel's lament about the "miserable war," missing his family, and the poor quality of Richmond coffee was only exacerbated by his worsening physical condition. "On the way home I was bleeding like a bull," he wrote, referencing his nagging hemorrhoids. "When I got home, I bathed in my own blood . . . the water was very cold, and I was frozen." He added, "There was no fire in the house . . . I pray constantly to the Blessed Virgin Mary to take pity on me. This is too much misery to bear." The available cleaning agents did not help. "The soap we are using has a lot to do with it. It is of very bad quality. Well, it is Confederate soap, and that says it all."[5]

These discomforts notwithstanding, Garidel kept up his normal routine of Mass and work. He also kept his ear to the ground for rumors. Maybe the One Big True One would come along and change everything. At the end of January, Garidel claimed a peace settlement was imminent. "Everyone in Richmond" was discussing it. He seems to have been referring to the Hampton Roads Conference. "We will see how all this turns out," he wrote. It did not turn out well for the South. On February 3, Lincoln and Seward met with three representatives of the Confederate government aboard a steamboat near Union-occupied Fort Monroe. The Confederate side was immediately disheartened to learn that full reunification of the Union was the only acceptable condition for peace.[6]

Poche, like Garidel, also kept hoping in rumors. On January 22, he mentioned a fantastic double rumor, confirming the conventional wisdom that the desperation of a situation correlates to a rise in the unbelievability of proposed remedies. This tale stated that George McClellan had assumed command of a rogue army numbering one hundred thousand men who did not believe Lincoln's reelection was valid and so were in "rebellion against the tyrant . . . disput[ing] the power of Abraham the 1st and begin[ning] to fight him." In addition, a coalition of "powerful foreigners," led by France and England, had just recognized the Confederacy.[7]

Poche was not alone in entertaining the latter part of this rumor. Wheeling, West Virginia's *Daily Register* reported that the "Catholic powers of Europe have formed a secret league to recognize the Confederacy." It credited Bishop Lynch for this breakthrough; it had been accomplished "through the agency of [Lynch], who was sent out by Jeff. Davis to intrigue for recognition." Another West Virginia paper also recognized Lynch. "It was not difficult for him to convince the master spirits of European reaction and absolution that the slaveholders' rebellion was identical in spirit with their cause and enlist their sympathy," the paper noted, adding that the bishop of Charleston "assured magnates of the Catholic church that its expansion and predominance throughout the hemisphere would be assured by the triumph of the rebels." Therefore, on March 4, a "secret league of the Roman Catholic powers of France, Spain and Austria, under the guidance of the Pope" was set to officially recognize the Confederate States of America.[8]

Southern newspapers carefully tracked these supposed developments.[9] But not all believed the predictions to be true. The *Alexandria Gazette* featured a reprint from the *New York Tribune* claiming Lynch's work had not been as successful as the gossip would imply and that on the contrary, there was no foundation to any of these stories other than "loose rumor." That Lynch had been busy "forming a plot with the Catholic powers, France, Spain, Austria, &c., to recognize the South after the 4th of March next, persuading them that such a recognition would be for the benefit of the Catholic Church, &c., &c." was pure fabrication. There was little more to the affair than "the sanguine hopes of the rebels and their European friends."[10]

Thoughts of European assistance eventually led Poche to reflect on the balance between slavery and independence. He explained that it was clear England and France would never allow a full reconstitution of America. Each did, however, desire two things preeminently: a divided, weaker America and the abolition of slavery. Poche explained that, like Lynch, he was a supporter of slavery as it existed. But if the question was slavery or independence, in a mutually exclusive fashion, the answer was simple. To secure Confederate independence, "I would sacrifice all, save honor"—above all, "separation from the vile Yankees." Poche believed his viewpoint was common. "Their motto [that of the Southern people] is 'Independence at any price even without Slavery' . . . the reconstruction of the Union, never, even with slavery and our previous rights."[11]

It was not long before yet another, and yet again desperate, plea for peace came from a Southern Catholic. Father L. P. O'Connell of Columbia, South Carolina, published an article in the Catholic journal the *Pacificator* advocating for immediate peace.[12] In the style of Pius's joint letter to Archbishops Jean-Marie Odin and John Hughes, O'Connell hoped the spiritual unity of American Catholics would translate into the political realm. This was fanciful, because while O'Connell was right that Catholics were largely of one mind on matters pertaining to their religion, they were at complete odds on the war. Also like Pius, who told Lynch that while he was willing to mediate peace talks the North would never consent, O'Connell worried about the "thousands of bigoted people in both sections of the country who would rather that the war should never cease, than that peace should come through the influence of the Catholic Church."[13]

The *Wilmington (North Carolina) Gazette* promoted O'Connell's views with a February 1865 feature article. O'Connell explained that because the combined Catholic population of the North and South was a hefty "three or four million," it possessed within itself the seeds of change. Should "this grand mass [be] put in motion, its momentum would be irresistible when espousing the great question of peace . . . all good citizens, without distinction, would fall into its ranks, no matter where they lived." O'Connell had no intention to "make the party a Catholic organization"; rather, the goal was to establish "a grand peace society, and invite all to join it. We could easily obtain passports from both Governments, consult together, and decide upon the modus operandi." Should this utopian project take shape, it would undoubtedly be "one of the grandest organizations this world ever saw." O'Connell concluded by explaining, "I do not wish it to be understood that I am a reconstructionist, a Unionist or anything else. I am a peace man, and with God's help and your co-operation, I will accomplish my purpose."[14]

O'Connell's plan, predictably, amounted to nothing. Rumors were proving not just *usually* false but false almost every time. The Confederacy could not help itself, and no one, not from Europe or anyplace else, was coming to help. On April 8, 1865, at Appomattox Court House in Virginia, Grant wrote Lee asking for terms. "I would say that *peace* being my great desire there is but one condition I insist upon," Grant wrote, "namely: that the men and officers surrendered shall be disqualified from taking up arms, against the Government of the United States, until properly exchanged." Lee consented. He surrendered the following day, Palm Sunday. While sporadic fighting would continue through the end of the month, the American Civil War had come to an end.[15]

The war's final major event occurred in the postscript, less than a week after Appomattox. When Lincoln was assassinated on April 14, Good Friday, the mainstream reaction from the Southern clergy, and Southern Catholics, was mostly one of anger about the crime and sympathy for the late president. Dooley, who, like Sheeran, called Lincoln "Abraham the First" and a "monster," wrote of the popular opinion toward the assassination, "There seems to pervade the minds of nearly all a horror for the crime." Archbishop Martin John Spalding spoke for many Southern Catholics when he wrote, "Words fail us for expressing detestation for a deed so atrocious, hither-to unparalleled in our history. Silence is, perhaps, the best and most appropriate expression for a sorrow too great for utterance." Pius IX sent his condolences via Cardinal Giacomo Antonelli, "begging" Rufus King to make known the Vatican's sympathy in Washington.[16]

It was around this time, naturally, that the assorted war narratives of the main characters of this book concluded as well. Sheeran was on a steamboat back to New Orleans on April 29. Poche, who surrendered to the Union on May 5, as news of Appomattox slowly trickled West, was back in New Orleans five days later. Bishop Elder would continue to minister to his Natchez congregation into the 1880s, until he was sent North to Cincinnati, serving as archbishop of that city from 1883 until his death in 1904. Bannon never came back to America, remaining in Ireland until his death in 1913.[17]

Dooley was paroled on February 27. When he heard of Lee's surrender, he wrote that this would surely be "the closing act of our bloody tragedy. Poor Richmond! Poor Lee! Poor Army! Poor Confederacy!" But sometime shortly after that, he assumed a different tone. It seemed as if Dooley had, by war's end, completely exhausted his Confederatization. He had given the fullest possible devotion to the Confederate cause; now, looking back, he wondered if it had been worth it.[18]

> Go to church in the evening and recite the Rosary. Why should I seek any longer to follow the fleeting vanities of the world? Has not everything that I set my heart upon turned out contrary to my desires and expectations? What has my religion always taught me but that worldly desires and pleasures bring with them only bitterness and remorse, and if I had followed the inspirations of my College days and entered the Society of Jesus, would I now be exposed to the misery, wretchedness and homeless wandering from which I now recoil and in vain endeavor to free myself? My anchor had been cast firmly and securely in a port that shall ever be calm and agitated by the outside storms and cares of life. Where I may live in happy seclusion while Republics fall, empires totter to their run and civil wars boil and seethe around my hallowed precincts![19]

Lynch was not able to secure a return to America until the autumn. And for this return, he had Spalding to thank, for Spalding's intervention with Seward secured him a pardon. Since Lynch's diplomatic service had been closely followed, his pardon and return to America made national news, covered in newspapers as far west as Montana, where the *Montana Post* explained to its readership that the bishop of Charleston was famous for his "bitter and most virulent opposition to the government and the Union." Nonetheless, one could understand the US government granting him forgiveness as the "tone of the petition is exceedingly humble and penitent."[20]

Unsurprisingly, Lynch, widely admired if not beloved in South Carolina and across denominational lines, received the warmest welcome at home, from Columbia's *Daily Phoenix* and the *Charleston Daily News*.[21] "There are none among us who are more highly esteemed for every quality that constitute the cultivated gentleman, elegant scholar, and true Christian" than Lynch, the *Daily News* began, before quoting an unnamed New York paper in which a glowing estimation of the bishop had recently appeared. Lynch had been held in high regard by "both Catholics and Protestants, North and South"; this was the prime reason for his speedy pardon. "Although belonging to the South," the article concluded, "his charity towards Union prisoners, black and white, for whom he exhausted his resources, and exposed his health in the hospitals and prisons to succor, have justly acquired for him the gratitude of the North."[22]

Lynch's pardon and celebrated return was not the only postwar Southern Catholic footnote. In Jefferson Davis, who was imprisoned in Fort Monroe, Virginia, while his family was out of America all together and living in Montréal, the connection between Catholicism and the Confederacy is highlighted a final time. The ex-president never did become a Catholic, but he retained a deep fondness for the Church. And so it is unsurprising that the man who enlisted Catholic clergymen as diplomatic envoys and never relinquished his warm boyhood memories of a Catholic education in Tennessee would want the same for his own family. "The family of Jefferson Davis are at the Donegana Hotel in Montréal," the Dallas Herald reported in October 1865. "His oldest daughter is to be placed at school at the Catholic convent in that city."[23]

Southern Catholics had passionately supported a push for independence that, after four years of plentiful bloodshed, had failed. One historian notes that sorrow for the Confederacy's defeat was not restricted to the Southern states. Because even "outside the border states" they had "enthusiastically supported the Confederacy," Catholics now, naturally, shared in its "pain, humiliation, and defeat." The very ardent nature of Catholic Confederatization only served to exacerbate the sense of loss. Perhaps it would be better to focus on other matters following surrender, for this was a painful reflection indeed.[24]

Three issues defined Southern Catholics' immediate postwar goals: maintain growth in rural areas, keep evangelizing Protestants, and baptize former slaves into the faith. Some passionately set to this work. Bishop Verot, author of the 1861 tract defending slavery, became, according to one historian, a "model abolitionist." Like Elder (who would dedicate significant "time, energy and concern" to his postwar African American ministry) and much of the Southern episcopate, Verot was a holder of the spiritual equal, societal inferior paradigm regarding slaves. But now the war was over and the Confederacy had lost, losing the "Old South" apparatus and slavery in kind. Therefore, Verot "set aside his proslavery doctrine . . . devot[ing] himself to the welfare of the freedmen with a zeal that looked like the excitement of a man convinced that the sudden emancipation of four million men was an undiluted blessing."[25]

One of the main issues at the Second Plenary Council in 1866, presided over by Archbishop Spalding, was black evangelization. The proposals could have been drawn directly from Bishop Elder's 1858 letter to the Propaganda Fide, wherein he had stated that because African Americans were "every one of them immortal, made to the image & likeness of God, redeemed by the Precious Blood of the Son of God," Catholics should put the "sickle into the abundant field" of souls.[26] The council bishops, while regretting that emancipation had not come about "more gradually," stated blacks were equivalently redeemed by Christ's salvific Death and Resurrection, hardly the common position across the multi-denominational Southern Christian landscape. They further recommended that black and white children be housed at orphanages together and attend schools together and that an office be created, a "special prefecture apostolic," that would assist bishops in finding missionaries for black communities. In the end, black evangelization would be left up to individual bishops' discretion.[27]

Four years later, at the First Vatican Council, famous for defining the doctrine of (ex cathedra) papal infallibility, Southern bishops were among the most warmly disposed toward questions concerning Protestants, owing, perhaps, to their many integrated years in the South and a Confederatized wartime experience that had made them see Protestant Christians more as beloved, separated brethren—and friends, too—than schismatic heretics. Protestants would only "listen to the truth if it were proposed to them in a kindly and sympathetic fashion," Bishop Elder noted, not when pronouncements were designed to "injure their sensibilities."[28]

Southern Catholics remained integrated members of their communities long after the war. Lynch, as mentioned, would spend the rest of his life, right up to his death in 1882, working to help Charlestonians rebuild from the devastating December 1861 fire. Elder remained bishop of Natchez for a decade and a half after the war, quitting the South only because of his promotion to the Archdiocese of Cincinnati in 1880 (becoming archbishop there three years later). When a yellow fever epidemic swept across New Orleans in 1867, Sheeran was in the midst of the suffering, helping, just as he had been among wounded soldiers during the war, proving the veracity of his 1864 claim that he "belonged to the South." Catholic sisters were on the front lines of the yellow fever epidemics that claimed more than five thousand lives in the Mississippi River Valley in the 1870s.[29]

Catholics in the South surely faced some discrimination in the postwar era, from the Ku Klux Klan in particular and perhaps most famously—but this was during the 1920s, when memories of Catholic Confederatization had worn thin for many. American anti-Catholicism was often a Northern phenomenon. It was a Northerner, conqueror of the South Ulysses S. Grant, who as president in 1875 denounced public funding for "sectarian" and "superstitious" private schools, a not too subtle attack against Catholic education. Conspicuous Northern anti-Catholicism led the bishops at the 1884 Third Plenary Council to all but demand Catholic parents send children to parochial schools. This Catholic-Protestant pedagogical animus was often found in Northern cities. The rabidly anti-Catholic American Protective Agency, founded in 1887, was established in the North, in Clinton, Iowa. The organization would grow strong across the Midwest, but due to the impression that it was a "Republican tool," it made "little headway in the South," with Southerners being "generally apathetic towards anti-Catholicism."[30]

In many ways, Catholicism continued to be present, even grow, in the postwar South, the devastating effects of four years of war notwithstanding. By 1870 there were 551 Catholic churches across the former Confederacy, 130 more than there had been a decade prior. Of all the Catholic churches in America, 60 percent were located in Kentucky, Maryland, and Louisiana. In 1870s Arkansas, a Benedictine abbey and Benedictine order of sisters was established, and Catholic growth was especially noticeable in the Louisville environs, where by the early 1890s more than one hundred thousand Catholics belonged to eighty-seven parishes, the city being added to the ranks of the long-standing major urban centers of Southern Catholicism in Baltimore, New Orleans, and Charleston. By the turn of the century, there were twenty Southern dioceses, four more than in 1870, with the number of priests serving these dioceses increasing from 730 to more than 1,500.[31]

Examples of postwar growth should not be misinterpreted. Confederatization provides a window into how integrated, and active, Southern Catholics were in the Confederacy. But the South did not become a "Catholic region" after the war, the many conversions won by sister-nurses notwithstanding. Catholics might have been more at home in the South, but they still remained far more numerous in the North. To understand Catholics in the South, one should place emphasis on *more at home,* on understanding how a long-standing antebellum acceptance in Southern society became more pronounced during the Civil War when Catholics found themselves deeply involved in an independence movement that returned their devotion in full.

Catholic Confederates has tried to understand this phenomenon. What has made this endeavor all the more exciting is that the testing ground was a time of war, when identities, allegiances, and the whole of life is brought into sharper focus, with clearer lines being drawn and more at stake. What can be stated with certainty is that between 1861 and 1865, Southern Catholics were deeply involved, integrated, and appreciated members of their society. Bishops quickly progressed from watchful reticence during the Secession crisis to outright endorsement of the Confederate cause once the first shots of the war were fired. Catholic soldiers and chaplains volunteered to fight for and serve the Confederacy on the battlefields, marching alongside and suffering with non-Catholic Confederates from start to finish; for some, "start to finish" meant going abroad in service of their new nation. And the sister-nurses, by way of their participation without politicization, demonstrated just how thorough the Catholic involvement in the Confederacy was.

This point precisely—how thorough Catholic involvement in the Confederacy was—is this book's most important point. The Confederatization thesis adds to the full meaning of Americanization, showing that more than one hundred years before Vatican II and JFK, Catholics in the South were fully integrated members of society who, save for their religion, believed the same things as and acted in similar fashion to their well-known Protestant neighbors. These Confederatized Catholics found themselves incorporated into the Southern societal body and called upon to contribute to that society's ultimate goal: the creation and sustenance of a new nation.

If a scholar of the Civil War South has learned something new about Civil War Southerners, a religious historian has learned something new about Confederate religiosity, a Catholic scholar can consider the importance of the South to the larger picture of American Catholicism with a fresh perspective, and if scholars of international relations can gain a new appreciation for the role of religion in Confederate, and Civil War diplomacy, then this book has been successful, especially in bringing to light previously overlooked material and starting long-overdue conversations.

APPENDIX

Brief Biographical Sketches

Father John Bannon (1829–1913)

John Bannon was born in Ireland in 1829. He was ordained a priest in 1853 and soon after moved to America. He settled in St. Louis, where he became pastor of the Church of the Immaculate Conception. In 1858 he was assigned to St. John's Parish. Bannon volunteered to join the Confederate cause early in the War and was assigned a chaplaincy with the First Missouri. He gained fame for his bravery on the battlefield and his tireless devotion to his men's souls. Most notably, Bannon served as a Confederate diplomatic agent to Europe and is credited with stemming some Irish immigration into the Union ranks. He was a virulent Southern nationalist. Via his diplomatic service, he showed that Catholic-Confederate commitment extended beyond the American continent. Having returned to Ireland on his diplomatic mission, Bannon stayed there for good following the war and became a Jesuit. He developed a reputation as one of the country's greatest preachers. He died in 1913.[1]

John Dooley (1842–1873)

John Dooley was born in Virginia, the son of Irish immigrants, in 1842. His family was wealthy and popular in a Richmond that was, he wrote, "a gracious and friendly place" to live in the 1840s and '50s. Dooley was enrolled at Georgetown University in 1861, but, like many fellow Southerners, he withdrew upon the commencement of hostilities. He enlisted in the Confederate army, joining the Old First Virginia Infantry Regiment, "the most famous regiment in the

history of the US Army" according to Lee biographer Douglas Southall Freeman. Dooley was wounded at Gettysburg, captured, and spent the remaining
war years as a prisoner. After the war, disillusioned with the world's vanities, he
entered the Novitiate of the Jesuit Order in 1865. Stricken with a lung condition
in 1868, he spent the rest of his life in and out of the infirmary. He died in 1873,
at the age of thirty, just nine months before the date of his priestly ordination.[2]

Bishop and Archbishop William Henry Elder (1819–1904)

Born in Baltimore in 1819 and ordained in Rome in the 1840s, Elder served
as a seminary professor in Emmitsburg, Maryland, before becoming bishop
of Natchez in 1857. He was a pastoral bishop with a deep commitment to his
congregation. Elder, as historian Charles Nolan notes, was continuously on
the road, ministering to his congregants via "long lonely trips by steamboat,
horse and/or carriage, or railroad; brief stays in communities or with individual families to administer the sacraments, offer religious instruction, con-
sole the bereaved, or simply visit isolated Catholic families; parish missions in
remote areas where the pastor could not afford to pay a visiting missionary.
His supportive visits were often the only clerical companionship a lonely missionary experienced for months." Elder's wartime ministry to Protestants and
African Americans was extensive. His refusal of the Union prayer demand,
discussed at length in chapter 3, remains the most remembered act of his life.
He remained bishop of Natchez until 1880, whereupon he was transferred to
Cincinnati. Elder became archbishop of Cincinnati three years later, and he
held this post until his death in 1904.[3]

Father Louis-Hippolyte Gache (1817–1907)

Louis-Hippolyte Gache was born in France in 1817. He became a chaplain in
the Tenth Louisiana Volunteer Regiment. He addressed much of his wartime
correspondence to his brother priests at Spring Hill College in Mobile, Alabama. His devotion to the Daughters of Charity, an order that contributed
significantly to Civil War sister-nurses, can be attributed to his love for his own
sister, Marie Therese, a Carmelite nun in France. The Jesuit Gache believed,
with his order, that the war, no matter how devastating, might improve the

position of Catholics in the South. He thought it would afford Catholics the opportunity to demonstrate their societal integration by way of the battlefield. Gache survived the war and the century, dying in 1907.[4]

Henri Garidel (1815–1878)

Henri Garidel was born in New Orleans in 1815. Descended from an old bourgeois French family on his mother's side, Garidel considered himself more French than American, and perhaps Catholic before all else. Before the war, he worked as an officer and bookkeeper for the State Bank of Louisiana. Garidel was a devout Catholic and a devoted Confederate, both of which are made patently clear in his diary, written between May 1863 and June 1865, while he was in self-imposed exile in Richmond, stemming from his refusal to take an oath of allegiance to the Union occupier. In Richmond, dogged by a "sense of alienation," he resided as "a devout Catholic in a largely evangelical Protestant city." Like Poche, Garidel was a family man, and his diary is filled with constant reverences to and prayers for his wife and children. Unlike Poche, Garidel never directly served in the Confederate forces. His services, which he volunteered, were judged not to be needed. Nonetheless, his lack of military involvement did nothing to hamper his rabid Confederatization. His diary is filled with equal parts Confederate cheerleading and anti-Yankee vitriol; there is also humor aplenty, as when he quipped that a Creole friend in Richmond was "a little too French for me." Garidel survived the war, exile, and a brief sojourn in New York City in the early 1870s and was eventually reunited with his family, dying, back home in New Orleans, at the age of sixty-three in 1878.[5]

Bishop Patrick Lynch (1817–1882)

Patrick Lynch was born in Ireland in 1817 and immigrated, with his family, to the United States shortly thereafter. At the age of seventeen, he was sent to Rome to study at the Urban College. By the time he had earned his doctorate in 1840, he had extensively studied theology, philosophy, physics, ethics, scripture, archaeology, liturgy, and canon law. Polyglot Lynch became fluent in Italian, could speak French and German, was skilled in Latin and Greek, and possessed some proficiency in ancient Syriac, Sanskrit, and Arabic. He won prizes for his achievements in theology, Church history, sacred scripture, and canon law. When Pope Gregory XVI visited from Rome, he was selected to give a lecture in Hebrew. Back in Charleston, he earned a national reputation for his work on drilling and maintaining artesian wells and was active in numerous scientific and philosophical societies throughout the city. Lynch, installed as bishop of Charleston in 1857, was the most politicized Southern bishop, a leading and outspoken voice supporting the Confederacy. Jefferson Davis appointed him a plenipotentiary to Europe and the Vatican late in the war. His diverse talents and erudition notwithstanding, his involvement in Confederate politics prevented him from advancing within the Church's hierarchy. Twice he was nominated for prestigious posts: archbishop of Baltimore in 1872 and coadjutor of New York in 1880. Both times he was passed over. Lynch died, bishop of Charleston, in 1882.[6]

Felix Pierre Poche (1836–1895)

Felix Pierre Poche was born in Convent, Louisiana, in 1836. He was working as lawyer when his state withdrew from the Union. Without rank, he joined a Confederate brigade commissary in 1863 and spent the next three years on scouting missions in western Louisiana, along the Arkansas border and into eastern Mississippi. Poche was a devout Catholic deeply loyal to his wife, Selima, with whom he had nine children. His Civil War journal is dominated by references to his faith and his family, often both together. Poche assumed leadership of a squad of scouts in 1864 and continued to lead one until May of 1865, when he surrendered to Union forces. He was home five days later. Poche died in New Orleans in 1895.[7]

Father James Sheeran (1819–1881)

James Sheeran was born in Ireland in 1819 and immigrated to Canada at the age of twelve, moving shortly thereafter to McConnellsville, Pennsylvania, by way of New York City. He moved once more, this time to Monroe, Michigan, where, now married and father to a son and a daughter, he operated a successful tailoring business. Sheeran became a widower in 1849. Six years later, he joined the Redemptorists, was ordained a priest in 1858, after which he was assigned to New Orleans. Although Sheeran had been in the South but three short years, he was, according to one author, "an ardent Southerner in his thoughts and affections." Sheeran became a chaplain in the Army of Northern Virginia in September 1861 and served throughout the war. Afterward, he aided many New Orleans citizens suffering from the 1867 yellow fever epidemic. He was transferred north to a parish in New Jersey later on and died there, at the age of sixty-two, in 1881.[8]

Bishop Augustin Verot (1804–1876)

Augustin Verot, born in France in 1804, was ordained to the priesthood in 1828. He served as a science professor in American seminaries of his order, the Society of Saint Sulpice, for the next three decades. In 1858, he was installed as the first vicar apostolic of Florida. Three years later, he was appointed bishop of Savannah, a post he held in conjunction with his Florida assignment. An added dimension to Verot's legacy is his 1861 tract on slavery. It was a seminal moment for American Catholics when a clergyman, uncharacteristically, provided widespread public commentary on an issue outside of the Church's direct scope (that is, something strictly theological). Verot, most remembered for his tract, was, like Elder, a man deeply committed to his congregation. A Protestant remembered him as a "saintly" man and, although a "thorough Catholic," someone of "too noble a heart to refuse love to those who differ from him in the matter of religion." Verot traveled constantly, seeking financial aid for his congregation as well as for nuns and impoverished brother bishops. He died in 1876.[9]

Notes

Introduction

1. A. Dudley Mann to Hon. J. P. Benjamin, Nov. 14, 1863, in James D. Richardson, *A Compilation of the Messages and Papers of the Confederacy*, 2 vols. (Nashville: US Publishing Co., 1905), 2:591–95.

2. *Memphis Daily Appeal*, Feb. 2, 1864.

3. Leo Francis Stock, "Catholic Participation in the Diplomacy of the Southern Confederacy," *Catholic Historical Review* 16 (Apr. 1930): 9–10. Numerous scholars have written about the prejudices Roman Catholics faced in the nineteenth-century Northern United States. See John Higham, *Strangers in the Land: Patterns of American Nativism* (New Brunswick, NJ: Rutgers Univ. Press, 1955); Jay P. Dolan, *In Search of American Catholicism: A History of Religion and Culture in Tension* (Oxford: Oxford Univ. Press, 2002); John T. McGreevy, *Catholicism and American Freedom: A History* (New York: Norton, 2003); and Jon Gjerde, *Catholicism and the Shaping of Nineteenth-Century America* (Cambridge: Cambridge Univ. Press, 2012).

4. The Irish were the South's largest ethnic group, with Louisiana, Tennessee, Virginia, Maryland, and Kentucky each having Irish populations exceeding ten thousand people. Maryland and Kentucky each had an Irish population of more than twenty thousand; in each state, nearly a third of all foreign-born immigrants were Irish. In Louisiana, approximately 35 percent of the eighty thousand–plus foreign-born population was Irish. The next three largest ethnic identities were German—a sprawling conglomerate listed on the 1860 Census as "Total Germany," which comprised Austria, Bavaria, Baden, Hesse, Nassau, Prussia, and Wurttemberg, along with "Germany non-specified"; the largest concentration of Germans could be found in Louisiana (only four thousand fewer than the Irish), Kentucky, and Maryland, the latter of which wherein more than half of the foreign-born population identified as German English (the largest concentration of Englishmen found in Virginia, Maryland, and Kentucky) and French. The highest concentrations of Frenchmen were found in Louisiana, Kentucky, Texas, and, possibly

surprisingly, Alabama, thanks in part to Mobile and the Gulf Coast. In perhaps the most Catholic of all Southern states, Louisiana, more than half of the foreign-born population—and 11 percent of the total state population—was of either French or Irish origin (US Department of the Interior, *Eighth Census* [1860], available online at https://www .census.gov/library/publications/1864/dec/1860a.html).

5. Booth's sister, Asia Booth Clarke, "a devout Roman Catholic, and very attentive to the duties of her church," claimed, in the wake of Lincoln's assassination, "John Wilkes was of that faith [Roman Catholicism]—preferably—and I was glad that he had fixed his faith on one religion for he was always of a pious mind." Asia Booth Clarke, *John Wilkes Booth: A Sister's Memoir*, ed. Terry Alford (Jackson: Univ. of Mississippi Press, 1996), 17; see also Asia B. Clarke to Jean Anderson, May 22, 1865, in the same volume, 127–28.

6. Robert McElroy, *Jefferson Davis: The Unreal and the Real* (New York: Smithmark, 1937), 7, 681. Confederate chaplain Louis-Hippolyte Gache once wrote to a fellow priest, "I know you are aware of the sentiments of our worthy president, but perhaps you didn't know about those of Mrs. Jefferson Davis." According to Gache, she only wanted "a practicing Catholic" babysitter for her children and at another time she said, "It's strange, but each time I go into a Catholic church or chapel, I seem to hear a voice deep down within me saying, 'this is where you ought to be.'" Gache to Rev. Father Phillip de Carriere, May 19, 1863, in *A Frenchman, a Chaplain, a Rebel: The War Letters of Pere Louis-Hippolyte Gache, S.J.*, trans. Cornelius M. Buckley (Chicago: Loyola Univ. Press, 1981), 169–87.

7. Michael Bedout Chesson and Leslie Jean Roberts, introduction to *Exile in Richmond: The Confederate Journal of Henri Garidel*, ed. Michael Bedout Chesson and Leslie Jean Roberts (Charlottesville: Univ. of Virginia Press, 2001), 6.

8. That same year, Steven E. Woodworth justified excluding Catholics from his book *While God Is Marching On: The Religious World of Civil War Soldiers* (Lawrence: Univ. Press of Kansas, 2001): "There were, of course, a fair number of Catholics [in the ranks] . . . but their numbers together constituted a small minority of the soldiers, and their beliefs and practices play little role in these pages" (ix).

9. Mark Noll, *The Civil War as a Theological Crisis* (Chapel Hill: Univ. of North Carolina Press, 2006); Michael Pasquier, *Fathers on the Frontier: French Missionaries and the Roman Catholic Priesthood in the United States, 1789–1870* (New York: Oxford Univ. Press, 2010); Andrew H. M. Stern, *Southern Crucifix, Southern Cross: Catholic-Protestant Relations in the Old* South (Tuscaloosa: Univ. of Alabama Press, 2012); David T. Gleeson, *The Green and the Gray: The Irish in the Confederate States of America* (Chapel Hill: Univ. of North Carolina Press, 2013); David C. R. Heisser and Stephen J. White Sr., *Patrick N. Lynch, 1817–1882: Third Catholic Bishop of Charleston* (Columbia: Univ. of South Carolina Press, 2014); William Kurtz, *Excommunicated from the Union: How the Civil War Created a Separate Catholic America* (New York: Fordham Univ. Press, 2015). Max Longley's *For the Union and the Catholic Church* (Jefferson, NC: McFarland, 2015) is a recent book as well. To date, no work has rendered so complete a treatment of Civil War religion as George Rable's *God's Almost Chosen Peoples: A Religious History of the American Civil War* (Chapel Hill: Univ. of North Carolina Press, 2010).

10. Noll dedicates one chapter to Catholics. Pasquier briefly discusses Confederate Catholics, but French missionaries are the prime focus of his book. Stern's work is set in the antebellum period. Kurtz's is about the North. Thanks to these scholars, a more nuanced picture of Civil War religion has been and is being constructed; but as relates to Southern Catholics specifically, more work remains.

11. Randall M. Miller and Jon L. Wakelyn, introduction to *Catholics in the Old South: Essays on Church and Culture,* ed. Randall M. Miller and Jon L. Wakelyn, 2nd ed. (Macon, GA: Mercer Univ. Press, 1999), xiv.

12. See Pope Leo XIII's 1899 encyclical *Testum Benevolentia Nostrae* and Pope Pius X's 1907 encyclical *Pascendi Dominici Gregis.*

13. In their introduction to *Catholics in the Old South,* Randall Miller and Jon Wakelyn write, "Southern Catholics wrestled with the sometimes conflicting demands of their religious culture and their regional one. This tension underscored Catholic life in the Old South, and indeed in all the New Souths that followed. Southern Catholics never resolved the dilemma of their double identity" (x). Other scholars agree, citing the nineteenth-century Catholic experience as one of tension and outsider status. R. Laurence Moore concludes that modern American religious toleration and pluralism is the product of conflict, not consensus, outsiders fighting for a place at the table of the mainstream Protestant American culture (*Religious Outsiders and the Making of Americans* [Oxford: Oxford Univ. Press, 1989], 205–10, 49, 57, 128). Jon Gjerde builds on Moore's work by arguing that the nineteenth century was a "contested space" between Protestants and Catholics (*Catholicism and the Shaping of Nineteenth-Century America,* viii, xv). When historian Phillip Gleason called Americanization the great theme of US Catholic history, he was arguing within the traditional Americanization paradigm, that Catholics only fully integrated into American society in the twentieth century (*Catholicism in America* [New York: Harper & Row, 1970], 10). This assimilation drew inspiration from, among others, the work of Father Isaac Hecker (1819–1888), founder of the Paulist Fathers, and *Nouvelle Theologie* thought (McGreevy, *Catholicism and American Freedom,* 1–12, 91, 196; Dolan, *In Search of American Catholicism,* 69). Jesuit priest John Courtney Murray (and, above all, the changes implemented by the Second Vatican Council, 1962–65) put the finishing touches on an Americanization project that had aimed to reconcile Catholicism with American society, arguing for a C. S. Lewis "Mere Christianity" approach to politics, coalitions built on Christian fundamentals held across denominational lines (*We Hold These Truths: Catholic Reflections on the American Proposition* [Lanham, MD: Sheed & Ward, 1960], 23, 29, 335, 36). Murray classified the United States as inherently pluralistic. Therefore, adherence to the natural law and a Christian understanding of freedom became the method for harmonizing the faith with American democracy. Within this Americanization model, US Catholics—having squared their religion with their democratic values—would no longer be outsiders nor find it necessary to take shelter in their own institutions. John F. Kennedy's election to the presidency was indisputable proof that Catholicism had Americanized.

Jay P. Dolan argues one must understand the reality of Catholic revivalism—fiery preaching, mass revivals, and devotions, such as to the Sacred Heart of Jesus—to grasp the full narrative of American Catholicism (*Catholic Revivalism: The American Experience 1830–1900* [Notre Dame, IN: Univ. of Notre Dame Press, 1978], 203). Because nineteenth-century America was a frontier "mission country," itinerant preaching and revival gatherings were a necessary component of growing the faith. Dolan traces the growth of Catholic revivalism from St. Alphonsus Liguori's founding of the Redemptorist Order in Italy in 1732 through the emergence of the parish mission at the turn of the century (3, 17, 53). "People had to be converted to religion before they could practice it," Dolan writes. "The key to the renewal of Catholic piety was the revival" (64, 186–87). Dolan's 1992 *The American Catholic Experience* raises interesting points about the growth of Catholic devotionalism (212–13, 220). His 2002 *In Search of an American Catholicism* reaffirms the growth of midcentury devotionalism and revivalism as crucially important (53). McGreevy's 2003 *Catholicism and American Freedom* argues that slavery was maintained in the South, and supported by Catholics, because societal order was held at a premium (51). And Gjerde's 2012 book, *Catholicism and the Shaping of Nineteenth-Century America*, places Catholic allegiance questions in similar terms to Moore's *Religious Outsiders* (x).

14. Catholics had to constantly balance devotion to the Church with the obligations of American citizenship. It did not help them that nineteenth-century America was saturated with an antiauthoritarian tenor, especially toward Europe and the Church. Michael Pasquier, in his 2010 *Fathers on the Frontier*, provides excellent commentary on Southern Catholic views on slavery, society, and wartime allegiance (133–66). Of additional interest are two recent works by Andrew Stern (2012) and William Kurtz (2015)—*Southern Crucifix, Southern Cross* and *Excommunicated from the Union*, respectively—to which *Catholic Confederates* directly responds, carrying the work Stern has done on antebellum Catholics into the Civil War and doing for Southern Catholics during the war what Kurtz has accomplished for Northern Catholics.

15. Examples of books within this purview that have received significant acclaim include John T. McGreevy, *Parish Boundaries: The Catholic Encounter with Race in the Twentieth-Century Urban North* (Chicago: Univ. of Chicago Press, 1998); Mark S. Massa, *The American Catholic Revolution: How the Sixties Changed the Church Forever* (Oxford: Oxford Univ. Press, 2010); Leslie Woodcock Tentler, *Catholics and Contraception: An American History* (Ithaca, NY: Cornell Univ. Press, 2009); Gerald E. Poyo, *Cuban Catholics in the United States, 1960–1980: Exile and Integration* (Notre Dame, IN: Univ. of Notre Dame Press, 2006); James P. McCartin, *Prayers of the Faithful: The Shifting Spiritual Life of American Catholics* (Boston: Harvard Univ. Press, 2010); Robert A. Orsi's field standards *Thank You, St. Jude: Women's Devotion to the Patron Saint of Hopeless Causes* (New Haven: Yale Univ. Press, 1996); and *The Madonna of 115 St.: Faith and Community in Italian Harlem, 1880–1950*, 3rd ed. (New Haven: Yale Univ. Press, 2010).

16. A brief primer begins with Emory Thomas's 1979 work *The Confederate Nation: 1861–1865* (New York: Harper & Row), in which he argued that the South and the Confederacy envisioned themselves as the best hope for Western Civilization, the true heirs to antiquity and the "European tradition" (9, 66). The South's Confederate revolution was therefore a reaction, a hoped return to a more glorious past. Thomas first explored these ideas in an earlier work, *The Confederacy as a Revolutionary Experience* (Engle-

wood Cliffs, NJ: Prentice Hall, 1971), arguing Confederates created the second of America's two revolutionary heritages (x, 1–2). Drew Gilpin Faust seconds this in *The Creation of Confederate Nationalism* (Baton Rouge: Louisiana State Univ. Press, 1988), citing the American Revolution as the prime influence for Confederates fighting to restore America's lost "true ideals" (14, 22). More recently, Anne Sarah Rubin (*A Shattered Nation: The Rise and Fall of the Confederacy, 1861–1868* [Chapel Hill: Univ. of North Carolina Press, 2005], 15, 7) has joined this conversation, along with Aaron Sheehan-Dean (*Why Confederates Fought: Family and Nation in Civil War Virginia* [Chapel Hill: Univ. of North Carolina Press, 2007], 187) and Jason Phillips (*Diehard Rebels: The Confederate Culture of Invincibility* [Athens: Univ. of Georgia Press, 2007], 2, 187–89). Gary Gallagher's most recent book, *Becoming Confederates: Paths to a New National Loyalty* (Athens: Univ. of Georgia Press, 2013), has added much as well. These scholars echo the foundational Confederate nationalism work of Thomas, Faust, and David Potter (especially his *The Impending Crisis, 1848–1861* [New York: Harper & Row, 1977]).

17. Thomas, *Confederate Nation*, 66.

18. Faust, *Creation of Confederate Nationalism*, 11–13, 22; Potter, *Impending Crisis*, 6, 13–17.

19. Thomas, *Confederate Nation*, 66; Faust, *Creation of Confederate Nationalism*, 31, 42. For more information on these themes, see Michael Burleigh, *Earthly Powers: The Clash of Religion and Politics in Europe, from the French Revolution to the Great War* (New York: Harper Perennial, 2007).

20. In *Fears and Fascinations: Representing Catholicism in the American South* (New York: Fordham Univ. Press, 2005), Thomas Haddox challenges the idea that Catholicism did not fit within Southern culture (3, 58, 81, 58, 126). He even goes beyond this, demonstrating that some believed it was the ideal Southern religion (3, 10). Haddox claims the faith was attractive to many in the South because of its immutable dogma, use of symbol and ritual, and otherworldly feel (58, 81). Southerners, to borrow Benedict Anderson's phrase coined in *Imagined Communities: Reflections on the Origin and Spread of Nationalism* (London: Verso, 1983), were or wanted to be citizens of an imagined community where agrarian values, the family, religion, and honor were given preeminent status, especially in contrast to what they believed to be a materialistic and secular North. Perhaps Catholicism, a faith "congenial to Southern conservatism," could provide the spiritual outlines of a feudal society some in the South wished to return to (58, 126).

21. James Woods, *A History of the Catholic Church in the American South, 1513–1900* (Gainesville: Univ. Press of Florida, 2011), 378.

1. The Bishops Respond to Secession and the First Year of the War, 1860–1861

A slightly different version of this chapter is currently forthcoming in the *Catholic Historical Review* under the title "Devout Catholics, Devoted Confederates: The Evolution of Southern Catholic Bishops from Reluctant Secessionists to Ardent Confederates."

1. "South Carolina," *United States Catholic Miscellany* (Charleston, SC), Dec. 22, 1860, Sisters of Charity of Nazareth, Kentucky (hereafter cited as MNAZ), University of

Notre Dame Archives (hereafter cited as UNDA); U.S. Catholic Miscellany collection, microfilm; Francis Patrick Kenrick, archbishop of Baltimore, to John McGill, bishop of Richmond, Dec. 1, 1860, 2, Diocese of Richmond records (hereafter cited as MDRI), microfilm UNDA; Martin John Spalding, Apr. 26, 1861, Civil War Journal, as bishop of Louisville, Apr. 5, 1860–Mar. 27, 1864, MNAZ, 3/12.

2. Woods, *History of the Catholic Church in the American South*, 278; US Department of the Interior, "Statistics of the United States (Including Morality, Property &c.,) in 1860," Eighth Census, 1860 (Washington, DC: GPO, 1866), 500.

3. Because of the considerable pro-Southern sentiment in and general Southern character of Kentucky and Maryland, these states—while never a part of the eleven-state Confederacy—are within this book often grouped in a "larger South," with the obvious qualification that they remained loyal to the Union. The Catholic Church in America viewed the situation similarly, as the Archdiocese of Baltimore's ecclesiastical oversight was directed southward, with jurisdiction over its five suffrage sees of Richmond, Charleston, Savannah, Wheeling, and the Vicariate Apostolic of Florida, which included the whole state of Georgia. At the start of the war, because there was no West Virginia yet, Wheeling was technically in the South too (Michael V. Gannon, *Rebel Bishop: Augustin Verot, Florida's Civil War Prelate* [Gainesville: Univ. Press of Florida, 1997], 60).

4. Woods, *History of the Catholic Church in the American South*, 285; US Department of the Interior, *Eighth Census*, 500, 403.

5. Baltimore, the prime US see, nicknamed "America's Rome," had direct jurisdiction over numerous Southern dioceses and itself claimed twenty-two Catholic churches, four better than New Orleans, valued at $1.1 million and with the ability to seat 22,300. US Department of the Interior, *Eighth Census*, 500.

6. Woods, *History of the Catholic Church in the American South*, 142; Dolan, *Catholic Revivalism*, 8.

7. Raymond H. Schmandt, "Overview of Institutional Establishments in the Antebellum Southern Church," and Randall Miller, "A Church in Cultural Captivity: Some Speculations on Catholic Identity in the Old South," both in Miller and Wakelyn, *Catholics in the Old South*, 53–76, 11–52; Stern, *Southern Crucifix, Southern Cross*, 4–5.

8. Stern, *Southern Crucifix, Southern Cross*, 57–66, 91, 101–2, 29, 128; Woods, *History of the Catholic Church in the American South*, 224.

9. Stern, *Southern Crucifix, Southern Cross*, 134–38, 178; *Dollar Weekly Bulletin* (Maysville, KY), Nov. 5, 1863.

10. Stern, *Southern Crucifix, Southern Cross*, 178.

11. Francis Patrick Kenrick was installed as archbishop of Baltimore in 1851, a year after John McGill became bishop of Richmond. In 1857, William Henry Elder and Patrick Neeson Lynch became the bishops of Natchez and Charleston. That same year, Augustin Verot was consecrated bishop of the Florida Vicariate Apostolic in Saint Augustine. John Quinlan was installed as bishop of Mobile in 1859. In 1861, Verot became the bishop of Savannah while maintaining his Florida episcopacy. Also in 1861, Jean Marie-Odin, formerly of Galveston, assumed the South's second most important see when he became archbishop of New Orleans. The primary see became vacant shortly thereafter, when

Archbishop Kenrick died unexpectedly in the summer of 1863. Martin John Spalding, the bishop of Louisville since 1850, became the archbishop of Baltimore in 1864.

12. The one exception is James Whelan (OP, 1823–78), bishop of Nashville from February 1860 until February 1864. Whelan is the only member of the Southern episcopate who did not fully support the Confederacy. He was accused of Northern sympathies, even of perhaps passing along important information to the Union army. This, presumably, was the reason he was removed from his Nashville post. He died in Ohio. Historical opinion on Whelan is hazy. In his recent book *A History of the Catholic Church in the South,* James Woods labels Whelan a "Unionist," adding that his relationship with Union general William Rosecrans "damaged his relationship with Tennessee's Catholics" (291). It is not made clear whether Whelan's friendship with Rosecrans was primarily because of the former's supposed "pro-Union views" or because the general was a devout Catholic. Earlier works are more reserved. In their edited volume *Catholics in the Old South,* Schmandt states only that Whelan was "at odds with his flock," in "Overview of Institutional Establishments," 65. At the same time, James Pillar, *The History of the Catholic Church in Mississippi, 1837–65* (New Orleans: Hauser, 1964), and Gannon, *Rebel Bishop,* all but exonerate him. Pillar claims Whelan did not support the Confederacy as "wholeheartedly" as did the other Southern bishops (166), and Gannon states that he was simply "reluctant" to support the South (62). Contemporary Southern newspapers writing about Whelan nearly fully exonerate him. In its March 4, 1863, edition, the *Yorkville (SC) Enquirer* called Whelan simply "the distinguished Catholic prelate of the Nashville disease." In a January 24, 1862, article, titled "The Catholic Bishop of Nashville," the *Memphis Daily Appeal* stated that reports labeling Whelan a unionist were false, that "upon inquiry, we are satisfied that the telegrapher from Louisville did him the greatest injustice—attributing to him statements which he never made." Furthermore, "the bishop was an early friend of the cause of southern independence and has constantly and consistently supported it."

13. Faust, *Creation of Confederate Nationalism,* 22.

14. Bishop William Henry Elder to Archbishop Francis Patrick Kenrick, undated letter, quoted in Willard E. Wright, ed., "Bishop Elder and the Civil War," *Catholic Historical Review* 44 (1958–59): 293.

15. Martin John Spalding, bishop of Louisville, to John Baptist Purcell, archbishop of Cincinnati, Nov. 12, 1860, quoted in Thomas W. Spalding, *Martin John Spalding: American Churchman* (Washington, DC: Catholic Univ. of America Press, in association with Consortium Press, 1973), 131; Kenrick to McGill, Dec. 1, 1860.

16. William Henry Elder, bishop of Natchez, circular letter to parish priests, given in Bay St. Louis, MS, Nov. 25, 1860, in Pillar, *History of the Catholic Church in Mississippi, 1837–65,* 158–59.

17. Elder, circular letter.

18. Elder, circular letter.

19. "A Declaration of the Immediate Causes Which Induce and Justify the Secession of South Carolina from the Federal Union," adopted Dec. 24, 1860, *The Avalon Project: Documents in Law, History and Diplomacy,* Yale Law School, Lillian Goldman Law Library, http://avalon.law.yale.edu/19th_century/csa_scarsec.asp.

20. Ralph Selph Henry, *The Story of the Confederacy* (Old Saybrook, CT: Konecky & Konecky, 1931), 22–23.

21. "South Carolina," *United States Catholic Miscellany* (Charleston, SC), Dec. 22, 1860.

22. "South Carolina."

23. Augustin Verot, *A Tract for the Times, Slavery and Abolitionism, Being the Substance of a Sermon, St Augustine, Florida, Jan. 4, 1861, day of public humiliation, fasting, and prayer,* new ed. (New Orleans: Printed at the "Catholic Propagator" Office, 1861).

24. Pope Gregory XVI, *In Supremo Apostolatus,* Rome, Dec. 3, 1839, in *American Catholics and Slavery, 1789–1866: An Anthology of Primary Documents,* ed. Kenneth J. Zanca (Lanham, MD: Univ. Press of America, 1994), 27–29. The pope "vehemently admonish[ed] and adjure[d] in the Lord all believers in Christ, of whatsoever condition, that no one hereafter may dare unjustly to molest Indians, Negroes, or other men of this sort; or to spoil them of their goods; or to reduce them to slavery . . . all the aforesaid actions as utterly unworthy of the Christian name . . . [and] by the same apostolic authority, do strictly prohibit and interdict that any ecclesiastic or lay person shall presume to defend that very trade in Negroes as lawful under any pretext or studied excuse."

25. Verot, "Tract for the Times."

26. Verot, "Tract for the Times."

27. Patrick Neeson Lynch, bishop of Charleston, to John Hughes, archbishop of New York, Jan. 6, 1861, item 25Y2, Lynch Administration Papers, 1858–66, Charleston Diocesan Archives (hereafter CDA).

28. Lynch to Hughes, Jan. 6, 1861.

29. Unlike South Carolina, which based its secessionist rationale on ideological defenses of 1776, Mississippi's delegates left no doubt as to their prime motives for secession. "Our position is thoroughly identified with the institution of slavery—the greatest material interest of the world," the declaration began. "Its labor supplies the product which constitutes by far the largest and most important portions of commerce of the earth. These products are peculiar to the climate verging on the tropical regions, and by an imperious law of nature, none but the black race can bear exposure to the tropical sun," the text continued. "A blow at slavery is a blow at commerce and civilization. That blow has been long aimed at the institution, and was at the point of reaching its consummation. There was no choice left us but submission to the mandates of abolition, or a dissolution of the Union, whose principles had been subverted to work out our ruin." See "A Declaration of the Immediate Causes Which Induce and Justify the Secession of the State of Mississippi from the Federal Union," *Avalon Project,* http://avalon.law.yale.edu/19th_century/csa_missec.asp.

30. *New Orleans Crescent,* Feb. 9, 2, 1861.

31. *Memphis Daily Appeal,* Feb. 14, Mar. 1, 1861; *Sugar Planter* (Port Allen, LA), Apr. 6, 1861.

32. John McGill, bishop of Richmond, pastoral letter, issued Feb. 4, 1861, in Richmond, reprinted and published in the *Charleston Catholic Miscellany,* Feb. 23, 1861.

33. McGill, pastoral letter, Feb. 4, 1861.

34. Wright, "Bishop Elder and the Civil War," 292; Elder to Fr. Napoléon-Joseph Perché, Feb. 4, 1861, quoted in Pillar, *Catholic Church in Mississippi, 1837–1865,* 162.

35. Kenrick to McGill, Feb. 14, 1861, 2, MDRI.

36. Jefferson Davis, "Inaugural Address of the President of the Provisional Government," Montgomery, AL, Feb. 18, 1861, in James D. Richardson, *A Compilation of the Messages and Papers of the Confederacy,* 2 vols. (Nashville: US Publishing Company, 1905), 1:32–36.

37. John Quinlan, bishop of Mobile, pastoral letter, issued Jan. 1, 1861, on the Feast of the Lord's Circumcision (today January 1 is celebrated as the Solemnity of Mary, the Holy Mother of God), Mobile, Alabama, reprinted and published in the *Charleston Catholic Miscellany,* Mar. 2, 1861.

38. Quinlan, pastoral letter.

39. Quinlan, pastoral letter.

40. Pillar, *Catholic Church in Mississippi,* 162–63; Elder to James Duggan, bishop of Chicago, Feb. 19, 1861, quoted in Wright, "Bishop Elder and the Civil War," 291.

41. Elder to Kenrick, undated letter, spring 1861, quoted in Wright, "Bishop Elder and the Civil War," 293.

42. Stephanie McCurry, "Women Numerous and Armed: Gender and the Politics of Subsistence in the Civil War South," in *Wars within a War: Controversy and Conflict over the American Civil War,* ed. Gary Gallagher and Joan Waugh (Chapel Hill: Univ. of North Carolina Press, 2014), 1.

43. Gary Gallagher, "Disaffection, Persistence, and Nation: Some Directions in Recent Scholarship on the Confederacy," *Civil War History* 55 (Sept. 2009): 340–41; Rubin, *Shattered Nation,* 246, 7; Sheehan-Dean, *Why Confederates Fought,* 187. For internal divisions in the Confederate South, also see William W. Freehling, *The South vs. the South: How Anti-Confederate Southerners Shaped the Course of the Civil War* (Oxford: Oxford Univ. Press, 2001).

44. Spalding to Purcell, Apr. 11, 1861, quoted in Spalding, *Martin John Spalding,* 131; Beauregard to Davis, Apr. 13, 1861, *The War of the Rebellion: A Compilation of the Official Records of the Union and Confederate Armies,* 128 vols. (Washington, DC: GPO, 1880–1901), ser. 1, vol. 1:309 (hereafter cited as *OR*); Henry, *Story of the Confederacy,* 30–33.

45. *Charleston Catholic Miscellany,* Apr. 13, 1861; *New South* (Port Royal, SC), Aug. 1, 1863; Heisser and White, *Patrick N. Lynch,* 78. There was a final, unfortunate, parting note from Fort Sumter. Major Anderson, upon surrender, asked permission to fire a hundred-gun salute as the US flag was lowered. The Confederates obliged. Midway through, a gun burst, wounding five Union soldiers and killing Pvt. Daniel Hough. The first casualty of the war was suffered not in battle but during a ceremony. See Henry, *Story of the Confederacy,* 32–33.

46. Reprint of "The Horrors of Civil War," *Catholic Mirror,* Apr. 13, 1861, originally in the *Richmond Whig.*

47. Kenrick to Lynch, Apr. 16, 1861, 26B4, and Wood to Lynch, Apr. 18, 1861, 26B6, both in CDA; Spalding to Purcell, Apr. 11, 1861, quoted in Spalding, *Martin John Spalding,* 131;

Spalding, Civil War Journal, Apr. 26, 1861, MNAZ, 3/12; Kenrick to Hughes, Apr. 26, 1861, in "Letters of Kenrick to Hughes and Lincoln," *Catholic Historical Review* 4 (Oct. 1918): 386.

48. Douglas Southall Freeman, *Lee: An Abridgement* (New York: Charles Scribner's Sons, 1935), 110; "From the Executive Journal of the State of Virginia," Apr. 20, 1861, *OR*, ser. 3, vol. 108:21; Kenrick to McGill, Feb. 14, 1861, 2, MDRI.

49. Elder to Lynch, May 9, 1861, 26D2, and Kenrick to Lynch, May 12, 1861, 26D3, both in CDA.

50. McGill to Lynch, May 15, 1861, 26D4, CDA.

51. McGill to Lynch, May 15, 1861.

52. William Henry Elder, bishop of Natchez, *Charleston Catholic Miscellany,* May 11, 1861.

53. Benjamin Blied, *Catholics and the Civil War* (Milwaukee: Privately printed, 1945), 37.

54. Quinlan to Lynch, May 18, 1861, 26D7, and Perché to Elder, May 19, 1861, 26E1, both in CDA; Elder to Lynch, July 16, 1861, quoted in Wright, "Bishop Elder and the Civil War," 293.

55. Gen. Thomas J. Jackson, Report of the Battle of First Manassas, July 23, 1861, *OR*, ser. 1, vol. 2:481–82; Henry, *Story of the Confederacy,* 57–58.

56. Jackson, Report of the Battle of First Manassas, 481–82.

57. *Catholic Mirror,* July 27, 1861.

58. Patrick Neeson Lynch, bishop of Charleston, "Letter of the Bishop of Charleston," Aug. 4, 1861, in John Tracy Ellis, *Documents of American Catholic History* (Milwaukee: Bruce, 1962), 347–56.

59. Lynch, "Letter of the Bishop of Charleston," Aug. 4, 1861.

60. Lynch, "Letter of the Bishop of Charleston," Aug. 4, 1861.

61. *Memphis Daily Appeal,* Jan. 29, 30, 1861.

62. That same day, a report appeared in the Mississippi newspaper *Eastern Clarion,* detailing the arrest of a New York city priest, "by a party of Dutch, who said he was a secessionist." *Eastern Clarion* (Paulding, MS), Aug. 23, 1861.

63. John Hughes, archbishop of New York, "Letter of the Archbishop of New York," Aug. 23, 1861, in *The Rebellion Record: A Diary of American Events,* ed. Frank Moore (New York: D. Van Nostrand, 1866), 381–84

64. In March 1861, Stephens remarked: "Its [the Confederate government] foundations are laid, its cornerstone rests, upon the great truth that the negro is not equal to the white man; that slavery . . . is his natural and normal condition." Quoted in James M. McPherson, *Battle Cry of Freedom: The Civil War Era* (New York: Oxford Univ. Press, 2003), 244. Augustin Verot, bishop of Savannah and St. Augustine, pastoral letter, issued Sept. 9, 1861, given in Charleston, reprinted and published in the *Charleston Catholic Miscellany,* Sept. 14, 1861.

65. Thomas Sim Lee to his father, from Rome, Nov. 21, 1861, collection 259, box 1, Col. 292, 1, F1, Thomas Sim Lee Papers, Catholic University of America Archives.

66. *Memphis Daily Appeal,* Oct. 23, 1862.

67. *Saint Mary's Beacon* (Leonard Town, MD), Sept. 5, 1861.

68. *Camden (SC) Confederate*, Dec. 20, 1861; Heisser and White, *Patrick N. Lynch*, 83.

69. *Smoky Hill and Republican Union* (Junction City, KS), Dec. 26, 1861; Heisser and White, *Patrick N. Lynch*, 83; Verot to Lynch, Dec. 23, 1861, 26T1, CDA.

70. James B. McPherson to E. P. Alexander, Apr. 20, 1861, quoted in Henry, *Story of the Confederacy*: "This war is not going to be the ninety days affair that papers and politicians are predicting. Both sides are in deadly earnest, and it is going to be fought out to the bitter end. . . . You have no army, no navy, no treasury . . . [nor] the manufactures and machine shops necessary for the support of armies, and for war on a large scale. You are but scattered agricultural communities, and you will be cut off from the rest of the world by blockade. Your cause is foredoomed to failure" (18).

2. Confederatization on the Battlefield

1. *Memphis Daily Appeal*, Nov. 28, 1862.

2. Phillip Thomas Tucker, *The Confederacy's Fighting Chaplain: Father John B. Bannon* (Tuscaloosa: Univ. of Alabama Press, 1992), 128.

3. William S. J. Faherty, *Exile in Erin: A Confederate Chaplain's Story* (St. Louis: Missouri History Museum Press, 2002), 71.

4. James M. McPherson, *For Cause and Comrades: Why Men Fought in the Civil War* (New York: Oxford Univ. Press, 1997), 28; David Potter, "The Historian's Use of Nationalism and Vice Versa, *American Historical Review* 67 (July 1962): 937.

5. Pillar, *History of the Catholic Church in Mississippi*, 189–90.

6. Joseph R. Frese, "The Catholic Press and Secession, 1860–1861," *American Catholic Historical Society of Philadelphia Records* 45 (1957): 79–106, 106; John Dooley, *Confederate Soldier, His War Journal*, ed. Joseph T. Durkin (Washington, DC: Georgetown Univ. Press, 1945), 1; T. Conn Bryan, "The Churches in Georgia during the Civil War," *Georgia Historical Quarterly* 33 (Dec. 1940): 287; Gary B. Mills, *The Forgotten People: Cane River's Creoles of Color* (Baton Rouge: Louisiana State Univ. Press, 1977), xxix; Cornelius M. Buckley, introduction to *Frenchman, a Chaplain, a Rebel*, 39–40; Woods, *History of the Catholic Church in the American South*, 291, 283; Randall M. Miller, "Catholic Religion, Irish Ethnicity, and the Civil War," in *Religion and the American Civil War*, ed. Randall M. Miller, Harry S. Stout, and Charles Reagan Wilson (Oxford: Oxford Univ. Press, 1998), 262.

7. A representative argument is better made with the bishops, as there were only 11. And even though in a slightly lesser degree, with chaplains: 28 served in the chaplaincy out of a pool of 278 priests living in the Confederacy at the start of the war. Pillar, *History of the Catholic Church in Mississippi*, 197.

8. Tucker, *Confederacy's Fighting Chaplain*, 39, 22, 44–45, 93, 47.

9. Brig. Gen. John B. Floyd to A. S. Johnston, Feb. 16, 1862, *OR*, ser. 1, vol. 7:256; Henry, *Story of the Confederacy*, 86; Jefferson Davis, "Inaugural Address," Richmond, Virginia, Feb. 22, 1862, in Richardson, *Compilation of the Messages and Papers of the Confederacy*, 1:183–88; Blied, *Catholics and the Civil War*, 123.; Pillar, *History of the*

Catholic Church in Mississippi, 198, 200. Northern chaplains were paid better, receiving eighty dollars per month.

10. Aug. 10, 1862, *The Civil War Diary of Father James Sheeran, Confederate Chaplain and Redemptorist,* ed. Patrick J. Hayes (Washington, DC: Catholic Univ. of America Press, 2016), 20.

11. Sept. 1, 1862, *Civil War Diary of Father James Sheeran,* 49–51.

12. Gache to Rev. Father Cornette, SJ, July 8, 1862, in Gache, *Frenchman, a Chaplain, a Rebel,* 119–27.

13. Rable, *God's Almost Chosen Peoples,* 115–16; Bruce Catton, preface to James B. Sheeran, *Confederate Chaplain, a War Journal,* ed. Joseph T. Durkin (Milwaukee: Bruce, 1960), v; Aug. 15–16, 1862, *Civil War Diary of Father James Sheeran,* 21–22.

14. May 30, 1864, *Exile in Richmond: The Confederate Journal of Henri Garidel,* ed. Michael Bedout Chesson and Leslie Jean Roberts (Charlottesville: Univ. of Virginia Press, 2001), 152; Feb. 8, 1865, *A Louisiana Confederate: Diary of Felix Pierre Poche,* ed. Edwin C. Bearss, trans. Eugiene Watson Somdal (Natchitoches: Louisiana Studies Institute, 1972), 214.

15. Oct. 26, 1862, *Civil War Diary of Father James Sheeran,* 106–8.

16. Gache to Carriere, Mar. 8, 1863, and Gache to Carriere, May 19, 1863, both in Gache, *Frenchman, a Chaplain, a Rebel,* 155, 169.

17. Sept. 1862, Sept. 2, 1863, both in Dooley, *Confederate Soldier,* 28, 140–41; May 29, Jan. 10, 1864, Nov. 24, Aug. 2, 1863, May 2, 29, Nov. 27, 1864, Jan. 22, Apr. 22, 1865, all in Poche, *Louisiana Confederate,* 127, 72, 44, 14, 118, 127, 186, 239.

18. May 2, 29, Nov. 27, Feb. 20, 1864, Sept. 20, 1863, Apr. 22, 1865, in Poche, *Louisiana Confederate,* 118, 127, 186, 86, 31, 239; Apr. 19, 1865, *John Dooley's Civil War: An Irish American's Journey in the First Virginia Infantry Regiment,* ed. Robert Emmett Curran (Knoxville: Univ. of Tennessee Press, 2012), 383.

19. After the war's conclusion, Butler recommended pardons and restitution of property in New Orleans. "Four ladies from New Orleans were also pardoned, and their confiscated estates returned to them. Gen. Butler, it is said, recommended yesterday that the latter step be taken." *Howard Union* (Glasgow, MO), Aug. 10, 1865.

20. Richardson, *Compilation of the Messages and Papers of the Confederacy,* 1:628, 615; Garidel, Aug. 6, 1864, *Exile in Richmond,* 193; *Catholic Mirror,* May 3, 1862; Sister Marietta, born Mary Ann Murphy, Sisters of Loretto, Nazareth, Kentucky, "Reminiscences of Civil War-Days at Nazareth Academy (1859–1864) at Nazareth, Kentucky," Civil War Book, MNAZ, 3/11; Garidel, Sept. 30, 1864, Jan. 3, 1865, May 9, 1864, *Exile in Richmond,* 222, 273, 134–35.

21. Henry, *Story of the Confederacy,* 151; *Memphis Daily Appeal,* Mar. 23, 21, 1862.

22. *Memphis Daily Appeal,* Mar. 23, Apr. 2, 1862.

23. Richardson, *Compilation of the Messages and Papers of the Confederacy,* 1:643; Gen. Nathaniel P. Banks to Edwin Stanton, Secretary of War, May 23, 1862, Banks to Stanton, May 25, 1862, Lt. Col. Thomas S. Garnett, Reports of the battle of Cross Keys and the engagement at Port Republic, June 15, 1862, *OR,* ser. 1, vol. 15:525, 528, 768.

24. Aug. 9, 1862, *John Dooley's Civil War,* 17; Gache to Carriere, Aug. 20, 1862, *Frenchman, a Chaplain, a Rebel,* 127–38.

25. Gache to Carriere, Aug. 20, 1862.

26. Richardson, *Compilation of the Messages and Papers of the Confederacy*, 1:583; Aug. 28, 1862, *John Dooley's Civil War*, 26–32.

27. Gache to Carriere, Aug. 20, 1862, 127.

28. Aug. 27, 1862, *Civil War Diary of Father James Sheeran*, 35–40.

29. Aug. 28, 1862, *Civil War Diary of Father James Sheeran*, 40–43.

30. Aug. 31, 1862, *Civil War Diary of Father James Sheeran*, 47–48.

31. Henry, *Story of the Confederacy*, 179; Davis, "Inaugural Address," 183–88.

32. Dooley, Sept. 1862, *Confederate Soldier*, 28.

33. *Daily Confederate* (Raleigh, NC), May 13, 1864; *Western Sentinel* (Winston, NC) Jan. 14, 1864.

34. *Daily Clarion* (Meridian, MS), Sept. 9, 1864; Sept. 6, 1862, *Civil War Diary of Father James Sheeran*, 57–62.

35. Sept. 6, 1862, *Civil War Diary of Father James Sheeran*.

36. Sept. 6, 1862, *Civil War Diary of Father James Sheeran*.

37. Richardson, *Compilation of the Messages and Papers of the Confederacy*, 1:575; Sept. 16, 1862, *John Dooley's Civil War*, 45.

38. Gache to Carriere, May 19, 1863, *Frenchman, a Chaplain, a Rebel*, 178; Dooley, Sept. 1862, *Confederate Soldier*, 56.

39. Sept. 17, 1862, *John Dooley's Civil War*, 45; Sept. 17, 1862, *Civil War Diary of Father James Sheeran*, 80–81.

40. Nov. 1, 1862, *John Dooley's Civil War*, 70–71.

41. Richardson, *Compilation of the Messages and Papers of the Confederacy*, 1:601; Dec. 13, 1862, *John Dooley's Civil War*, 103; Henry, *Story of the Confederacy*, 212; Tucker, *Confederacy's Fighting Chaplain*, 173.

42. Dec. 16, 1862, *Civil War Diary of Father James Sheeran*, 135–36.

43. Dec. 20, 1862, *Civil War Diary of Father James Sheeran*, 138; Gache to Rev. Father Jourdan, Rector of Spring Hill College, Dec. 5, 1861, and Gache to Carriere, Jan. 17, 1862, both in *Frenchman, a Chaplain, a Rebel*, 87, 91–96; Dooley, Christmas Day 1862, *Confederate Soldier*, 82.

44. Garidel, Christmas Day 1863, *Exile in Richmond*, 626; Christmas Day 1862, *Civil War Diary of Father James Sheeran*, 139.

45. John Quinlan, bishop of Mobile, to Stephen Mallory, Confederate secretary of the navy, Jan. 7, 1863, quoted in Tucker, *Confederacy's Fighting Chaplain*, 99–100.

46. Ulysses S. Grant to Henry Halleck, May 25, 1863, Grant Papers, ser. 4, Ulysses S. Grant Presidential Library, Starkville, MI; Garidel, May 18, 1863, June 17, 1864, *Exile in Richmond*, 41–47, 163.

47. Garidel, May 18, 1863, *Exile in Richmond*, 41–47.

48. Richardson, *Compilation of the Messages and Papers of the Confederacy*, 1:584; Freeman, *Lee*, 295, 298; Gache to Carriere, May 19, 1863, *Frenchman, a Chaplain, a Rebel*, 177.

49. Gache to Carriere, May 19, 16, 1863, *John Dooley's Civil War*, 145; May 6, 1863, *Civil War Diary of Father James Sheeran*, 165–66.

50. Tucker, *Confederacy's Fighting Chaplain*, 128; *Sugar Planter* (Port Allen, LA), Mar. 30, 1861.

51. *Dollar Weekly Bulletin* (Maysville, KY), July 20, 1863.

52. Col. Joshua Chamberlain, Twentieth Maine Infantry, Report of the Battle of Little Round Top, *OR*, ser. 1, vol. 43:622–26; Henry, *Story of the Confederacy*, 279; Joshua Lawrence Chamberlain Resources at Bowdoin College Library, George J. Mitchell Department of Special Collections and Archives, available online at https://library.bowdoin.edu/arch/subject-guides/joshua-lawrence-chamberlain-resources.shtml.

53. July 3, 1863, *John Dooley's Civil War*, 157–62.

54. July 3, 1863, *John Dooley's Civil War*. Sheeran once recounted a similar story from camp. It is natural to assume that soldiers who were constantly on the march, fatigued from battle and lack of food and shelter, would take any moment's break from action as a time to dedicate to mental and physical recuperation. But one spring morning, a foot and a half of snow had fallen. Naturally, it was a great opportunity for a snowball fight. These soldiers, it appears, could not get enough of military exercise. Sheeran reported that "some 8,000" men from two divisions formed standard lines and proceeded to fight a "regular scientific battle with snow balls." He wrote that the battle, complete with flank movements, charges and counter-charges, lasted a good two hours. At its conclusion, the winning side "came home as proud as if they had gained a victory over the Yankees" (Mar. 23, 1864, *Civil War Diary of Father James Sheeran*, 330).

55. July 3, 1863, *John Dooley's Civil War*, 157–62.

56. July 3, 1863, *John Dooley's Civil War*.

57. Grant to Pemberton, July 3, 1863, Ulysses S. Grant Papers.

58. In *The Age of Lincoln* (New York: Hill & Wang, 2007), Orville Vernon Burton points out that "not only had Lee's forces been sent reeling back toward Virginia," never again to attempt a Northern invasion, but, the loss at Vicksburg was so important that "west of the [Mississippi] river, Texas, Arkansas, and portions of Missouri would fight on for nearly two years, but essentially they had been knocked out of the war . . . with the subsequent Union victory at Port Hudson, the heart of cotton's kingdom and the Mississippi River were now firmly under Federal control" (181).

59. Rubin, *Shattered Nation*, 80, 246.

60. July 4, 1863, *Civil War Diary of Father James Sheeran*, 204.

61. The Mr. Mitchel to whom Dooley refers is John, leader of the 1848 movement. July 5, 1863, *John Dooley's Civil War*, 174.

62. *Memphis Daily Appeal*, Jan. 14, 1864, July 27, 29, 1863; *Daily Confederate* (Raleigh, NC), May 13, 1864.

63. *Western Democrat* (Charlotte, NC), Mar. 10, 1863.

64. Some works on this subject include Susannah J. Ural, ed., *Civil War Citizens: Race, Ethnicity, and Identity in America's Bloodiest Conflict* (New York: New York Univ. Press, 2010); Jeff Strickland, *Unequal Freedoms: Ethnicity, Race, and White Supremacy in Civil War–Era Charleston* (Gainesville: Univ. Press of Florida, 2015); Gleeson, *Green and the Grey*; and Miller and Wakelyn, *Catholics in the Old South*, with special attention paid to Randall Miller's chapter, "A Church in Cultural Captivity: Some Speculations on Catholic Identity in the Old South," 11–52.

65. Dooley, July 13, July 21, July 9, 1863, Feb. 27, 1865, Aug. 23, 1863, *Confederate Soldier*, 123–25, 168, 135.

66. July 27, 1864, *John Dooley's Civil War*, 281.

67. Garidel, Sept. 11, 21, 1863, *Exile in Richmond*, 62, 80.

68. Garidel, Sept. 11, 21, 24 1863, Apr. 14, Sept. 13, 1864, *Exile in Richmond*, 62, 80, 85, 116, 209. Chesson and Roberts, the editors of Garidel's diary, note that *cafiot* was "a colloquialism for bad, weak coffee" (116). Gache to Carriere, Sept. 11, 1861, *Frenchman, a Chaplain, a Rebel*, 52.

69. Garidel, Sept. 23, 1863, Sept. 24, 1864, Oct. 1, 1863, Sept. 29, 1863, Oct. 9, 1863, Apr. 14, Mar. 24, 1864, *Exile in Richmond*, 82, 215, 91, 89, 99, 116, 104. Gache also counted Davis as a friend and claimed that he possessed "influence with the President of the Confederacy." Gache to Fr. Francis Gautrelet, June 1, 1863, *Frenchman, a Chaplain, a Rebel*, 189.

70. Garidel, May 6, 1864, *Exile in Richmond*, 131.

71. Garidel, May 7, 1864, *Exile in Richmond*, 133.

72. Garidel, May 8, 14, 15, 16, 1864, *Exile in Richmond*, 134, 136–38, 139–40.

73. Garidel, May 16, 1864, *Exile in Richmond*, 140.

74. Garidel, May 17, 1864, *Exile in Richmond*, 142.

75. Garidel, May 17, 1864, *Exile in Richmond*, 141–43.

76. Garidel, June 1, May 26, 1864, *Exile in Richmond*, 153, 148.

77. Just in Louisiana, Poche traveled the road between Washington and Opelousas six times, a distance of 25 miles one way and 150 miles in sum. He journeyed from Columbia to Monroe four times, for a total distance of 122 miles. And he took the sixty-odd mile road from French Settlement up to Clinton at least seven times, for a total of 420 miles. His excursion out of Magnolia, Mississippi, to Meridian, Mississippi, by way of Jackson, amounted to an approximately 150-mile jaunt one way. Poche, *Louisiana Confederate*, 113–15.

78. Poche, Oct. 24–26, 1863, *Louisiana Confederate*, 44.

79. Poche, Nov. 24, Dec. 4, 8, 9, 1863, *Louisiana Confederate*, 55–61.

80. Poche, Apr. 1, 2, 1864, *Louisiana Confederate*, 103, 104.

81. Poche, Apr. 8, 1864, *Louisiana Confederate*, 105–8.

82. Poche, Apr. 9, 22, 1864, *Louisiana Confederate*, 110–11, 114.

83. Poche, Apr. 20, 21, July 31, 1864, *Louisiana Confederate*, 114, 148.

84. Poche, Apr. 20, 1864, *Louisiana Confederate*, 114.

85. Oct. 31, Nov. 1, 8, 1864, *Civil War Diary of Father James Sheeran*, 490–94, 502–3.

86. Northern Confederate sympathizers—often and especially Northern Catholic Confederate sympathizers—constantly played up censorship and potential imprisonment as evidence against a supposed tyrannical American government. For example, on October 21, 1863, the *Memphis Daily Appeal* reported that Lincoln had suppressed Baltimore's *Catholic Mirror* and imprisoned its editors at Fort McHenry. Their crime was publishing a pamphlet titled "Fourteen Months in a Federal Bastille." Nov. 17, 28, 1864, *Civil War Diary of Father James Sheeran*, 517–18, 524–25; James McMaster, "A Great and Cruel Wrong: Arrest and Imprisonment of a Confederate Catholic Chaplain," *Freeman's Journal*, Nov. 19, 1864.

87. Sheeran to McMaster, printed as part of McMaster, "A Great and Cruel Wrong."

88. McMaster believed Sheridan would give Sheeran a fair hearing, as he had the "reputation of an able and gallant soldier" and was "a Catholic in religion, and, almost

certainly, as a student under the good Dominican Fathers [would know that he could not receive absolution for the chaplain's unfair imprisonment] . . . till he makes reparation for the outrage he has committed on Father Sheeran." McMaster, "Great and Cruel Wrong."

89. Sheeran to Sheridan, Nov 1, 1864, sent from Military Prison, Winchester, Virginia, printed as part of McMaster, "Great and Cruel Wrong."

90. Dec. 4, 1864, *Civil War Diary of Father James Sheeran,* 529–30.

91. Dec. 4, 30–31, 1864, *Civil War Diary of Father James Sheeran,* 529–30, 545–50.

92. The Northern Peace Democrats had failed to win the White House. Lincoln succeeded in gaining a second term. While Grant and Lee waged their brutal war of attrition in the East, the former having taken command of the Union forces in March 1864, Sherman, having taken Atlanta in September 1864, embarked on his famous "March to the Sea." Nine days before Sheeran was discharged from prison, Savannah was in the hands of the Union army. Lee's Army had twice failed in Northern invasions. The Mississippi River, Atlanta, and most of the South were in Union hands; so, too, were major Southern railroads. The Confederacy's Army of Tennessee was broken beyond repair at the Battle of Franklin, in November 1864. Richardson, *Compilation of the Messages and Papers of the Confederacy,* 1:580, 627, 601.

93. Jason Phillips, "The Grape Vine Telegraph: Rumors and Confederate Persistence," *Journal of Southern History* 72 (Nov. 2006): 753–88; see also Phillips, *Diehard Rebels,* 189, 2.

94. Phillips, *Diehard Rebels,* 189, 2.

95. Poche, July 23, 28, 29, Sept. 3, 1863, *Louisiana Confederate,* 7, 10, 24–26; Garidel, Sept. 22, 27, 1863, *Exile in Richmond,,* 81, 87–88.

96. Poche, July 30, Nov. 7, 1863, Jan. 22, June 5, 1864, *Louisiana Confederate,* 11, 48, 75, 128–29.

97. Poche, July 1, 10, 1864, *Louisiana Confederate,* 136, 139.

98. Garidel, July 18, 19, May 30, Sept. 11, 1864, *Exile in Richmond,* 180, 181, 152, 209.

99. Poche, Sept. 13, 19, Oct. 20, 1864, July 26, 1863, July 20, 1864, *Louisiana Confederate,* 164, 165, 174, 9, 143.

3. Catholicity on the Battlefield

1. Sept. 2, 1862, *Civil War Diary of Father James Sheeran,* 53.

2. Tucker, *Confederacy's Fighting Chaplain,* 33, 44–45

3. Pillar, *History of the Catholic Church in Mississippi,* 212–15

4. Drew Gilpin Faust, *This Republic of Suffering: Death and the American Civil War* (New York: Knopf, 2008), 7; Elder to Mouton, Dec. 28, 1862, quoted in Pillar, *History of the Catholic Church in Mississippi,* 232; Gache to Carriere, Aug. 20, 1862, and Gache to Cornette, Apr. 5, 1862, both in *Frenchman, a Chaplain, a Rebel,* 136, 106.

5. Elder to Boeheme, Mar. 13, 1862, and Elder to Elia, Apr 5, 1862, both quoted in Pillar, *History of the Catholic Church in Mississippi,* 219, 223.

6. Aug. 15, 1862, *Civil War Diary of Father James Sheeran,* 21.

7. Gache to Cornette, July 8, 1862, *Frenchman, a Chaplain, a Rebel,* 117–20.

8. Tucker, *Confederacy's Fighting Chaplain*, 138, 146.

9. Fr. John Bannon, "Experiences of a Confederate Army Chaplain," from Letters and Notices, Oct. 1867, in William B. Faherty, *The Fourth Career of John B. Bannon: St. Louis Pastor, Southern Chaplain, Confederate Agent, and Irish Jesuit Orator* (Portland, OR: C&D Publishing, 1994), 92.

10. Bannon, "Experiences of a Confederate Army Chaplain."

11. Gache to Cornette, May 22, 1861, *Frenchman, a Chaplain, a Rebel*, 117–20.

12. Gache to Rev. Father D. Yenni, SJ, Nov. 22, 1861, *Frenchman, a Chaplain, a Rebel*, 59.

13. Gache to Yenni, Nov. 22, 1861, *Frenchman, a Chaplain, a Rebel*, 65; Sheeran, Sept. 18, 1862, *Confederate Chaplain*, 33.

14. Jan. 17, 1864, *Civil War Diary of Father James Sheeran*, 296–97.

15. Aug. 15, 1862, May 7, 1864, *Civil War Diary of Father James Sheeran*, 21–22, 359.

16. Gache to Rev. Father Cornette, SJ, Apr. 5, 1862, *Frenchman, a Chaplain, a Rebel*, 101; Apr. 24, Apr. 26, 1863, *Civil War Diary of Father James Sheeran*, 152–54.

17. *Memphis Daily Appeal*, June 18, 1862; *Weekly Ottumwa (IA)*, July 24, 1861.

18. Feb. 6, 7, 21, Mar. 19, 20, 1864, Reverend Jesse L. Henderson Civil War Diary; B. F. Gentry to his parents, W. R. and Mariah, Apr. 1864, B. F. Gentry Collection, and T. G. Clark to his wife, Margery, Dec. 9, 1861, Clark Family Letters, all in Digital Collections: Civil War Archive, University of Mississippi, University of Mississippi Libraries, http://clio.lib.olemiss.edu/cdm/landingpage/collection/civil_war.

19. Sheeran, Apr. 26, 1863, Feb. 24, 1864, Sept. 5, 1863, *Confederate Chaplain*, 40, 76–77, 55.

20. Gache to Yenni, Nov. 22, 1861, *Frenchman, a Chaplain, a Rebel*, 59.

21. Gache to Carriere, Jan. 17, Sept. 11, 1862, *Frenchman, a Chaplain, a Rebel*, 91, 52.

22. Gache to Francis Gautreet, Lynchburg, June 1, 1863, *Frenchman, a Chaplain, a Rebel*, 190.

23. Gache to Gautreet, June 1, 1863.

24. Gache to Yenni, Nov. 22, 1861, *Frenchman, a Chaplain, a Rebel*, 65.

25. Gache to Carriere, Aug. 20, 1862, *Frenchman, a Chaplain, a Rebel*, 127.

26. Gache to Carriere, Sept. 11, 1861, *Frenchman, a Chaplain, a Rebel*, 41–52.

27. Gache to Carriere, Sept. 11, 1861. The Latin verse is Luke 10:2: "Therefore ask the Lord of the harvest to send workers to his harvest."

28. Gache to Carriere, Sept. 11, 1861, and Gache to Rev. Yenni, Nov. 22, 1861.

29. Gache to Cornette, Nov. 18, 1862, *Frenchman, a Chaplain, a Rebel*, 144–45.

30. Rable, *God's Almost Chosen Peoples*, 145.

31. Dooley, Nov. 1, 1862, *Confederate Soldier*, 70; Aug. 27, 1863, *Civil War Diary of Father James Sheeran*, 228; Gache to Carriere, Sept. 11, 1861.

32. *The Soldiers Journal* (Rendezvous of Distribution, VA), Dec. 21, 1864; Rable, *God's Almost Chosen Peoples*, 121; May 7, 1864, *Civil War Diary of Father James Sheeran*, 359; Gache to Yenni, Nov. 22, 1861, 65.

33. Gache to Cornette, Apr. 5, 1862, 101.

34. Apr. 5, 1863, *Civil War Diary of Father James Sheeran*, 146.

35. Gache to Carriere, May 15, 1861, *Frenchman, a Chaplain, a Rebel*, 28.

36. Aug. 9, 1862, *John Dooley's Civil War*, 18–19.

37. Dooley, Nov. 1, 1862, *Confederate Soldier*, 70.

38. Mar. 24, 1864, *Civil War Diary of Father James Sheeran*, 335; Pillar, *Catholic Church in Mississippi*, 190; Father Francis Burlando to Superior General Father Etienne, Emmitsburg, Apr. 10, 1868, Daughters of Charity Province of St. Louise Archives, Emmitsburg, Maryland, 7-5-1 Civil War Annals, 1866; Oct. 1862, *John Dooley's Civil War*, 61.

39. Poche, Aug. 2, 1863, *Louisiana Confederate*, 13.

40. Poche, July [?], May 8, July 15, 1864, Aug. 9, 1862, Feb. 19, Jan. 5, 1864, *Louisiana Confederate*, 119, 141, 139–148, 18, 85, 70–71.

41. Garidel, Oct. 10, 1863, Apr. 8, Aug. 15, May 1, 1864, *Exile in Richmond*, 101, 112, 197–98, 127.

42. Garidel, Dec. 7, 1864, Sept. 23, 1863, *Exile in Richmond*, 256, 82.

43. Garidel, Apr. 4, 1864, *Exile in Richmond*, 110. The Feast of the Annunciation is normally celebrated on March 25, nine months before Christmas Day. Garidel noted "it's observance here [in Richmond]" on April 4.

44. Garidel, Apr. 3, Mar. 24, 1864, Oct. 3, 1863, *Exile in Richmond*, 110, 105, 93.

45. Garidel, Apr. 3, May 29, 1864, *Exile in Richmond*, 110, 150–51.

46. Gache to Cornette, Apr. 5, 1862, 105.

4. The Ambiguities of Peace

1. Martin John Spalding, Jan. 15, 20, 1862, Civil War Journal, MNAZ, 3/12. Spalding's biographer claims the bishop largely abstained from political issues and that he was unlike Protestant ministers who were "conspicuous at party conventions and political rallies." Spalding was undoubtedly focused on spiritual matters, but he was simultaneously a Confederate sympathizer and aligned with the Confederacy on all the basic Southern positions concerning war guilt, slavery, preferred economic models, and societal structure. But while Spalding was in favor of the South, he seemed to honestly despise politics, and to not like war much better. Much of the Southern episcopate— save for the fanatical Lynch and Quinlan—assumed this general outlook: Confederatized, often deeply so, yet looking first toward episcopal duties. Spalding, *Martin John Spalding*, 121; Rable, *God's Almost Chosen Peoples*, 197.

2. Odin to Lynch, Jan. 18, 1862, 26Y6, Verot to Lynch, Feb. 1, 1862, 27A3, and Elder to Lynch, Oct. 16, 1862, 28A4, all in CDA.

3. Odin to Lynch, Jan. 18, 1862, 26Y6.

4. Spalding, Feb. 26, 1862, Civil War Journal.

5. Harry S. Stout, *Upon the Altar of the Nation: A Moral History of the Civil War* (New York: Viking, 2006).

6. Spalding, Feb. 26, 1862, Civil War Journal. The Catholic practice of praying for the dead is rooted in the Second Book of Maccabees 12:46: "It is therefore a holy and wholesome thought to pray for the dead, that they may be loosed from their sins," a part of the Catholic Old Testament, which contains forty-six books, compared to the

Protestant thirty-nine (for an overall difference of seventy-three to sixty-six books). This passage, along with Christ's words in Matthew 12:32—"But whoever speaks against the Holy Spirit will not be forgiven, either in this age or in the age to come"—forms the Scriptural basis for the Catholic belief in purgatory—a place where souls who are saved, although not fully perfected so as to enter Heaven, are purified. Catholic doctrine, which Spalding explained, holds that the prayers and sacrifices of those on earth, on behalf of those in purgatory, expedite the latter's purification process and admittance into Heaven.

Southern newspapers questioned the war's justice, too, but, as an excerpt from the *Avolleyes Pelican* of Louisiana demonstrates, the rationale was often skewed fully toward Southern subjugation in a supposed connection between Northern barbarism and a special aim of eradicating religion in the South with the target here—as was often the case—Roman Catholicism specifically. "A more unholy war was never waged against any people, and the ultimate result of it, [in the event of our subjugation,] will be and inveterate religious intolerance. The Puritan elements of the North will combine in the effort to destroy the Roman Catholic worship, and if you will not fight for the free and liberal institutions under which you have lived, you may yet have to join the bannered hosts of the South for the privilege of worshipping God to the dictates of your own conscience." *Ayolleyes Pelican* (Marksville, LA), Mar. 1, 1862.

7. In the October 7, 1862, entry of his Civil War journal, Spalding reported the collection for Pius IX netted $1,310.

8. *Catholic Mirror,* June 7, 1862, UNDA, MNEW; Spalding, [Nov. ?], 1, Dec. 15–30, 1862, Civil War Journal.

9. Lynch, "To the Clergy and Laity of the Diocese of Charleston," Feb. 11, 1863, 28N6, CDA.

10. Lynch, "To the Clergy and Laity of the Diocese of Charleston."

11. Lynch, "To the Clergy and Laity of the Diocese of Charleston."

12. Oct. 17, Apr. 12, 1863, *Civil War Diary of Bishop William Henry Elder, Bishop of Natchez (1862–1865),* ed. Richard Gerow (Natchez, MS: Most Reverend Richard Gerow, 1960), 67, 27.

13. Blied, *Catholics and the Civil War,* 38; *Evening Star* (Washington, DC), July 9, 1863; *Semi-Weekly Standard* (Raleigh, NC), July 21, 1863.

14. Heisser and White, *Patrick N. Lynch,* 90.

15. McGill to Lynch, July 23, 1863, 29G6, and Lynch to McGill, July 26, 1863, 29H1, both in CDA.

16. Lynch to McGill, July 26, 1863, 29H1; Spalding, *Martin John Spalding,* 149; Spalding, July 8, 1863, Civil War Journal.

17. Woods, *History of the Catholic Church in the American South,* 174.

18. Verot to Lynch, Oct. 5, 1863, 29R2, CDA; Heisser and White, *Patrick N. Lynch,* 96.

19. Pope Pius IX to Archbishops John Hughes, of New York, and Jean-Marie Odin, of New Orleans, Oct. 18, 1862, Rome, reprinted in *Daily Ohio Statesman* (Columbus, OH), Aug. 11, 1863.

20. Pope Pius IX to Archbishops Hughes and Odin, Oct. 18, 1862.

21. *Wilmington (NC) Journal,* Jan. 21, 1864; Frank L. Owsley, *King Cotton Diplomacy: Foreign Relations of the Confederate States of America,* 2nd ed., rev. Harriet Chappell Owsley (Chicago: Univ. of Chicago Press, 1959), 499–500; Spalding, *Martin John Spalding,* 144–45.

22. Jean Marie Odin, Archbishop of New Orleans, pastoral letter, Aug. *Freeman's Journal,* Sept. 26, 1863, cited in Blied, *Catholics in the Civil War,* 54. Earlier in 1862, Odin had been in Rome to make his *ad limina* visit the required visit of bishops to report, in person, to Rome on the state of their dioceses. During his trip, he also campaigned for peace and an end to the war.

23. *Semi-Weekly Standard* (Raleigh, NC), Nov 10, 27, 1863; *Memphis Daily Appeal,* Jan. 15, 1864.

24. *Richmond Enquirer,* Dec. 1, 1863; *Yorkville (SC) Enquirer,* Dec. 9, 1863.

25. Lynch, "Pastoral Prayers for Peace," Nov. 26, 1863, 29Y7, CDA.

26. Lynch, "Pastoral Prayers for Peace."

27. Lynch, "Pastoral Prayers for Peace."

28. Lynch, "Pastoral Prayers for Peace"; Verot to Lynch, Dec. 16, 1863, 30B4, CDA.

29. Concerning two examples among many, the *Memphis Daily Appeal* once encouraged Northerners to disavow New England–based puritanical "plots" and the Confederacy go its separate way. The Reverend John P. Campbell declared his intention to publish a series of articles aimed at a "speedy and most honorably" established peace and to encourage supplication to God from "all ministers and all Christian churches, both Catholic and Protestant, in behalf of peace." *Memphis Daily Appeal,* Sept. 1, Apr. 17, 1863.

30. *Memphis Daily Appeal,* Oct. 26, 1863; *Daily Dispatch* (Richmond, VA), Feb. 26, 1864. The following is a March 31, 1864, account from a *Wilmington (NC) Journal* newspaper correspondent who heard Lynch preach at a Confederate hospital in Montgomery, Virginia:

> Bishop Lynch, the eminent Catholic divine from Charleston, SC, has been at this place for over a week, and I have been fortunate enough to have enjoyed the pleasure of listening to his eloquent discourses on the two preceding Sabbaths. He is a very fine specimen of manhood, not overdone with years, with a fine eye and pleasant countenance, finely balanced bead, features of his face what are termed handsome, and his elocution is easy as his language is classic, graceful and elegant . . . very interesting and seems perfectly devoid of all ostentation so common to some highly educated men . . . we could perceive none of that austerity of manner germane to the underlings who generally crucify Christ more than they preach Christ crucified.

31. Nov. 7, 12, 1862, Feb. 23, 1863, Elder Diary, 3, 4, 18.

32. Dec. 10, 1862, Elder Diary, 8.

33. Dec. 10, 13, 14, 1862, Elder Diary, 8.

34. May 14, July 18, 1863, Elder Diary, 30, 46.

35. Bishop William Henry Elder, "Apostolate to the Negro Slaves in Mississippi," to the Society for the Propagation of the Faith, 1858, in Ellis, *Documents of American Catholic History,* 325–29.

36. Sept. 4, 5, 8, 12, 18, 21–24, Oct. 10, 19, 1863, Jan. 1, 1864, Elder Diary, 63–64, 67, 69, 72.

37. Elder, "Apostolate to the Negro Slaves in Mississippi"; Dec. 14, 1862, Mar. 16, 19–20, Apr. 14, July 26, 1863, Elder Diary, 9, 22–23, 28, 51.

38. Cyprian Davis, *The History of Black Catholics in the United States* (New York: Crossroad, 1990), 45–46.

39. Madeleine Hooke Rice, *American Catholic Opinion in the Slavery Controversy* (Gloucester, MA: Peter Smith, 1964), 12.

40. Elder Diary, May 15, Aug. 3, 1863, 34, 55.

41. Elder Diary, Nov. 1, 1862, 2; "Divine Origins of the Church." Elder was speaking of the Catholic belief that the Church has been personally and divinely instituted by Jesus Christ (Matthew 16:16–19): Simon Peter replied, "You are the Christ, the Son of the living God." And Jesus answered him, "Blessed are you, Simon Bar-Jonah! For flesh and blood has not revealed this to you, but my Father who is in heaven. And I tell you, you are Peter, and on this rock I will build my church, and the gates of hell shall not prevail against it. I will give you the keys of the kingdom of heaven, and whatever you bind on earth shall be bound in heaven, and whatever you loose on earth shall be loosed in heaven."

42. Mar. 27, Apr. 5, 1863, Elder Diary, 24, 26.

43. June 4, 1864, Elder Diary, 84.

44. Spalding, *Martin John Spalding,* 135.

45. Gleeson, *Green and the Grey,* 89; Poche, Aug. 13, 1864, *Louisiana Confederate,* 154; Nov. 9, 1864, *Civil War Diary of Father James Sheeran,* 503; Eric Foner, *A Short History of Reconstruction, 1863–1877* (New York: HarperCollins, 2010), 15, 85. Lincoln's address, titled "Proclamation of Amnesty and Reconstruction," Dec. 8, 1863, is available online at the *Freedman and Southern Society Project,* www.freedmen.umd.edu/procamn.htm. When a Southern state reached a loyalist population of 10 percent, it was granted permission to create a new government.

46. Pillar, *History of the Catholic Church in Mississippi,* 157.

47. Pillar, *History of the Catholic Church in Mississippi,* 295–96.

48. Elder to Lincoln, Apr. 7, 1864, quoted in Pillar, *History of the Catholic Church in Mississippi,* 307.

49. July 6, 1864, Elder Diary, 91.

50. Elder to Farrar, July 13, 1864, Diocese of Natchez Collection, UNDA. The Union did not appreciate prayers being said specifically for Southern leaders. The April 1, 1862, *Memphis Daily Appeal* recounted such a story that took place in Florida that year, in which an episcopal minister and a Catholic priest were threatened with arrest and deportation "unless they desisted from praying for Jeff. Davis and the Southern Confederacy."

51. Elder to Farrar, July 13, 1864.

52. Elder to Farrar, July 13, 1864.

53. July 13, 16, 1864, Elder Diary, 92–93.

54. July 18, 1864, Elder Diary, 95.

55. *Dollar Weekly Bulletin* (Maysville, KY), Jan. 1, 1863; *Memphis Daily Appeal,* May 14, 1864; *Democrat* (Tunkhannock, PA), Mar. 29, 1865.

56. July 25, 26, 1864, Elder Diary, 97–99; *Daily Dispatch* (Richmond, VA), Aug. 25, 1864.

57. *Daily Dispatch* (Richmond, VA), Aug. 25, 1864.

58. *Alexandria (VA) Gazette,* Aug. 19, 1864; *Wilmington (NC) Journal,* Aug. 18, 1864.

Just as the bishop of St. Louis, Peter Richard Kenrick, had refused to place the US flag over his cathedral because he believed only the flag of the Church could fly there, Whelan rejected the same invitation, telling a "Union mob" that "they must pass over his dead body" in order to mount the flag. Whelan did not stop at refusals, however. Rather, as reported in the March 31, 1862, *New Orleans Daily Crescent,* he asked the crowd,

> Why is it, if this be a "wicked rebellion" . . . why is it that the best citizens, as well as the clergy, the men who are known and respected as the most reliable, pure, unselfish members of society are loyal to a man? Why is it that the women—the mothers, wives and daughters—of the South place the cause of the South only second in their devotion to that of their God? If this be a "wicked rebellion" if it be not in fact the best and noblest cause that ever summoned a people to the field, it is strange that the good and noble people of the South should all be found among its friends, and only the false and doubtful in private life among its enemies.

59. July 18, 27, 1864, Elder Diary, 95, 99; Spalding, *Martin John Spalding,* 161.

60. Spalding, *Martin John Spalding,* 161.

61. *Yorkville (SC) Enquirer,* Sept. 9, 1864.

62. Concerning the Elder affair, Pillar wrote in *The History of the Catholic Church in Mississippi:* "Determined from the start of the War not to become politically involved, Bishop Elder would not have encountered ordinarily any difficulty in exercising his spiritual ministry during the Federal occupation of Mississippi. Once, however, the United States military authorities overextended themselves by interfering in purely ecclesiastical affairs, the Bishop of Natchez resisted. In so doing he defended not only the rights of the Catholic Church, but also the religious liberty of all Americans" (343).

63. Gleeson, *Green and the Grey,* 155; Raymond H. Schmandt, "An Overview of Institutional Establishments in the Antebellum Southern Church," in Miller and Wakelyn, *Catholics in the Old South,* 65.

64. July 31, Aug. 12, 1864, Elder Diary, 100, 102–3; *Weekly National Intelligencer* (Washington, DC), Sept. 15, 1864.

65. *Manitowoc (WI) Pilot,* Sept. 16, 1864; *Daily Chattanooga Rebel* (Griffin, GA), Sept. 14, 1864; *Democrat and Sentinel* (Ebensburg, PA), Dec. 14, 1864.

66. *Idaho World* (Idaho City, Idaho Territory), Nov. 12, 1864.

67. Aug. 12, 15, 1864, Elder Diary, 102–5.

5. Healing

1. James R. Rada Jr., *Battlefield Angels: The Daughters of Charity Work as Civil War Nurses* (Gettysburg, PA: Legacy Publishing, 2011), 22; Mary Denis Maher, *To Bind Up the Wounds: Catholic Sister Nurses in the U.S. Civil War* (Westport, CT: Greenwood, 1989), 69–70, 15; Sr. Frances Jerome Woods, CDP, "Congregations of Religious Women in the Old South," in Miller and Wakelyn, *Catholics in the Old South,* 112.

2. Maher, *To Bind Up the Wounds,* 27.

3. Maher, *To Bind Up the Wounds,* 27, 105, 109. William B. Faherty highlights this fact: "The country only had 600 trained nurses at the start of the Civil War. All were Catholic nuns. This is one of the best-kept secrets in our nation's history." Rada, *Battlefield Angels,* 5; Woods, "Congregations of Religious Women in the Old South," 119, 122–23.

4. Sister Coskery to unknown recipient, from Antietam, Civil War Annals, 1866.

5. Woods, "Congregations of Religious Women in the Old South," 122–23.

6. Rada, *Battlefield Angels,* 35; Maher, *To Bind Up the Wounds,* 127.

7. *Wilmington (NC) Journal,* Mar. 31, 1864; *Daily Chattanooga Rebel* (Griffin, GA), June 30, 1864.

8. Verot to Lynch, Oct. 5, 1863, 29R2, CDA; Rada, *Battlefield Angels,* 199.

9. McGill to Lynch, Sept. 2, 1862, 27R4, CDA; "War Letters of the Bishop of Richmond," ed. Willard Wright, *Virginia Magazine of History and Biography* 67 (July 1959): 260; Spalding, Oct. 1, 1862, Civil War Journal, MNAZ, 3/12; Faust, *This Republic of Suffering,* 27.

10. Kate Cumming, Apr. 18, 1862, Dec. 8, 1863, *Kate: The Journal of a Confederate Nurse,* ed. Richard Barksdale (Baton Rouge: Louisiana State Univ. Press, 1959), 22, 178; Bryan, "Churches in Georgia during the Civil War," 289. Rable, in *God's Almost Chosen People,* pointing out that Catholic nuns made up a majority of the war's trained nurses, writes of the sisters' wide acclaim, "If there was one thing that many Federals and Confederates agreed upon, it was that the Catholic Sisters of Charity—along with nuns from eleven other orders—performed these tasks [ministering physically and spiritually to men in hospitals] as anyone" (211).

11. In the words of historian Father James Pillar, in Pillar, *History of the Catholic Church in Mississippi:* "Through their nursing these nuns accomplished two things: seeing neither gray nor blue, they performed efficient and heroic service in the cause of charity, and they did much to better understanding of the Catholic Church and all it stands for" (253). Maher writes, in *To Bind Up the Wounds:* "To them the fundamental purpose for serving was to care for the sick and suffering as Jesus Christ would, bringing sick and dying men to think of God in their suffering and to be baptized if they were not" (120).

12. Sr. Lauretta Maher, "Reminiscences of the Civil War," Civil War Book, MNAZ 3/11, UNDA.

13. Maher, "Reminiscences of the Civil War."

14. Maher, "Reminiscences of the Civil War."

15. Maher, "Reminiscences of the Civil War."

16. Father Francis Burlando to Superior General Father Etienne, Emmitsburg, Apr. 10, 1868, Civil War Annals, 1866.

17. Burlando to Fr. Etienne, Apr. 10, 1868.

18. Sister Euphemia to Mother Elizabeth Montcellet, Superioreess of the Daughters of Charity, from Central House, St. Joseph's, Aug. 16, 1862, Civil War Annals, 1866.

19. Rable, *God's Almost Chosen Peoples,* 115–16; Sister Euphemia to Montcellet, Aug. 16, 1862.

20. Gache to Rev. P. Phil de Carierre, June 11, 1862, and Gache to Rev. Father Cornette, SJ, Nov. 18, 1862, *Frenchman, a Chaplain, a Rebel,* 109, 143; Woods, "Congregations of

Religious Women in the Old South," 121; Sister Euphemia to Montcellet, Aug. 16, 1862; Burlando to Fr. Jean-Baptiste Etienne, CM (Superior General of the Congregation of the Mission and the Daughters of Charity), Apr. 10, 1865, quoted in Rada, *Battlefield Angels*, 199–202.

21. Maher, *To Bind Up the Wounds*, 117–18; Bannon, "Experiences of a Confederate Army Chaplain," 92.

22. Gache to Cornette, Nov. 18, 1862, *Frenchman, a Chaplain, a Rebel*, 147.

23. Gache to Cornette, Nov. 18, 1862.

24. Gache to Cornette, Nov. 18, 1862; Burlando to Fr. Etienne, Apr. 10, 1868; Kenrick to Hughes, Sept. 23, 1862, 387, in "Letters of Kenrick to Hughes and Lincoln," *Catholic Historical Review* 4 (Oct, 1918): 385–88; Rada, *Battlefield Angels*, 108.

25. Maher, "Reminiscences of the Civil War"

26. Maher, "Reminiscences of the Civil War."

27. Sister Regina to Mother Elizabeth Montcellet, Superioreess of the Daughters of Charity, from New Orleans, Charity Hospital, Aug. 11, 1862, and "Ward A, To the Honor of the Holy Virgin, St. Louis Hospital," Dec. 9, 1866, both in Civil War Annals, 1866.

28. Gache to Cornette, Nov. 18, 1862, 148–49.

29. Bannon, "Experiences of a Confederate Army Chaplain," in Faherty, *Fourth Career of John B. Bannon*, 83–92, originally published in *Letters and Notices of the English Jesuit Province* 34 (1866–68): 201–10.

6. Across the Sea

1. Patrick N. Lynch, bishop of Charleston, commission from President Jefferson Davis, Apr. 4, 1864, MSS 9031, oversize box 2, folder 2, Special Commission, CDA.

2. Stock, "Catholic Participation in the Diplomacy of the Southern Confederacy," 9–10.

3. Pope Leo X (1513–21) upheld the Dominican position that "not only the Christian religion, but Nature herself cried out against a state of slavery." In 1639, Pope Urban VIII condemned the slave trade and expressly forbid Catholics to participate in it. In his December 3, 1839, encyclical *In Supremo Apostolatus*, Pope Gregory XVI stated that it was not "lawful under any pretext or studied excuse" to deprive people of their goods or reduce them to slavery and that such actions were "utterly unworthy of the Christian name" (in Zanca, *American Catholics and Slavery*, 27–29). Rice, *American Catholic Opinion in the Slavery Controversy*, 16, 20.

4. Walter Johnson, *Soul by Soul: Life Inside the Antebellum Slave Market* (Cambridge, MA: Harvard Univ. Press, 1999), 19, 21, 114, 189, 217.

5. Owsley, *King Cotton Diplomacy*; D. P. Crook, *Diplomacy during the American Civil War* (New York: Wiley, 1975); Charles M. Hubbard, *The Burden of Confederate Diplomacy* (Knoxville: Univ. of Tennessee Press, 2000); Howard Jones, "History and Mythology: The Crisis over British Intervention in the Civil War," in *The Union, the Confederacy, and the Atlantic Rim*, ed. Robert E. May (West Lafayette, IN: Purdue Univ. Press, 1995). The international theater's importance is best encapsulated by historian

Allan Nevins: "No battle, not Gettysburg, not the Wilderness, was more important than the contest waged in the diplomatic arena and the forum of public opinion" (Nevins quoted in May, introduction to *Union, the Confederacy, and the Atlantic Rim,* 23).

6. Between 1820 and 1860, Britain acquired three-fourths of its cotton from the South. In the wake of the 1860 bumper crop, the figure was as high as 85 percent. Owsley, *King Cotton Diplomacy,* 1–2; Crook, *Diplomacy during the American Civil War,* 9; Hubbard, *Burden of Confederate Diplomacy,* 7, 27; James McPherson, "The Whole Family of Man: Lincoln and the Last Best Hope Abroad," in May, *Union, the Confederacy, and the Atlantic Rim,* 142; Davis, "Inaugural Address," Feb. 22, 1862, in Richardson, *Compilation of the Messages and Papers of the Confederacy,* 1:183–88

7. Robert Toombs, CSA secretary of state, to William L. Yancey, Pierre A. Rost, A. Dudley Mann, Department of State, Montgomery, Alabama, March 16, 1861, in Richardson, *Compilation of the Messages and Papers of the Confederacy,* 2:3–11; Hubbard, *Burden of Confederate Diplomacy,* 34; Owsley, *King Cotton Diplomacy,* 76.

8. May, introduction, 4; Crook, *Diplomacy during the American Civil War,* 29; James Mason to Judah P. Benjamin, Apr. 27, 1863, and W. L. Yancey and A. D. Mann to Robert Toombs, Aug. 1, 1861, both in Richardson, *Compilation of the Messages and Papers of the Confederacy,* 2:476, 53.

9. The ongoing events on the Italian peninsula held his full attention. Italy was "pregnant with menace and danger," the *New York Herald* explained. "She is now, as she has almost always been, the key to the political troubles and difficulties of Europe." On April 15, 1861, Giacomo Cardinal Antonelli, Pius IX's secretary of state, informed the US minister that the pontiff was busy dealing with "all [the] sacrilegious usurpation already consummated" by Victor Emmanuel. Letter included in Leo Francis Stock, ed., *United States Ministers to the Papal States: Instructions and Despatches, 1848–1868* (Washington, DC: Catholic Univ. Press, 1933), 232–33; *New York Herald,* Jan. 4, 1863.

10. Seward to Rufus King, Washington, Apr. 29, 1861, and John P. Stockton to William H. Seward, Washington, Sept. 14, 1861, both in Stock, *United States Ministers to the Papal States,* 238, 236; George M. Blackburn, *French Newspaper Opinion on the American Civil War* (Westport, CT: Greenwood, 1997), 23, 36, 58; Crook, *Diplomacy during the American Civil War,* 42.

11. W. L. Yancey and A. D. Mann to Robert Toombs, Aug. 1, 1861, in Richardson, *Compilation of the Messages and Papers of the Confederacy,* 2:53; Owsley, *King Cotton Diplomacy,* 78; Blackburn, *French Newspaper Opinion,* 47; Mann to Hunter, from London, Dec. 2, 1861, in Richardson, *Compilation of the Messages and Papers of the Confederacy,* 2:123–24; Rost to Davis, from Paris, Dec. 24, 1861, and Walker Fearn, Confederate Secretary of Legation to Spain, to Hunter, from London, Jan. 1, 1862, both in Richardson, *Compilation of the Messages and Papers of the Confederacy,* 2:133–34, 147.

12. W. M. M. Browne, CSA asst. secretary of state, to J. A. Quintero, Esq., etc., Monterey, Mexico, care of F. W. Latham, Collector of Customs, Brownsville, Texas, Jan. 14, 1862, in Richardson, *Compilation of the Messages and Papers of the Confederacy,* 2:151–52. Just a few examples of when the Confederacy avoided potential, seemingly inevitable, disasters include George McClellan finding Special Order No. 191 at Antietam, the 1863 New York Draft Riots not evolving into another civil war within the war, and

Atlanta falling precisely when it did and so stymieing the momentum of Clement Vallandigham and the Northern Peace Democrats heading into the 1864 election, which directly contributed to Lincoln's reelection and the final prosecution of the war unto total victory. The final result being a saved Union, and one restored to its antebellum geographical integrity.

13. In June 1862, US diplomat Alexander Randall claimed to Seward that in the wake of the Hughes mission the Holy See had been "very open and unreserved, in favor of supporting our Government, and maintaining its stability" (Alexander W. Randall to Seward, US legation, Rome, June 11, 1862, in Stock, *United States Ministers to the Papal States*, 236, 247–48). Lincoln praised Hughes effusively, saying that he had been "a mountain of strength to us in the time when our emergencies were greatest, and a grateful people should remember him and his" (Blied, *Catholics and the Civil War*, 84–87; *Diplomacy during the American Civil War*, 39). The US president hoped he could lobby Pius IX to appoint Hughes cardinal.

14. McGill to Lynch, Sept. 2, 1862, 27R4, CDA; St. Vincent's Asylum, New Orleans, to Mother Elizabeth Montcellet, Superioreess of the Daughters of Charity, June 11, 1862, Civil War Annals, 1866; Patrick Foley, *Missionary Bishop: Jean-Marie Odin in Galveston and New Orleans* (College Station: Texas A&M Univ. Press, 2013), 162; Heisser and White, *Patrick N. Lynch*, 96.

15. The British prime minister, Palmerston, believed as early as July 1861, following Confederate victory at First Manassas, that the separation of the United States was a permanent fact. The blockade was as much a physical hardship as a point of derision for Southerners. One bishop claimed that the blockade was both unconstitutional and immoral, with its aim being to "crush the South completely" (Augustus Marie Martin, bishop of Natchitoches, "Pastoral Letter Regarding the War of Southern Independence," Aug. 21, 1861, published in the *Charleston Catholic Miscellany*, Sept. 28, 1861). Some Catholics in Europe felt similarly. The Reverend John McCloskey, rector of the American College in Rome, wrote to Bishop Lynch that he was aware of Charleston's sufferings, ranging from the fire to general impoverishment, and that as he saw it, the biggest problem was the blockade as it was preventing critical help from reaching the diocese (McCloskey to Lynch, Nov. 28, 1863, 30A2, CDA). Hubbard, *Burden of Southern Diplomacy*, 66; Jones, "History and Mythology," 31, 36; Inclosure B., "Memorandum of an Interview of Mr. Slidell with the Emperor at St. Cloud on Tuesday, October 28, 1862," in Richardson, *Compilation of the Messages and Papers of the Confederacy*, 2:345–51.

16. Two examples of failed emancipatory declarations are Gen. John C. Frémont's issue concerning Missouri in August 1861 and Gen. David Hunter's proclamation in Florida in April 1862. When denouncing Hunter's actions, Lincoln claimed that no Union official, not even the president, had the authority to emancipate slaves. Daniel L. Schafer, *Thunder on the River: The Civil War in Northeast Florida* (Gainesville: Univ. Press of Florida, 2010), 133.

17. Jones, "History and Mythology," 37; Burton, *Age of Lincoln*, 170; Eric Foner, *Reconstruction: America's Unfinished Revolution, 1863–1877*, updated ed. (New York: Harper Perennial Modern Classics, 2014); Blackburn, *French Newspaper Opinion*, 95, 57, 69; Jones, "History and Mythology," 41, 42, 47.

18. Blackburn, *French Newspaper Opinion*, 57, 66.

19. McPherson, "Whole Family of Man," 144.

20. Spalding wrote the following in his Civil War journal on January 1, 1863, the day the proclamation came into effect, arguably his most explicit signaling of his true views on the war:

> While our brethren are thus slaughtered in hecatombs, Ab. Lincoln cooly issues his Emancipation Proclamation, letting loose from three to four millions of half-civilized Africans to murder their Masters and Mistresses! And all this under the pretense of philanthropy!! Puritan hypocrisy never exhibited itself in a more horrible or detestable attitude. Puritanism, with its preachers and Common Schools, has at length ruined the Country, as we all foresaw & predicted it would. May God grant that at length the eyes of America may be opened to its wickedness, & may see that their only salvation is to be found in Conservative Catholicity! This may be the result of this unhallowed war, thus, in God's Providence, bringing good out of evil. (35)

Episcopal criticism of Lincoln was not restricted to America. Alexander Gross, bishop of Liverpool, seems to have taken a page directly from Southern Catholics such as Gache, Dooley, Sheeran, and Poche when posing the following question, published in the December 1, 1864, edition of Richmond, Virginia's *Daily Dispatch*: "Think you that the imperialism of Russia is more tyrannical, or that it crushes more people than Abraham Lincoln, who is the representative of a Liberal Government in the Republic across the ocean?" "No," he continued, "there is no tyranny more terrible than that which bears the banner of liberty—that banner which crushes the liberty of others whilst it raises up itself, which brings itself into dame because it has trodden down almost everything else that may be near it."

21. Blackburn, *French Newspaper Opinion*, 136; McPherson, "Whole Family of Man," 145; Félix Dupanloup, "To His Clergy on the Subject of American Slavery," 1862, in Zanca, *American Catholics and Slavery*, 121–25.

22. Judah P. Benjamin to John Slidell, Aug. 17, 1863, in Richardson, *Compilation of the Messages and Papers of the Confederacy*, 2:543–45; Crook, *Diplomacy during the American Civil War*, 154.

23. Benjamin to Hotze, Sept. 5, 1863, in Richardson, *Compilation of the Messages and Papers of the Confederacy*, 2:562–63; Tucker, *Confederacy's Fighting Chaplain*, 158.

24. Tucker, *Confederacy's Fighting Chaplain*, 166.

25. Heisser and White, *Patrick N. Lynch*, 111; Jefferson Davis to Pope Pius IX, "Most Venerable Chief of the Holy See, and Sovereign Pontiff of the Roman Catholic Church," Sept. 23, 1863, in Richardson, *Compilation of the Messages and Papers of the Confederacy*, 2:571–72.

26. Davis to Pope Pius IX, Sept. 23, 1863.

27. Davis to Pope Pius IX, Sept. 23, 1863.

28. Jefferson Davis to A. Dudley Mann, Sept. 24, 1863, in Richardson, *Compilation of the Messages and Papers of the Confederacy*, 2:570.

29. A. Dudley Mann to Hon. J. P. Benjamin, Nov. 14, 1863, in Richardson, *Compilation of the Messages and Papers of the Confederacy*, 2:591–95.

30. Mann to Benjamin, Nov. 14, 1863.

31. Mann to Benjamin, Nov. 14, 1863.

32. Mann to Benjamin, Nov. 14, 1863.

33. Mann to Benjamin, Nov. 21, 1863, 600–601, and Pope Pius IX to Jefferson Davis, Dec. 3, 1863, both in Richardson, *Compilation of the Messages and Papers of the Confederacy*, 2:600–601, 603–4.

34. *Daily Confederate* (Raleigh, NC), Jan. 26, 1864; *Daily Dispatch* (Richmond, VA), Feb. 7, 1865; Mann to Benjamin, Dec. 9, 1863, in Richardson, *Compilation of the Messages and Papers of the Confederacy*, 2:602; Heisser and White, *Patrick N. Lynch*, 99; Crook, *Diplomacy during the American Civil War*, 79.

35. Newspapers in the North, naturally, covered the story of the pope's letter as well, and not just major outlets but regional and local ones. One such example is the *Ashland (Ohio) Union*, which on February 3, 1864, reprinted the exchanges between Davis and Pius IX under the headline "Interesting Correspondence between Jeff Davis and Pope Pius IX." *Alexandria (VA) Gazette*, Jan. 18, 1864; *Daily Confederate* (Raleigh, NC), Jan. 26, 1864; *Western Democrat* (Charlotte, NC), Jan. 26, 1864; *Staunton (VA) Spectator*, Jan. 26, 1864.

36. *Memphis Daily Appeal*, Feb. 11, 1864.

37. *Memphis Daily Appeal*, Feb. 11, 18, 1864.

38. Stock, "Catholic Participation in the Diplomacy of the Southern Confederacy," 8, 9; *Daily Confederate* (Raleigh, NC), May 3, 1864; Haddox, *Fears and Fascinations*, 58; Faust, *Creation of Confederate Nationalism*, 31, 42.

39. *New Orleans Daily Crescent*, Apr. 22, 1862; *Spirit of the Age* (Raleigh, NC), Feb. 9, 1863; *Memphis Daily Appeal*, Nov. 14, 1862.

40. *Memphis Daily Appeal*, Feb. 24, 1863; *Memphis Daily Appeal*, June 18, 1862.

41. *Yorkville (SC) Enquirer*, Mar. 20, 1863; *Southern Enterprise* (Greenville, SC), Mar. 21, 1863; *Camden (SC) Confederate*, Mar. 22, 1863; *Edgefield (SC) Advertiser*, Apr. 13, 1864; *Wilmington (NC) Journal*, Apr. 30, 1863; *Memphis Daily Appeal*, May 7, 1863.

42. *Richmond Enquirer*, June 19, 1863.

43. Stock, "Catholic Participation in the Diplomacy of the Southern Confederacy," 9; Judah P. Benjamin to Henry Hotze, Sept. 5, 1863, 562–63.

44. Stock, "Catholic Participation in the Diplomacy of the Southern Confederacy," 12, 4; Tucker, *Confederacy's Fighting Chaplain*, 178.

45. Tucker, *Confederacy's Fighting Chaplain*, 178; Judah Benjamin to James Mason, July 6, 1863, in Richardson, *A Compilation of the Messages and Papers of the Confederacy*, 2:562–63.

46. *Wilmington (NC) Journal*, Oct. 1, 1864.

47. *Wheeling (WV) Register*, June 1, 1865; *Idaho World* (Idaho City, Idaho Territory), Aug. 5, 1865.

48. *Memphis Daily Appeal*, May 4, 1862.

49. Tucker, *Confederacy's Fighting Chaplain*, 177, 176. The number of immigrants fell from 63,533 in 1864 to 29,722 in 1865. Stock, "Catholic Participation in the Diplomacy of the Southern Confederacy," 14.

50. Tucker, *Confederacy's Fighting Chaplain*, 177, 176. In opposition to both Tucker and Stock, historian David T. Gleeson argues that Bannon's mission had little effect on the war's outcome. Bannon did not prevent enough Irishmen from entering the Union service in a way that could have contributed to ultimate Confederate victory (Gleeson, *Green and the Grey*, 173). But this would have been at least a minor miracle, probably a major one. Bannon did accomplish the task he had been given and was as successful as he or the Confederate government could have hoped. This book therefore concurs with Tucker and Stock and also with historian D. P. Crook, who claims that during the war the Irish people became disillusioned with the idea of America as a promised land of democratic opportunity, believing instead that it had become a place of Irish exploitation (Tucker, *Confederacy's Fighting Chaplain*, 177, 176; Stock, "Catholic Participation in the Diplomacy of the Southern Confederacy," 14; Crook, *Diplomacy during the American Civil War*, 149). These were Bannon's views exactly. Crook likewise argues that Ireland came to be a stronghold of pro-Confederate sympathy throughout the war, remaining so to the end (Crook, *Diplomacy during the American Civil War*, 149).

For these reasons, the statistical drop in emigration and the widespread acknowledgement that pro-Southern sympathies tended to rise alongside anti-Union feeling in the wake of Bannon's mission, and against the claim that Bannon's mission could only be judged successful if it would have contributed to Confederate victory—it is difficult to claim that one man should have completed something large armies could not accomplish—this book states that not only was Bannon's mission successful but most likely more than Davis and the Confederate government could have realistically hoped for. Furthermore, Bannon's Ireland mission, in conjunction with his mission to the pope, well illustrates Confederatization's bidirectional consensus, as well as Catholic appropriation of and involvement in Confederate nationalism and the Confederacy's appreciation and utilization of its Catholic citizens. Bannon was supporting the Confederate nation in one of the most obvious ways possible, as a diplomatic agent, and the Confederacy was placing political hope in an envoy whose first duties were to his priesthood.

51. Stock, "Catholic Participation in the Diplomacy of the Southern Confederacy," 14; *Wilmington (NC) Journal*, Sept. 29, 1864.

52. Lynch to Benjamin, Mar. 3, 1864, 30K1, CDA.

53. Lynch to Benjamin, Mar. 3, 1864; Patrick N. Lynch, bishop of Charleston, "Draft of temporary administration plans for Diocese," Mar. 4, 1864, 30R4, CDA. Fillion died from smallpox the following year; see *Columbia (SC) Phoenix*, Apr. 1, 1865. Verot to Lynch, Mar. 22, 1864, 30N2, CDA.

54. Verot to Lynch, Mar. 22, 1864.

55. Lynch to Benjamin, Mar. 25, 1864, 30N5, and P. G. T. Beauregard to Lynch, Mar. 30, 1864, 30P7, both in CDA; Benjamin to Lynch, Apr. 4, 1864, in Richardson, *Compilation of the Messages and Papers of the Confederacy*, 2:470–73.

56. Benjamin to Lynch, Apr. 4, 1864; Stock, "Catholic Participation in the Diplomacy of the Southern Confederacy," 17; *Daily National Republican* (Washington, DC), Dec. 19, 1864.

57. Hubbard, *Burden of Confederate Diplomacy*, 66. Benjamin to Lynch, Apr. 4, 1864.

58. Benjamin to Lynch, Apr. 4, 1864.

59. Lynch, commission from President Jefferson Davis, Apr. 4, 1864; Jefferson Davis to members of his cabinet and assorted Confederates on the appointments of Lynch, Apr. 4, 1864, 30T2, CDA; *Burlington (IA) Hawkeye,* Dec. 31, 1864; Heisser and White, *Patrick N. Lynch,* 104.

60. Lynch to Benjamin, from St. George's, Bermuda, Apr. 15, 1864, 30W2, CDA; *Alexandria (VA) Gazette,* May 20, 1864; *Yorkville (SC) Enquirer,* May 25, 1864; Stock, "Catholic Participation in the Diplomacy of the Southern Confederacy," 17.

61. Paul Cullen, archbishop of Dublin, to Lynch, May 16, 1864, 30Y6, CDA; Heisser and White, *Patrick N. Lynch,* 104, 106; Stock, "Catholic Participation in the Diplomacy of the Southern Confederacy," 17.

62. Heisser and White, *Patrick N. Lynch,* 106–7.

63. *Wilmington (NC) Journal,* Aug. 18, 1864.

64. Heisser and White, *Patrick N. Lynch,* 107; McCloskey to Lynch, July 1, 1864, 31D6, CDA; Stock, "Catholic Participation in the Diplomacy of the Southern Confederacy," 18.

65. Heisser and White, *Patrick N. Lynch,* 109.

66. Pope Pius IX to Lynch et al., in Rome, July 4, 1864, quoted in Heisser and White, *Patrick N. Lynch,* 111.

67. *Wilmington (NC) Journal,* July 28, 1864; *Richmond Enquirer,* Mar. 16, 1863, quoted in Faust, *Creation of Confederate Nationalism,* 13.

68. *Wilmington (NC) Journal,* July 28, 1864; *Richmond Enquirer,* Aug. 24, 1864.

69. Stock, "Catholic Participation in the Diplomacy of the Southern Confederacy," 17; King to Seward, July 30, Aug. 16, 22, Oct. 25, 1864, all in Stock, *United States Ministers to the Papal States,* 313, 314, 315–15, 321.

70. *New York Herald,* Feb. 3, 1865.

71. Pope Pius IX to Lynch et al., July 4, 1864; Patrick N. Lynch, bishop of Charleston, "A Few Words on the Domestic Slavery in the Confederate States of America." This piece appeared in full text, with opening remarks, thanks to David C. R. Heisser, over two issues in the *Avery Review:* "A Few Words on the Domestic Slavery in the Confederate States of America," part 1, in vol. 2 (Spring 1999): 64–103, and part 2, in vol. 3 (Spring 2000): 93–123.

72. Lynch, "Few Words on Domestic Slavery," pt. 1:71.

73. Lynch, "Few Words on Domestic Slavery," pt. 1:73–75, 79–80.

74. Lynch, "Few Words on Domestic Slavery," pt. 2:101–2.

75. Lynch, "Few Words on Domestic Slavery," pt. 2:87–88.

76. Lynch, "Few Words on Domestic Slavery," pt. 2:94. Lynch described the services as "generally rude and impassioned; and where, at times, each member of the Church, man or woman, is allowed to rise up in turn and preach a ludicrous exhortation, or to scream forth a wild untutored extempore prayer, as often blasphemous in its phraseology, as it is hypocritical in its meaning. The audience in the meantime is in a tumult of sobs and groans, and shrill hysterical exclamations" (94).

77. Lynch, "Few Words on Domestic Slavery," pt. 2:93–96.

78. Lynch, "Few Words on Domestic Slavery," pt. 2:95–96, 117.

79. Lynch, "Few Words on Domestic Slavery," pt. 1:88–90, 74–82, 94, pt. 2:98–99, 109–14.

80. Heisser and White, *Patrick N. Lynch,* 124.

81. Loretta Clare Feiertag, *American Public Opinion on the Diplomatic Relations between the United States and the Papal States, 1847–67* (Washington, DC: Catholic Univ. of America Press, 1933), 174.

Conclusion

1. Poche, Jan. 1, 1865, *Louisiana Confederate,* 201; Jan. 3, 1865, *Civil War Diary of Father James Sheeran,* 550–52.

2. On March 28, 1865, the *Columbia* (South Carolina) *Phoenix* ran an article 1865 titled "Sherman Not a Catholic," which reported that while the Union general's wife had converted to Catholicism, he was an Episcopalian. Then the paper derisively noted, "He is probably of no profession but that general one of the Yankee, which involves all manner of freedom with law, right, virtue and civilization."

3. *Daily Dispatch* (Richmond, VA), Jan. 5, 1865.

4. *Daily Dispatch* (Richmond, VA), Jan. 5, 1865.

5. Garidel, Jan. 3, 16, 28, 1865, *Exile in Richmond,* 273, 284, 296.

6. Garidel, Jan. 29, Feb. 3, 1865, *Exile in Richmond,* 297–306.

7. Poche, *Louisiana Confederate,* Jan. 22, 1865, 207.

8. Poche, *Louisiana Confederate,* Jan. 22, 1865, 207; *Daily Register* (Wheeling, WV), Jan. 31, 1865; *Daily Intelligencer* (Wheeling, WV), Jan. 31, 1865;

9. *Nashville Daily Union,* Jan. 31, 1865; *Brownlow's Knoxville (TN) Whig and Rebel Ventilator,* Feb. 1, 1865; *Edgefield (SC) Advertiser,* Feb. 8, 1865.

10. *Alexandria (VA) Gazette,* Feb. 1, 1865.

11. Poche, Jan. 22, 1865, *Louisiana Confederate,* 207. That Confederates would be willing to give up their societal cornerstone in order to secure independence is a long discussed issued. As Poche explained, the balance between slavery and/or independence came into sharp focus most especially at war's end. Recent scholarship has continued to investigate the phenomenon of the Confederate independence project's value system. What were Confederates willing to sacrifice to achieve their ultimate aim? One such historian is Robert E. May, who, in "The Irony of Confederate Diplomacy: Visions of Empire, the Monroe Doctrine, and the Quest for Nationhood," *Journal of Southern History* 133 (Feb. 2017), an article treating Confederate empirical designs, states that Confederates moved from an initial position of "separation mainly to preserve slavery" to, by war's end, dealing with the "reluctant decision by Davis and his cabinet to consider giving up slavery to win the war" (69, 104). This is all the more startling, as May explains, because the Confederacy had not seceded *just* to preserve its own domestic slavery but rather with the intention of imposing "the South's system of coerced labor on Latin American populations that had outlawed slavery for decades" (106).

12. The *Pacificator,* founded in Augusta, Georgia, in 1864, was "devoted to the interests of the Roman Catholic Church, which Church, until the inception of the Pacificator, was

without a representative organ in the Southern Confederacy . . . in this great struggle they are with the South heart and soul—head and hands." The editors excitingly claimed Bishops McGill and Verot—"Christian prelates of the most exalted character and magnificent attainments"—as contributors. The local South Carolina newspaper the *Edgefield Advertiser* noted on November 30, 1864, "It gives us much pleasure to recommend the *Pacificator* to all liberal and enlightened men, be they Catholic or Protestant."

13. *Lancaster (SC) Ledger,* Jan. 24, 1865.

14. *Wilmington (NC) Gazette,* Feb. 8, 1865.

15. Grant to Lee, Apr. 8, 1865, Grant Papers, ser. 4.

16. Apr. 19, 1865, *John Dooley's Civil War,* 383; Spalding, *Martin John Spalding,* 166; King to William Hunter, May 6, 1865, in Stock, *United States Ministers to the Papal States,* 336–37.

17. *Civil War Diary of Father James Sheeran,* 554; Poche, *Louisiana Confederate,* 114–15.

18. Feb. 27–28, 1865, *John Dooley's Civil War,* 337–39; Dooley, Apr. 1865, *Confederate Soldier,* 180.

19. Apr. 23, 1865, *John Dooley's Civil War,* 387–89.

20. Lynch to Seward, from Rome, Sept. 9, 1865, 32Q15, CDA; *Daily Ohio Statesman* (Columbus, OH), Aug. 7, 1865; *Daily Phoenix* (Columbia, SC), Dec. 17, 1865; *American Citizen* (Canton, MS), Nov. 28, 1865; *Dodgeville (WI) Chronicle,* June 29, 1865; *Daily Clarion* (Meridian, MS), Aug. 16, 1865; *Montana Post* (Virginia City, Montana Territory), July 15, 1865.

21. According to the December 12, 1865, issue of Columbia, South Carolina's *Daily Phoenix,*

the high respect in which Monsignor Lynch has always been held by both Catholics and Protestants of both of the sections with which the late unfortunate conflict divided his country, caused the President of the United States to permit his immediate return, as soon as the war was ended. . . . The departure of Bishop Lynch from Rome, where he has become so much venerated as a pious and learned prelate and devoted missionary, excites from the highest to the lowest universal regret, especially as he returns to his diocese to find his cathedral burnt [and the] convents and institutions of charity under his jurisdiction, either reduced to ashes or shattered to pieces, and with no future hope, excepting in the mercy of God and benevolence of the faithful elsewhere.

22. *Charleston Daily News,* Dec. 6, 1865.

23. *Dallas (TX) Herald,* Oct. 14, 1865.

24. Woods, *History of the Catholic Church in the American South,* 295, 319.

25. Woods, *History of the Catholic Church in the American South,* 319; Gannon, *Rebel Bishop,* 116.

26. Elder, "Apostolate to the Negro Slaves in Mississippi," in Ellis, *Documents of American Catholic History,* 325–29.

27. Woods, *History of the Catholic Church in the American South,* 299.

28. Woods, *History of the Catholic Church in the American South,* 303.

29. Joseph T. Durkin, postscript to Sheeran, *Confederate Chaplain*, 163; Woods, *History of the Catholic Church in the American South*, 353.

30. Woods, *History of the Catholic Church in the American South*, 354–55; Higham, *Strangers in the Land*, 60–62; McGreevy, *Catholicism and American Freedom*, 7–42.

31. Woods, *History of the Catholic Church in the American South*, 349, 354, 370.

Appendix

1. Tucker, *Confederacy's Fighting Chaplain*, 14, 1, 181.

2. Durkin, preface and postscript to Dooley, *Confederate Soldier*, xiv, 209.

3. Charles E. Nolan, *The Catholic Church in Mississippi, 1865–1911* (Lafayette: Univ. of Louisiana at Lafayette and the Catholic Diocese of Jackson, MS, 2002), 11.

4. Cornelius M. Buckley Jr., introduction to *Frenchman, a Chaplain, a Rebel*, 7, 24, 39–40.

5. Michael Bedout Chesson and Leslie Jean Roberts, introduction to Garidel, *Exile in Richmond*, 6.

6. Heisser and White, *Patrick N. Lynch*, 21, 32, 24, 35, 125.

7. Bearss, introduction to *Louisiana Confederate*, and 114–15 (map), same volume.

8. Joseph T. Durkin, "Father Sheeran and His Journal," and epilogue, both in Sheeran, *Confederate Chaplain*, ix, 163.

9. Gannon, *Rebel Bishop*, 18, quoting Gallow Glass, in *Savannah Daily Herald*, Jan. 19, 1865.

Bibliography

Primary Sources

ARCHIVAL SOURCES

Clark Family. Letters. University of Mississippi, Civil War Archive.

Daughters of Charity. Civil War Annals, 1866. Province of St. Louise Archives, Emmitsburg, MD.

———. "Lives of the Deceased Sisters." Notice on Our Sisters of the Province of the United States, 1862. Province of St. Louise Archives, Emmitsburg, MD.

Gentry, B. F. Collection. University of Mississippi, Civil War Archive.

Grant, Ulysses S. Papers, series 4. Ulysses S. Grant Presidential Library, Starkville, MS.

Hay-Ray-Webb Papers. Special Collections, Mississippi State University Libraries, Starkville, MS.

Henderson, Rev. Jesse L. Civil War Diary. University of Mississippi, Civil War Archive.

Lee, Thomas Sim. Papers. American Catholic History Research Center and University Archives, Washington, DC.

Lofton, John Guy. Collection. University of Mississippi, Civil War Archive.

Lynch, Bishop Patrick N. Papers. Lynch Administration Papers, 1858–66. Charleston Diocesan Archives, Charleston, SC.

Natchez, Diocese of. Collection. University of Notre Dame Archives. Hesburgh Library, Notre Dame, IN.

Newspapers. University of Notre Dame Archives. Hesburgh Library, Notre Dame, IN.

Richmond, Diocese of. Records. University of Notre Dame Archives. Hesburgh Library, Notre Dame, IN.

Sisters of Charity of Nazareth, Kentucky. MNAZ 3/3: Baptisms, Confirmations, List of Slaves, Retreats at Nazareth. University of Notre Dame Archives. Hesburgh Library, Notre Dame, IN.

———. MNAZ 3/11: Civil War Book. University of Notre Dame Archives. Hesburgh Library, Notre Dame, IN.

————. MNAZ 3/12: Writings of Bishop Martin John Spalding, Civil War Journal. University of Notre Dame Archives. Hesburgh Library, Notre Dame, IN.

PUBLISHED PRIMARY SOURCES

Bannon, John. "Experiences of a Confederate Chaplain." In William Barnaby Faherty, *The Fourth Career of John B. Bannon: St. Louis Pastor, Southern Chaplain, Confederate Agent, and Irish Jesuit Orator*, 183–92. Portland, OR: C&D Publishing, 1994.

Clarke, Asia Booth. *John Wilkes Booth: A Sister's Memoir*. Jackson: Univ. of Mississippi Press, 1996.

Cumming, Kate. *Kate: The Journal of a Confederate Nurse*. Edited by Richard Barksdale. Baton Rouge: Louisiana State Univ. Press, 1959.

"A Declaration of the Immediate Causes Which Induce and Justify the Secession of South Carolina from the Federal Union," adopted Dec. 24, 1860. *The Avalon Project: Documents in Law, History and Diplomacy*. Yale Law School, Lillian Goldman Law Library, http://avalon.law.yale.edu/19th_century/csa_scarsec.asp.

"A Declaration of the Immediate Causes Which Induce and Justify the Secession of the State of Mississippi from the Federal Union," adopted Jan. 9, 1861. *The Avalon Project: Documents in Law, History and Diplomacy*. Yale Law School, Lillian Goldman Law Library, http://avalon.law.yale.edu/19th_century/csa_missec.asp.

Dooley, John. *Confederate Soldier: His War Journal*. Edited by Joseph T. Durkin. Washington, DC: Georgetown Univ. Press, 1945.

————. *John Dooley's Civil War: An Irish American's Journey in the First Virginia Infantry Regiment*. Edited by Robert Emmett Curran. Knoxville: Univ. of Tennessee Press, 2012.

Elder, William Henry. *Civil War Diary of Bishop William Henry Elder, Bishop of Natchez (1862–1865)*. Edited by R. O. Gerow. Natchez, MS: Most Reverend R. O. Gerow, 1960.

Ellis, John Tracy. *Documents of American Catholic History*. Milwaukee: Bruce, 1962.

Gache, Pere Louis-Hippolyte. *A Frenchman, a Chaplain, a Rebel: The War Letters of Pere Louis-Hippolyte Gache, SJ*. Translated and edited by Cornelius M. Buckley. Chicago: Loyola Univ. Press, 1981.

Garidel, Henri. *Exile in Richmond: The Confederate Journal of Henri Garidel*. Edited by Michael Bedout Chesson and Leslie Jean Roberts. Charlottesville: Univ. of Virginia Press, 2001.

"Letters of Kenrick to Hughes and Lincoln." *Catholic Historical Review* 4 (Oct. 1918): 385–88.

Lynch, Patrick N. "A Few Words on the Domestic Slavery in the Confederate States of America." Edited by David C. R. Heisser. *Avery Review* 2 (Spring 1999): 64–103, and 3 (Spring 2000): 93–123.

McMaster, James. "A Great and Cruel Wrong: Arrest and Imprisonment of a Confederate Catholic Chaplain." *Freeman's Journal*, Nov. 19, 1864.

Moore, Frank, ed. *The Rebellion Record: A Diary of American Events*. New York: D. Van Nostrand, 1866.

Poche, Felix Pierre. *A Louisiana Confederate: Diary of Felix Pierre Poche.* Edited by Edwin C. Bearss. Translated by Eugiene Watson Somdal. Natchitoches: Louisiana Studies Institute, 1972.

Richardson, James D., ed. *A Compilation of the Messages and Papers of the Confederacy.* 2 vols. Nashville: US Publishing Company, 1905.

Sheeran, James. *Confederate Chaplain, a War Journal.* Edited by Joseph T. Durkin. Milwaukee: Bruce, 1960.

———. *The Civil War Diary of Father James Sheeran, Confederate Chaplain and Redemptorist.* Edited by Patrick J. Hayes. Washington, DC: Catholic Univ. of America Press, 2016.

Stock, Leo Francis, ed. *United States Ministers to the Papal States: Instructions and Despatches, 1848–1868.* Washington, DC: Catholic Univ. Press, 1933.

US Department of the Interior. *Eighth Census, 1860.* Washington, DC: GPO, 1866.

Verot, Augustine. *A Tract for the Times, Slavery and Abolitionism, Being the Substance of a Sermon.* New ed. New Orleans: Printed at the Catholic Propagator Office, 1861.

The War of the Rebellion: A Compilation of the Official Records of the Union and Confederate Armies, 128 vols. Washington, DC: GPO, 1880–1901.

Wright, Willard E., ed. "Bishop Elder and the Civil War." *Catholic Historical Review* 44 (1958–59): 290–306.

———. "War Letters of the Bishop of Richmond." *Virginia Magazine of History and Biography* 67 (July 1959): 259–70.

Zanca, Kenneth J., ed. *American Catholics and Slavery, 1789–1866: An Anthology of Primary Documents.* Lanham, MD: Univ. Press of America, 1994.

SECONDARY SOURCES

Anderson, Benedict. *Imagined Communities: Reflections on the Origin and Spread of Nationalism.* London: Verso, 1983.

Blackburn, George M. *French Newspaper Opinion on the American Civil War.* Westport, CT: Greenwood, 1997.

Blied, Benjamin. *Catholics and the Civil War.* Milwaukee: Privately printed, 1945.

Bryan, T. Conn. "The Churches in Georgia during the Civil War." *Georgia Historical Quarterly* 33 (Dec. 1940): 283–302.

Burleigh, Michael. *Earthly Powers: The Clash of Religion and Politics in Europe, from the French Revolution to the Great War.* New York: Harper Perennial, 2007.

Burton, Orville Vernon. *The Age of Lincoln.* New York: Hill & Wang, 2007.

Crook, D. P. *Diplomacy during the American Civil War.* New York: Wiley, 1975.

Davis, Cyprian. *The History of Black Catholics in the United States.* New York: Crossroad, 1990.

Dolan, Jay P. *The American Catholic Experience: A History from Colonial Times to the Present.* Notre Dame, IN: Univ. of Notre Dame Press, 1992.

———. *Catholic Revivalism: The American Experience, 1830–1900.* Notre Dame, IN: Univ. of Notre Dame Press, 1979.

———. *In Search of American Catholicism: A History of Religion and Culture in Tension.* Oxford: Oxford Univ. Press, 2002.

Faherty, William. *Exile in Erin: A Confederate Chaplain's Story.* St. Louis: Missouri History Museum Press, 2002.

Faust, Drew Gilpin. *The Creation of Confederate Nationalism: Ideology and Identity in the Civil War South.* Baton Rouge: Louisiana State Univ. Press, 1988.

———. *This Republic of Suffering: Death and the American Civil War.* New York: Knopf, 2008.

Feiertag, Loretta Clare. *American Public Opinion on the Diplomatic Relations between the United States and the Papal States, 1847–67.* Washington, DC: Catholic Univ. Press, 1933.

Foley, Patrick. *Missionary Bishop: Jean-Marie Odin in Galveston and New Orleans.* College Station: Texas A&M Univ. Press, 2013.

Foner, Eric. *Reconstruction: America's Unfinished Revolution, 1863–1877.* Updated ed. New York: Harper Perennial Modern Classics, 2014.

———. *A Short History of Reconstruction, 1863–1877.* New York: HarperCollins, 2010.

Freehling, William W. *The South vs. the South: How Anti-Confederate Southerners Shaped the Course of the Civil War.* Oxford: Oxford Univ. Press, 2001.

Freeman, Douglas Southall. *Lee: An Abridgement.* New York: Charles Scribner's Sons, 1935.

Frese, Joseph R. "The Catholic Press and Secession, 1860–1861." *American Catholic Historical Society of Philadelphia Records* 45 (1957): 79–106.

Gallagher, Gary. *Becoming Confederates: Paths to a New National Loyalty.* Athens: Univ. of Georgia Press, 2013.

———. "Disaffection, Persistence, and Nation: Some Directions in Recent Scholarship on the Confederacy." *Civil War History* 55 (Sept. 2009): 329–53.

Gallagher, Gary, and Joan Waugh, eds. *Wars within a War: Controversy and Conflict over the American Civil War.* Chapel Hill: Univ. of North Carolina Press, 2014.

Gannon, Michael. *Rebel Bishop: Augustin Verot, Florida's Civil War Prelate.* Gainesville: Univ. Press of Florida, 1997.

Gjerde, Jon. *Catholicism and the Shaping of Nineteenth-Century America.* Cambridge: Cambridge Univ. Press, 2012.

Gleason, Phillip. *Catholicism in America.* New York: Harper & Row, 1970.

Gleeson, David T. *The Green and the Gray: The Irish in the Confederate States of America.* Chapel Hill: Univ. of North Carolina Press, 2013.

Haddox, Thomas F. *Fears and Fascinations: Representing Catholicism in the American South.* New York: Fordham Univ. Press, 2005.

Heisser, Michael C. R., and Stephen J. White Sr. *Patrick N. Lynch, 1817–1882: Third Catholic Bishop of Charleston.* Columbia: Univ. of South Carolina Press, 2014.

Henry, Ralph Selph. *The Story of the Confederacy.* Old Saybrook, CT: Konecky & Konecky, 1931.

Higham, John. *Strangers in the Land: Patterns of American Nativism.* New Brunswick, NJ: Rutgers Univ. Press, 1955.

Hubbard, Charles M. *The Burden of Confederate Diplomacy.* Knoxville: Univ. of Tennessee Press, 2000.

Johnson, Walter. *Soul by Soul: Life Inside the Antebellum Slave Market.* Cambridge, MA: Harvard Univ. Press, 1999.

Kurtz, William. *Excommunicated from the Union: How the Civil War Created a Separate Catholic America.* New York: Fordham Univ. Press, 2015.

Longley, Max. *For the Union and the Catholic Church.* Jefferson, NC: McFarland, 2015.

Maher, Mary Denis. *To Bind Up the Wounds: Catholic Sister Nurses in the U.S. Civil War.* Westport, CT: Greenwood, 1989.

Massa, Mark S. *The American Catholic Revolution: How the Sixties Changed the Church Forever.* Oxford: Oxford Univ. Press, 2010.

May, Robert E. "The Irony of Confederate Diplomacy: Visions of Empire, the Monroe Doctrine, and the Quest for Nationhood." *Journal of Southern History* 133 (Feb. 2017): 69–106.

———, ed. *The Union, the Confederacy, and the Atlantic Rim.* West Lafayette, IN: Purdue Univ. Press, 1995.

McCartin, James P. *Prayers of the Faithful: The Shifting Spiritual Life of American Catholics.* Boston, MA: Harvard Univ. Press, 2010.

McElroy, Robert *Jefferson Davis: The Unreal and the Real.* New York: Smithmark, 1937.

McGreevy, John T. *Parish Boundaries: The Catholic Encounter with Race in the Twentieth-Century Urban North.* Chicago: Univ. of Chicago Press, 1998.

———. *Catholicism and American Freedom: A History.* New York: Norton, 2003.

McPherson, James. M. *Battle Cry of Freedom: The Civil War Era.* New York: Oxford Univ. Press, 2003.

———. *For Cause and Comrades: Why Men Fought in the Civil War.* Oxford: Oxford Univ. Press, 1997.

Miller, Randall, and Jon L. Wakelyn, eds. *Catholics in the Old South.* 2nd. ed. Macon, GA: Mercer Univ. Press, 1999.

Miller, Randall M., Harry S. Stout, and Charles Reagan Wilson, eds. *Religion and the American Civil War.* Oxford: Oxford Univ. Press, 1998.

Mills, Gary B. *The Forgotten People: Cane River's Creoles of Color.* Baton Rouge: Louisiana State Univ. Press, 1977.

Moore, R. Laurence. *Religious Outsiders and the Making of Americans.* Oxford: Oxford Univ. Press, 1989.

Murray, John Courtney. *We Hold These Truths: Catholic Reflections on the American Proposition.* Lanham, MD: Sheed & Ward, 1960.

Nolan, Charles E. *The Catholic Church in Mississippi, 1865–1911.* Lafayette: Univ. of Louisiana at Lafayette and the Catholic Diocese of Jackson, MS, 2002.

Noll, Mark A. *The Civil War as a Theological Crisis.* Chapel Hill: Univ. of North Carolina Press, 2006.

Orsi, Robert A. *The Madonna of 115 St.: Faith and Community in Italian Harlem, 1880–1950.* 3rd ed. New Haven: Yale Univ. Press, 2010.

————. *Thank You, St. Jude: Women's Devotion to the Patron Saint of Hopeless Causes.* New Haven: Yale Univ. Press, 1996.

Owsley, Frank L. *King Cotton Diplomacy: Foreign Relations of the Confederate States of America.* 2nd ed. Revised by Harriet Chappell Owsley. Chicago: Univ. of Chicago Press, 1959.

Pasquier, Michael. *Fathers on the Frontier: French Missionaries and the Roman Catholic Priesthood in the United States, 1789–1870.* New York: Oxford Univ. Press, 2010.

Phillips, Jason. *Diehard Rebels: The Confederate Culture of Invincibility.* Athens: Univ. of Georgia Press, 2010.

————. "The Grape Vine Telegraph: Rumors and Confederate Persistence." *Journal of Southern History* 72 (Nov. 2006): 753–88.

Pillar, James. *The History of the Catholic Church in Mississippi, 1837–1865.* New Orleans: Hauser, 1964.

Potter, David. "The Historian's Use of Nationalism and Vice Versa." *American Historical Review* 67 (July 1962): 924–50.

————. *The Impending Crisis, 1848–1861.* New York: Harper Perennial, 1976.

Poyo, Gerald E. *Cuban Catholics in the United States, 1960–1980: Exile and Integration.* Notre Dame, IN: Univ. of Notre Dame Press, 2006.

Rable, George C. *God's Almost Chosen Peoples: A Religious History of the American Civil War.* Chapel Hill: Univ. of North Carolina Press, 2010.

Rada, James R., Jr. *Battlefield Angels: The Daughters of Charity Work as Civil War Nurses.* Gettysburg, PA: Legacy Publishing, 2011.

Rice, Madeleine Hooke. *American Catholic Opinion in the Slavery Controversy.* Gloucester, MA: Peter Smith, 1964.

Rubin, Anne Sarah. *A Shattered Nation: The Rise and Fall of the Confederacy, 1861–1868.* Chapel Hill: Univ. of North Carolina Press, 2005

Schafer, Daniel L. *Thunder on the River: The Civil War in Northeast Florida.* Gainesville: Univ. Press of Florida, 2010.

Sheehan-Dean, Aaron. *Why Confederates Fought: Family and Nation in Civil War Virginia.* Chapel Hill: Univ. of North Carolina Press, 2007.

Spalding, Thomas W. *Martin John Spalding: American Churchman.* Washington, DC: Catholic Univ. of America Press, in association with Consortium Press, 1973.

Stern, Andrew H. M. *Southern Crucifix, Southern Cross: Catholic-Protestant Relations in the Old South.* Tuscaloosa: Univ. of Alabama Press, 2012.

Stock, Leo Francis. "Catholic Participation in the Diplomacy of the Southern Confederacy." *Catholic Historical Review* 16 (1930): 1–18.

Stout, Harry S. *Upon the Altar of the Nation: A Moral History of the Civil War.* New York: Viking, 2006.

Strickland, Jeff. *Unequal Freedoms: Ethnicity, Race, and White Supremacy in Civil War-Era Charleston.* Gainesville: Univ. Press of Florida, 2015.

Tentler, Leslie Woodcock. *Catholics and Contraception: An American History.* Ithaca, NY: Cornell Univ. Press, 2009.

Thomas, Emory M. *The Confederacy as a Revolutionary Experience*. Englewood Cliffs, NJ: Prentice Hall, 1971.

————. *The Confederate Nation: 1861–1865*. New York: Harper Perennial, 1979.

Tucker, Phillip Thomas. *The Confederacy's Fighting Chaplain: Father John B. Bannon*. Tuscaloosa: Univ. of Alabama Press, 1992.

Ural, Susannah J., ed. *Civil War Citizens: Race, Ethnicity, and Identity in America's Bloodiest Conflict*. New York: New York Univ. Press, 2010.

Woods, James. M. *A History of the Catholic Church in the American South, 1513–1900*. Gainesville: Univ. Press of Florida, 2011.

Woodworth, Steven E. "The Church and the Confederate Cause." *Civil War History* 6 (Dec. 1960): 361–73.

————. *While God Is Marching On: The Religious World of Civil War Soldiers*. Lawrence: Univ. Press of Kansas, 2001.

Index

Abolitionists, 28, 43, 86, 99; agitation, 9, 11; churches, 89; Southern Catholics' duty to rebuke, 17

African Americans: baptisms, 83–84; black evangelization, 139; Catholic Church and, 20, 83–85, 129–30; clergy interactions with, 83; education, 95; Elder, interactions with, 82–84, 91; freedmen, 138; human rights and, 8–9; hypocrisy regarding, 9, 84–85; paternalistic view of, 84, 128–29; slavery, 8–9, 20, 83–85; soldiers, 83–84; spiritual equality of, 9, 84–85, 139; religion, 9, 129–30; suffrage, 120

Alabama: Catholic churches in, 2; Catholic population of, 2; Diocese of Mobile, 3; Mobile, 29, 96; secession from union, 10; Union occupation of, 30

Alexander, E. P., 22

Alexandria Gazette: on Elder's imprisonment, 90; on Lynch's diplomatic visit to Europe, 124; on papal presidential salutation, 116; rumors spread in, 134–35

Algeria, 109

All Saints Day, 75

Alonzo, 84

American College at Rome, 21, 125

American Protective Agency, 140

American Revolution, 7, 11, 119

Anderson, Robert, 14, 15

Antonelli, Giacomo, 108, 125, 127, 136

Appomattox Court House, 136

Archbishop of Baltimore. *See* Kenrick, Francis Patrick (archbishop of Baltimore, MD); Spalding, Martin John (bishop of Louisville, KY/archbishop of Baltimore, MD)

Archbishop of Cincinnati. *See* Elder, William Henry (bishop of Natchez, MS); Purcell, John Baptist (archbishop of Cincinnati, OH)

Archbishop of New Orleans. *See* Odin, Jean-Marie (archbishop of New Orleans, LA)

Archdiocese of Baltimore, 14

Archdiocese of Cincinnati, 139

Arkansas: Benedictines, 140; Catholic population of, 3, 140; Diocese of Little Rock, 3; Monticello, 48

Armistead, Louis, 42

Army and Navy Gazette, 130

Army of Northern Virginia, 31, 39

Army of Tennessee, 133

augusterlebnts, 1

Augustine (saint), 8, 88

Austria, 134–35

Bannon, John, 24–25, 40, 45, 65, 78, 111, 120; "Address to the Catholic Clergy and the People of Ireland," 117; Catholic religious experience, 56; chaplaincy, official 38; confessions, 58–59, 66, 67; death, 137; dedication to the Civil War, 40, 99; diplomatic visit to Ireland, 19, 37, 54, 105, 111–12, 114, 117, 119–21, 124, 131, 132; duties on the battlefield, 57, 58, 71; ethnic identity, 44; exchange with Private McGolfe, 58–59, 67, 101; "Experiences of a Confederate Army Chaplain," 58–59; joining First Missouri as its chaplain, 26–27; meeting with Pius IX, 112–13; religious duties in camp, 40, 56, 61, 66, 71; siege of Vicksburg, 24, 40, 58; sister-nurses, praise for, 104; state of grace, 69; view of the Civil War as a "holy war," 26; Union soldiers and, 58